VIRGIL'S GAZE

VIRGIL'S GAZE

NATION AND POETRY IN THE *AENEID*

J. D. Reed

PRINCETON UNIVERSITY PRESS

PRINCETON AND OXFORD

Copyright © 2007 by Princeton University Press

Published by Princeton University Press, 41 William Street, Princeton,
New Jersey 08540

In the United Kingdom: Princeton University Press, 3 Market Place,
Woodstock, Oxfordshire OX20 1SY

Library of Congress Cataloging-in-Publication Data

Reed, J. D.

Virgil's gaze : nation and poetry in the Aeneid / J. D. Reed.

p. cm.

Includes bibliographical references and index.

ISBN-13: 978-0-691-12740-8 (hardcover : alk. paper)

ISBN-10: 0-691-12740-9 (hardcover : alk. paper)

1. Virgil. Aeneis.   2. National characteristics, Roman, in literature.

I. Title.

PA6825·R385 2007

873′ .01—dc22

2006013965

British Library Cataloging-in-Publication Data is available

This book has been composed in Adobe Caslon

Printed on acid-free paper. ∞

pup.princeton.edu

Printed in the United States of America

1 3 5 7 9 10 8 6 4 2

10 9 8 7 6 5 4 3 2 1

CONTENTS

PREFACE

This book studies the way Virgil's *Aeneid* defines a nationality—one that the poem invites us to understand as Roman—out of a play of contrasts between nationalities. It is intended for a broad literary audience: not only specialists in Latin poetry, but anyone who has read the *Aeneid* at least in translation. In the bibliography, names of journals in classical studies have the standard abbreviations found in the *American Journal of Archaeology*. In footnotes I abbreviate a few ancient titles that I cite often: *Ad(onis)*, *Aen(eid)*, *Georg(ics)*, *Il(iad)*, *Met(amorphoses)*, *Od(yssey)*. *A.P.* means the *Anthologia Palatina* (the Greek Anthology, minus the Planudean Anthology). It is customary, when writing on the *Aeneid*, to own one's keen awareness of being unable to take into account more than a part of the immense and ever-increasing critical literature; I am no exception, and I can only hope that my references make my debts plain and ultimately permit readers to make up my inadvertent omissions.

I wrote and rewrote this book over many years, traditionally finishing a new draft toward the end of the year. What will Christmastime be without a turn through these gilt and empurpled halls? I am particularly grateful to audiences at Stanford in December 1992 and February 2001, in Atlanta in December 1994, in Dallas in December 1999, and at more job talks than I care to remember. For enlightening conversations and correspondance I owe a debt of gratitude to Fred Ahl, Alessandro Barchiesi, Will Batstone, Pamela Bleisch, Ruth Caston, Joy Connolly, Basil Dufallo, Mark Edwards, Denis Feeney, Kris Fletcher, Marcus Folch, David Halperin, Brent Hannah, Albertus Horsting, Richard Janko, Geoff Maturen, James O'Hara, Hayden Pelliccia, Piero Pucci, Susan Stephens, Richard Thomas, Tobias Torgerson, Michael Wigodsky; and to the students in my undergraduate and graduate classes on the *Aeneid*.

Ann Arbor
December 2005

ABBREVIATIONS

CIS   *Corpus Inscriptionum Semiticarum.* Paris 1881–1951.

CLE   F. Buecheler and E. Lommatzsch, *Carmina Latina Epigraphica.* Leipzig 1895–1926.

EV   *Enciclopedia Virgiliana.* Rome 1984–91.

FGrH F. Jacoby, *Die Fragmente der griechischen Historiker.* Berlin 1923–55.

KAI   H. Donner and W. Röllig, *Kanaanäische und aramäische Inschriften.* 4th ed. Wiesbaden, 1979.

PMG D. L. Page, *Poetae Melici Graeci.* Oxford 1962.

SH   H. Lloyd-Jones and P. Parsons, *Supplementum Hellenisticum.* Berlin 1983.

RE   *Real-Encyclopädie der classischen Altertumswissenschaft.* Stuttgart 1893–.

TLL   *Thesaurus Linguae Latinae.* Leipzig 1900–.

VIRGIL'S GAZE

INTRODUCTION

I

In composing the *Aeneid*, Virgil had inherited the peculiar task of tracing the Roman nation from a group of Trojan refugees. The possibilities for an epic of national foundations are rich. Not only does the westward shift from the eastern Mediterranean world suggest self-defining contrasts with other nations (nations over which the Romans had gained dominion); an origin in the world of Greek mythology, but in a city opposed to the Greeks, makes the mediation of Hellenism in any such account—and in the very form it takes—necessary but complicated. Virgil's poem, in fact, represents (among other things) a Roman version of a specific type of Greek poetry: the *ktisis* or foundation myth (the word literally means the foundation of a city or colony), celebrating a *ktistês* or founder; and its narrative engages in detail with Greek ktistic or foundational mythology. The present study, through close readings of the text, looks at the way the *Aeneid* offers the readerly subject a national identity—which the teleology of the poem invites us to read as Roman—through comparisons and contrasts between other nationalities (especially Trojan, Carthaginian, Italian, and Greek). In speaking of nationalities, I mean the unities that the poem may designate by the terms *gens*, *genus*, or *populus*, and by the myriad of ethnic groupings that it names, opposing some to others (for example, Trojans versus Greeks) and including some within others (as the Rutulians are part of the Italians). The *Aeneid* uses ethnic boundaries to organize and mold into new ideological shapes the disorderly wealth of facts (mythological, historical, and so on) that Virgil inherited; the schema that results complicates a simpler one (based on the *Catalogue of Women* attributed to Hesiod) that it also offers, whereby the Italian-derived descendants of Dardanus are opposed to the Greco-Oriental lineage of Inachus.[1] The whole process necessarily involves Virgil's poetics of nationality in a dialogue between other Greek and Latin poets.

Other paradigms of identity and alterity—those offered by gender and age, for example—are also relevant to the poem's representations of nationality, and we shall take account of these as well. Sometimes characters (particularly those who oppose Aeneas' Trojans) equate Eastern ethnicity with effeminacy, in formulations that the poem may confirm or explode by turns. Gender abets the poem's constructions of nationality, perhaps most conspicuously in the case of the female and Phoenician Dido and the female and Italian Camilla, but also in unexpected ways. The poem's evaluation of the national claims of Turnus

---

[1] See Hannah 2004.

must be viewed alongside his assimilation, at crucial moments in his story, to the literary model of the distressed mythological heroine; at the end of the book we return to this model as it touches the central case of Aeneas himself. The book introduces its nexus of themes by discussing a group of peculiar descriptions of battle deaths that erotically objectify warriors of both sexes and different ethnicities (all of which will ultimately be subsumed into the Roman); the erotic gaze not only suggests certain oppositional constructions of gender, but in the desirous viewer (whether conceived as narrator, character, or reader), we can explore the way that alterity can posit a lack, a need, even an urge to assimilate one's object to oneself (or vice versa).

Indeed, the gaze is a central trope of the study, one of whose principal concerns is the narratology of the poem, understood broadly as its chains of viewing or perceiving personae that assimilate poet, narrator, reader, and character. Hence the book's title; and hence also (as reflected in chapter titles) characters are often the focus of individual chapters. Identity implies a shared viewpoint that discloses certain contrasts and boundaries—or to put it conversely, any contrast that the poem draws between nations demands that we attend to the coordinates under which that contrast appears. What emerges is a schema that shifts with the narratology of the poem: the ethnic affinities of a character, national group, or motif—and the ethnic identity produced by opposition to an Other—can change depending on the changing perspectives that the poem, reconfiguring its great mass of inherited comparanda into meaningful patterns, offers its readers.

For this book will not attempt to characterize in definitive terms the Roman identity that the *Aeneid* offers; rather, its working hypothesis is that that identity is always provisional and perspectival—that the pairs of opposites that mark it out are never fixed. The moving boundaries between Greek, Oriental, and Italian carve out a standpoint—a persona assimilable to the Roman—so that the poem constructs the self as empty of nationality except as defined against a foil, or a series of foils. Roman identity—always reducible to some other nationality, depending on where the poem draws the boundary between nations—emerges as a synthesis (in a dialectical sense) of other national identities (analogous to the dialogue conducted by the *Aeneid* with its literary forerunners); there is no essence, no absolute center, no origin that exclusively authorizes Romanness. One recalls the *Eclogues*, where the literal, geographic boundaries of the Italian landscape, scumbled and shadowy, already prompt Connolly to discern a "revelation of fictionality at work," a fragmented quality that "draws readerly attention to extratextual—which is to say political and social—efforts to make landscape whole."[2] In the later poem, too, with its grander scale and vaster sense of a national self, a unity that one perspective asserts will only beg, from another perspective, the question of what figure, what stance, enforces that unity.

[2] Connolly 2001:113.

Like much other recent work on the *Aeneid*, the present readings accept the anomalies and discrepancies that appear when one passage or level of discourse is tested against another,[3] and they suggest an approach (at least where national identity is concerned) to the ambiguity that critics of the past half-century have found to be of especial interpretive interest in the poem: Roman identity is an ambiguous figure, a *problêma* without a single solution. The polycentrism that many have detected in the *Aeneid* will thus deny the reading subject a positive or definitive ethnic identity, but rather involve him or her in a play of ethnic identities. The Roman has an ambivalent place wherever in the world he stands, even in Latium: belonging everywhere, he belongs nowhere. Yet the ideology that is produced by this narrative incoherence as we try to make the parts fit is not necessarily negative. We are free to recuperate the poem's provisionality as less ambivalent than multivalent, and as serving a capacious imperialism consistent with the claims of the Roman Empire generally and of Augustan imperial culture specifically[4] (though it can also serve other, conflicting ends). "The *Aeneid*," warns Toll in a paper titled "The *Aeneid* as an Epic of National Identity," "was not made to express any simple partisanship, but precisely to deter partisan splintering from hindering its dream of ideological unity and ethical endeavor for the whole of Roman Italy."[5] This is as true on the level of multinational empire as it is on that of Roman politics and Italian relations with Rome. Mere difference is uninteresting; what is interesting is difference disguised as sameness. The uniformity imposed by an empire can be analyzed. There is no essential Roman in the *Aeneid*; the ethnicity that unavoidably, historically, is to be attached to the "self" in the poem is endlessly reducible, both conceptually and as represented by the poem as a historical reality. It is constantly deferred to other, mediating representations of ethnicity. Rome is simply not defined by what is present.

This is most crudely true on the topographical plane, where the site of Rome in Book 8 is said to empty repeatedly between arrivals by different outsiders (Saturn, Evander, Romulus). At 8.310–12 the site already has a past, intriguing to Aeneas:

> miratur facilisque oculos fert omnia circum
> Aeneas capiturque locis et singula laetus
> exquiritque auditque virum monimenta priorum.

---

[3] Cf. Feeney's metaphor of the "pair of binoculars with incompatible lenses" for scenes in the *Aeneid* where irreconcilable interpretations seem equally compelling (Feeney 1991:168). Hexter 1990:121–2 describes Virgilian inconsistency as a reflective surface in which readers see only their own desire for a solution. On taking inconsistencies in the *Aeneid* seriously as an integral part of the text, rather than explaining them away, see O'Hara 2005 (describing his forthcoming book, with a summary of this direction in Virgil criticism).

[4] In this regard Galinsky's sense of Augustan *ambiguitas* as a practice of calculated multivalence (cf. 1996:258) is most congenial to the present readings.

[5] Toll 1991:3. See also Toll 1997:49: "[t]he *Aeneid* does not envision the expansion of Rome as the extension of dominion over aliens, but rather as their gradual amalgamation . . ."; cf. 52–53.

Aeneas stares in wonder, sending his ready glances everywhere. He is captivated by the scene, and joyfully inquires about and hears tales about each and every reminder of earlier men.

According to his host, Evander, this human past is uncanny: "These woodlands were inhabited by native-born fauns and nymphs and a race of men born of the tough wood of tree trunks" (314–15 *haec nemora indigenae fauni nymphaeque tenebant / gensque virum truncis et duro robore nata*). These native, autochthonous beings have none of the arts of civilization, in particular agriculture and settled living, until Saturn, in flight from the wrath of Jupiter, arrives to rule them (8.319). He too, like Aeneas, is an exile from his kingdom (also like Metabus or Mezentius, among the poem's latter-day Italian kings). But Saturn and his subjects have no direct relation to the later inhabitants apart from dwelling place. The next inhabitants of the place are Italians arriving from the south ("an Ausonian band and Sicanian peoples" [328]), who themselves yield to Evander's "Greek city" (as the Sibyl provocatively calls it at 6.97). Each population is replaced or displaced by another; the very names keep changing (329). Any identity that can be claimed among the different settlements will, as a metaphor based only on the sameness of their place, disintegrate readily into metonymy. Romulus' accomplishment will be to orchestrate a fresh convergence from various directions on the newly built Rome (note 342 *asylum*). There is an emptiness at the geographic heart of identity, waiting to be—not exactly filled, but given outward shape, by a play of contrasts.

In the *Aeneid*'s version of Roman foundations, Aeneas' settlement will include not only Trojan colonists and Latin indigens, but representatives of other peoples: Cretans whom Aeneas' men married during their sojourn on that island (3.136; the slave Pholoe, awarded as a prize at 5.285, may be one such), a few Epirotes picked up at Buthrotum, and even various Greeks, like Salius and Patron at 5.298. The opposing sides of the Italian war in Books 9–12, the bloody prerequisite to Aeneas' settlement, are not cleanly defined ethnically, but include each other's characteristic ethnic components (note the Greek-Italian ancestry of both Pallas and Turnus, for example). The presence among the Italian army of Greek figures like Aventinus, Virbius, and Halaesus approximates it to the Greek army that fought against Aeneas in the Trojan War; but the Trojan army, too, includes Evander's Arcadians and other mainland Greeks. One is Antores, one-time companion of Hercules, who, felled by an "alien" wound (that is, by the Etruscan king Mezentius, fighting on the Latin side), famously "looks to heaven and, dying, remembers sweet Argos" (10.781–82 *caelumque / aspicit et dulcis moriens reminiscitur Argos*). Both the broad narrative of the poem and the smaller genealogies and stories of origin, inserted with the passing mention of a name like that of Antores, make Italy a sink of many peoples, a destination not only for Aeneas and his followers.[6]

[6] On the uses of these foundation myths cf. Bickerman 1952, Malkin 1998:156–209, Fletcher 2006.

The war, characterized as a proleptic civil war between peoples meant to become one, dramatizes our sense of the Roman not just as the combination of Trojan and Latin, but as forged out of cross-cultural exchanges from many sides. The ethnic presences they bring to a cumulative Roman identity, I suggest, prevent that identity from ever being fixed or independent of the multiple oppositions that inhere among its components.

Beyond the actual, narrated movements of the poem's persons we have the symbolic ethnic identifications produced by extra-textual allusions of various kinds. Here we enter the shadowy realm of meaningful etymology, so beloved of Latin poets: *nomen* as *omen*. Names of warriors, for example, introduce overtones, at least, of blurred national identity.[7] To be sure, warriors on the Trojan side may have clearly Asiatic names like Asius, Assaracus, and Thymbris (10.123–24), overflowing with Anatolian geographical and mythological connotations. Others, like Tyres (10.403) and Aeneas' captain Orontes point to a broader Oriental sphere (in these cases recalling the city Tyre and the river Orontes in the Levant). Sometimes names allegorize national transition, as when at 10.145 another Trojan warrior, Capys, is said to have given his name to "the Campanian city" (Capua). This old etymology not only recapitulates the ethnic trajectory from Troy to Italy, but, in this poem, etiologizes the dominion of the Romans over Campania in central Italy (specifically through the city that served as the Italians' capital during the Social Wars) in a way that nevertheless evokes or preserves the ethnic boundaries that separated the Trojan-descended Romans from the rest of the Italians.[8] This case is both like and unlike the etymologies of Roman clan names from followers of Aeneas in Book 5 (the Memmii from Mnestheus, the Sergii from Sergestus, the Cluentii from Cloanthus), which also emphasize the transition from Trojan to Roman, but which direct that trajectory toward Rome itself.

But this sense of national transition is sometimes not historical, but synchronic. At 10.337 a Rutulian Maeon—a poetic synonym for "Lydian"—bears a name elsewhere used of the "Lydian" Etruscans, his enemies. At 10.399 an Italian named Rhoeteus dies in the place of an Italian named Ilus—both bear names associated with the toponymy of Troy. At 9.344–45 the name of a Rutulian Rhoetus could be etymologized from either Trojan Rhoet- or Italian Rut- (analogically to the alternation Poenus/Punicus, among others). This blurs the boundary line of nationality in a way reminiscent of Virgil's almost exclusive use for the river Tiber of the name Thybris, which recalls both the

---

[7] Saunders 1940 and Zaffagno 1973 catalogue the connotations of warriors' names in the *Aeneid*.

[8] The story is first found around 500 B.C.E.: Hecataeus *FGrH* 1 F 62 = Stephanus of Byzantium s.v. Καπύα. Capys' homonymy with the father of Anchises (in *Il.* 20.239) affirms this meaning from an intertextual perspective. A later Capys, carrying on this tradition, appears as a king of Alba Longa at *Aen.* 6.768.

Tiber and the Trojan river Thymbris.[9] Personal names connected with this last specimen recur in significant ways. We hear of both an Italian Thymber (10.391–94) and a Trojan Thymbraeus (12.458); there is also a Trojan Thymbris (10.124). And Evander at 8.330–32 reports that the Tiber took its Trojan-sounding name from a local king named Thybris. One message here is that these peoples belong together: the near-homonymies allegorize an identification that lies in the future—and attest one that lies in the past, when we remember that the poem makes Dardanus originate in Etruria.[10] But what are we to make of Italians with blatantly Egyptian names like Pharos (10.322: the Ptolemies' famous lighthouse), Lagus (10.381: the founder of the Ptolemy family),[11] and Osiris (12.458: the Egyptian god)? Here one message might be of eventual Roman—that is to say, Trojan-Italian—conquest of Egypt (subtly correcting the Trojans' own status as "Orientals," capable of being classed together as such with Egypt). The last-named, for example, is slain by Thymbraeus in a foreshadowing of Octavian's victory over Antony and Cleopatra.[12] But other, conflicting messages are also latent; in our discussion of Turnus we shall explore the way Oriental features—like names—given to Aeneas' Italian enemies repeatedly estrange them from the land they are fighting to keep the Trojans out of.

We would find a geographical opposition between East and West only partially useful. To be sure, "East" suggests the boundary line between the poem's implied self and the nations of the eastern Mediterranean ("barbarian" nations, according to the Hellenocentric discourse that Romans adopted for certain purposes—but potentially, as seen from the west, including the Greeks). We see versions of this delineation in the picture of the Battle of Actium on Aeneas' Shield (8.675–713), and already in the *Georgics* (for example, in the prooemium to Book 3). But this schema breaks down if we try to identify the self with the "West." As geography, that would be unhelpful, since apart from Italy, western Mediterranean nations (Spain, Gaul) hardly signify in the *Aeneid*. The poem's most prominent "Eastern" nation, Carthage, founded by Phoenicians from Tyre and repeatedly qualified by epithets like Tyrian,

---

[9] See Reed 1998:401–403. The form Thybris may have been suggested by the name Thebris, which Varro *L.L.* 5.30 says was an old Etruscan name for the river; it may have a precedent in line 5 of a Sibylline oracle (in Zosimus 2.6, Phlegon of Tralles *FGrH* 257 F 37 [p. 1190.2])—whose line 3 contains a well-known parallel to *Aen.* 6.851 *Romane memento*—if it predates the *Aeneid* (cf. Horsfall 1989b:10, Zetzel 1989:277–79). If it does not, Virgil's is the first known use of this nomenclature.

[10] Note that poetic etymology and related types of wordplay are now being studied from semantic and ideological angles; see, for a recent example, the papers in Nifadopoulos 2003.

[11] The "a," short here, is long in the Ptolemaic ancestral name. Ancient literary wordplay freely connects words with different vowel quantities, as in Virgil's implicit connection between Cācus in Book 8 and Gk. *kăkos*, "evil" (see Servius on 8.190, O'Hara 1996:204; more generally his pp. 61–62 and Ahl 1985:56–57).

[12] Reed 1998.

Sidonian, and Phoenician, in fact lies west of Rome. Moreover, the *Aeneid* by no means consistently identifies Italy itself, the poem's most conspicuous Western land (indeed, called "Hesperia" at key moments, identified—from a Hellenophone standpoint—as "Land of the Evening Star"), with the ethnic self, or with any unified identity. For similar reasons I shall often employ the term "Oriental" rather than "Eastern," since it has more than directional connotations, and tends to lump Near Eastern, "barbarian" peoples together in opposition to Greek and Roman (as the *Aeneid* sometimes does; for example, on the shield in Book 8, where Egyptian, Indian, and so on constitute a "barbarian force" opposed to Roman Italy).[13] The poem aims at no "Western" identity; there is an implied "self," assimilable to the "Roman" as the poem presents it, in perpetual contrast with other ethnic constructions. The problems with a clean geographical opposition between East and West here are not just practical, but symptomatic of the poem's ethnic constructions.

II

The poem's opening announces its field of oppositions in spatial and temporal terms. The *Aeneid* presents itself as the story of a Trojan refugee who brought his ancestral deities to Italy and founded the nation that was to become Rome (1.1–7):

> Arma virumque cano, Troiae qui primus ab oris
> Italiam fato profugus Laviniaque venit
> litora, multum ille et terris iactatus et alto
> vi superum, saevae memorem Iunonis ob iram;
> 5 multa quoque et bello passus, dum conderet urbem
> inferretque deos Latio, genus unde Latinum
> Albanique patres atque altae moenia Romae.

I sing of arms and of a man, the first one who came from the shores of Troy to Italy and the Lavinian beaches, exiled by fate, much buffeted both on land and on the deep by the force of the gods above, because of the remembering anger of savage Juno; and enduring much in war as well, until he could found a city and introduce his gods to Latium: and from this came the Latin race, the elders of Alba, and the ramparts of high Rome.

Trojan and Latin shores demarcate Aeneas' transition.[14] Before arriving at Rome, the teleology runs through the Latin race (representing Aeneas'

[13] The trope occurs on a smaller scale at 3.297, where Helenus is Andromache's *patrius maritus*: "Asiatics" are one big national group, sharing an ancestry.

[14] Compare the way shores demarcate Rome's future empire at 3.97 *domus Aeneae cunctis dominabitur oris* ("the house of Aeneas will be master of all shores"), where *oris* is Virgil's addition to the (tendentious, pro-Roman) variant reading at *Il.* 20.307–308 Αἰνείαο βίη πάντεσσιν [for Τρώεσσιν] ἀνάξει / καὶ παίδων παῖδες, "the might of Aeneas and his children's children will be master over all [for "over the Trojans"]" (Strabo 13.1.53; cf. Gruen 1992:12–13).

settlement in Italy, into which the already existing Latins are curiously folded, as if they originated with it) and the "elders of Alba" (literally "Alban fathers," encompassing both the local elders of Rome's mother city and the emperor's Julian clan, which had historical and legendary ties to Alba Longa). The latter are crucial for filling in the gap between Aeneas himself and the foundation of Rome;[15] they will appear, with slight but significant slippage, as the Alban kings (not precisely the elders—senators or quasi-senators—that are implied by *patres*), direct descendants of Aeneas, prophesied at 1.272 and 6.760–70.

The trouble Aeneas and his people underwent to achieve this aim, we are told, was caused by Juno, specifically on account of the threat the Trojan refugees—or their Roman posterity—were fated to present her favorite city, Carthage (12–22):

> Urbs antiqua fuit (Tyrii tenuere coloni),
> Karthago, Italiam contra Tiberinaque longe
> ostia, dives opum studiisque asperrima belli;
> 15 quam Iuno fertur terris magis omnibus unam
> posthabita coluisse Samo; hic illius arma,
> hic currus fuit; hoc regnum dea gentibus esse,
> si qua fata sinant, iam tum tenditque fovetque.
> progeniem sed enim Troiano a sanguine duci
> 20 audierat, Tyrias olim quae verteret arces;
> hinc populum late regem belloque superbum
> venturum excidio Libyae: sic volvere Parcas.

There was an ancient city (colonists from Tyre possessed it): Carthage, far opposed to Italy and the mouths of the Tiber, rich in resources and most keen in zeal for war. This city alone Juno is said to have cultivated more than all others, even Samos. Here were her weapons, here her chariot; this land the goddess then already intended and nurtured to be kingdom over the nations—should the fates allow. For yet she had heard that generations were being drawn forth from Trojan blood to overturn that Tyrian citadel one day; that hence to Libya's destruction would come a people widely sovereign and proud in war: the goddesses of fate so unwound their tale.

More shores, marking out further ethnic oppositions. The wording sets us on the Latin shore at the mouth of the Tiber, Aeneas' eventual landfall and ultimately Rome's entrance to the Mediterranean, looking far across to Carthage—figures us, that is, as Romans by an immediate prolepsis. The geographical opposition (13 *contra*) between the two countries makes them archenemies, even antitheses; and the epic, which mentions the Punic Wars only rarely, will implicitly set up

---

[15] This historical expediency is found as early as Fabius Pictor *FGrH* 809 F 2 and Cato fr. 13 Peter, around 200 B.C.E.

the struggle between them as the defining event in Roman history from the time before there was even a Rome, by tracing (as we shall explore) the gradual differentiation of two originally Oriental peoples. Yet this prologue makes the similarity between Rome and Carthage persist fundamentally: both are devoted to war (1.14 *studiisque asperrima belli*, 21 *belloque superbum*) and intended to hold sway over many lands (17 *regnum . . . gentibus*, 21 *late regem*). This is a contest for military empire.[16] We begin the poem with the vision of a nation rising out of a play of contrast with and likeness to another nation.

Greece is already introduced, in Samos and Argos, as alongside Carthage in Juno's affections (and in opposition to Troy—and proleptically to Rome). This is the beginning of an unstable ethnic triangle that will replace a Greek-derived ethnic polarity (self versus "barbarian") with a less determined one and thus supersede, in the cause of Rome, the Greek worldview and the Greek authors who expounded it, from Homer onward. The schema Trojan-Italian-Greek replicates the ethnic composition of Rome's environment during its early formative period, when Easterners (like Phoenician and Carthaginian traders), Italians (like other Latins, Etruscans, and the more distant Sabellan peoples), and South Italian Greeks were the most conspicuous "Others." (For that matter, we might also read in this composition a reanalysis of what never explicitly appears in the *Aeneid*, the multiethnic city of Virgil's time, filled with Greeks and Hellenized Easterners.) The poem can assimilate any one of these three to a self, or set it apart as an Other: Trojans can represent either origins or a past existence, now abandoned and assimilable to such aliens as Carthaginians and Egyptians; Italians can represent either the homeland Virgil had exalted in the *Georgics* or hostile neighbors to be subdued. And Greeks—who in Anchises' prophecy of the Roman future are still cast as an anti-Trojan enemy—can finally either be lumped together with the Orientals whose neighboring lands they came to rule, or be identified with as the alter ego with whom Romans had so strenuously elaborated cultural parallels over the centuries, and especially as the source of the literature that the *Aeneid* itself is simultaneously extending and revising.[17]

---

[16] The discussion in chapter 4 and elsewhere will suggest that these characterizations cannot simply be referred to and contained by the viewpoint of Juno, implied in 20 *audierat* and the succeeding dependent infinitives (cf. Fowler 2000b:47–48 on *superbum*, citing Jackson Knight 1933:57 n. 6 and, on 28 *genus invisum*, Henry 1873:217–18).

[17] See Gruen 1992:31 on how the myth of Trojan origins both "enabled Rome to associate itself with the rich and complex fabric of Hellenic tradition" and "announced Rome's distinctiveness from that world." Cf. Malkin 1998:29, 171–72, 202–207 (who emphasizes, in the case of Aeneas' founding of Rome, his eventual disjunction from the Greek Odysseus, whom an earlier legend—apparently Etruscan in origin—had made his cofounder). Erskine 2001 cautions that an anti-Trojan bias is far from inevitable in the attested Greek outlook on populations that claimed Trojan descent. Note O'Hara 1990:83 n. 50: "An important development in recent Vergilian scholarship has been the recognition of Vergil's ambivalence and uneasiness about the Romans' legendary Trojan heritage" (with citations).

The narrative parallels Greek foundational legends, as formulated especially in the Hesiodic *Catalogue of Women* and mythological texts that depend on it. There the Greek Io, driven by the wrath of Juno, wanders to the lands of the East; generations later her descendants (the Inachids, so called from Io's father Inachus) make their way back west—following Europa—and settle in Greek lands, sometimes with conflict and bloodshed. Hellenistic Greek poets—Apollonius, Euphorion, Lycophron—had performed their own versions of this story with special application to the broadened Hellenic world after Alexander; and colonization myths—some involving Inachid descendants like Heracles, Europa, and Danae—extend it to Italy and the western Mediterranean. It significantly articulates the ancestries of the characters of the *Aeneid*, particularly those who in some way oppose the mission of Aeneas. Dido and Turnus are chief examples: the first is descended from Belus (1.729–30), great-grandson of Io in Greek tradition; the second, according to Amata, is a descendant of Inachus and Acrisius (7.372), the fathers of Io and Danae. The myth figures explicitly as the *argumentum ingens*, the "immense narrative" of Io, on the shield of Turnus (in an allusion to Moschus of Syracuse's *Europa*). But it also appears in mirror fashion in the story told by the poem: the Italian-born Dardanus migrates to the lands of the East; his progeny found Troy; after the fall of Troy his descendants—led by Aeneas—make their way back in accordance with fate and settle in Italian lands, with much conflict and bloodshed. In our testimony, this story is new with Virgil: other authors make Dardanus originally Arcadian (the *Aeneid* in effect displaces this origin onto Evander, whose connection with the foundation of Rome is more tangential).[18] In Italy Dardanids and Inachids—two dynasties tracing their origins back to Jupiter—come into conflict.

The justification that the *Aeneid* offers for this schema and this migration furnishes a concrete example of the way the poem avoids the positive sense of a national identity—indeed, the overarching and primordially significant example, as expounding the deepest origin of Aeneas' people and the reason for his divinely ordained settlement in Italy. The Trojan Penates, in their exegesis of Apollo's charter-oracle to Aeneas, tell him to settle in Italy because Dardanus came from that land: specifically, Anchises is immediately to lead the group to Corythus (3.167–71 *Corythum terrasque requirat Ausonias*). This is a city of legend; the *Aeneid* identifies it with no historical place. King Latinus supplements the Penates' explanation in his welcoming speech to Ilioneus:

---

[18] Hellanicus *FGrH* 4 F 23, Servius Auctus on 5.167, Strabo 8.3.19 Inscriptional evidence may suggest that Virgil's tracing Dardanus to Italy is borrowed from an Etruscan ktistic myth; cf. Horsfall 1987:99–104, Jocelyn 1991. For a detailed account of Virgil's use of Dardanus' Italian origin, see Cairns 1989:114–18; Kvíčala 1878:76–83 neatly reviews the passages where the Aeneadae's "return" to Italy is ordained, esp. as regards the question of Aeneas' increasing awareness of his destination.

Dardanus, he states, originally set out "from the Etruscan place of Corythus" (7.209 *Corythi Tyrrhena ab sede*). When Iris summarizes the Trojan menace for Turnus at 9.10–11, she stresses Aeneas' quest for alliances even to "the furthest cities of Corythus and the Etruscan forces" (*extremas Corythi penetravit ad urbes, / Lydorumque manum*). The place referred to by the Penates, Latinus, and Iris is represented as both the origin and immediate destination of the Trojan dynasts.

In tracing Aeneas' lineage back to this place, Virgil awakens the possibility that his ancestry is Etruscan—in conformity, one might suppose, with the generally sympathetic treatment of Etruscans in the poem. But that sympathetic treatment must also be read alongside the Etruscans' originally being Lydian or Maeonian—Asiatic, Oriental like the Trojans—in this poem, in accordance with an account first read in Herodotus 1.94.[19] Etruscans cannot claim Italian soil by virtue of their origins. If Dardanus was Etruscan, and the Etruscans are originally Lydian, we are sent back to Anatolia and the Trojan sphere. Another dilemma arises against the report by Dionysius of Halicarnassus that Cortona in Etruria was once a "Pelasgian" (that is, prehistoric Greek) city:[20] if Cortona is the legendary Corythus (an old identification),[21] we meet with Greek identity at a certain point in its past, and the Dardanids' opposition to their Greek enemies becomes more ambiguous. Indeed, the *Aeneid* then starts to abet the programmatic assimilation of Romans to Greeks that is characteristic of one strain of ethnographical polemic (including the work of Dionysius).[22] We thus return, circuitously, to the more widespread tradition that Dardanus was originally Greek. It is noteworthy that at 10.719 one Acron, a "Greek man" (720 *Graius homo*), is said to come from Corythus. But perhaps Dardanus was a native Italian, sprung from autochthons before the Etruscans' ancestors arrived from Lydia or the Pelasgians from Greece. In that case we arrive all the sooner at the fundamental, unavoidable dilemma, for neither Etruria as a whole nor the city of Corythus in particular is in fact Aeneas' revealed or eventual destination; rather, according to two new prophecies (3.389–93, 8.42–48), his people will settle where he finds the omen of a nursing pig: in Latium, in the event. Rome itself, the end of all Aeneas' efforts, will lie a little upriver in the same country. Aeneas, despite Iris' warning to Turnus, does not in fact follow the Penates'

---

[19] See *Aen.* 8.479–80, 499; 9.11; 10.155; 11.759. This is the background to the wordplay at 10.697, where the exiled Etruscan king Mezentius kills a Trojan named Palmus, whose name echoes a Lydian word for king, *palmus* (cf. Janko 1992:143 on *Il.* 13.792): we have the conceit of one "Lydian" king killing another.

[20] Dionysius of Halicarnassus *A.R.* 1.26.1.

[21] Upheld by Harrison 1976; cf. Harrison 1991 on 10.719. See Silius Italicus 4.718–21, 5.122, and 8.472–73 with Horsfall 1987:93–94.

[22] Gruen 1992:7–8.

order to seek out Corythus specifically; he gets new instructions that have nothing to do with his ancestral place.

As Dardanus' origin and the justification of Aeneas' destination, Corythus should refer to Rome or at least Rome's corner of Latium (where Aeneas will build his settlement, Lavinium); yet however the name is understood, it rather leads us away from Rome.[23] What does it mean for the prophecies to say, "The human founder of your race originated in the city of Corythus, in Etruscan country, so you must return to settle in Latium" (let alone "... so your descendants will found Rome")? It is not as if Virgil were bound by a universal consensus to trace the Dardanid line to this place; again, the story appears first in the *Aeneid*. The justification for Aeneas' westward migration—or homecoming—quite arbitrarily mismatches its outcome. An uncompleted circle leaves unanswered questions. Corythus, as a *problêma*, is a figure. It can be solved, and the grounds for Aeneas' mission justified, by treating it as a metaphor for Italy, another "ancient" Italian city like the ones Rome will conquer and subsume—or as a metonymy, part of the Italian world that will come under the sway of Rome. But as such it will always threaten to come apart; the discrepancy within the identity is always near to hand.[24] More fundamentally, on the level of narrative, metaphor is reduced to metonymy: what on the terms accepted by the poem should have been a replication, a return to the same, turns out to be a contingency, a near return to something adjacent. Any solution works only provisionally; the problem of Corythus can be solved only by raising other interpretive problems.[25]

The poem's riddling justification for Trojan settlement in Italy, and Roman origins, is comparable to its depiction of the early history of the site of Rome. Each case presents an emptiness, a gap, an incommensurateness begging to be made up, where a central presence could have provided stability. The indeterminacy goes even deeper, if origins count: why is Dardanus' line privileged over Teucer's in Trojan ancestry (and future)? The logic of the *Aeneid* privileges origins, but the poem presses national origins only to find that they yield, in every case, to another differentiation, or to aporia. The Roman is predicated on oppositions, contrasts, and foils that are impossible to fix or define except provisionally. So the *Aeneid* is endlessly rereadable: every angle from which we

---

[23] The phrases exchanged by Latinus and Ilioneus, *his ortus ut agris Dardanus* (7.206–207) and *vestras exquirere terras . . . hinc Dardanus ortus* (239–40), must be taken broadly of Italy, not narrowly of Latium; aside from the force of qualifications like *Tyrrhena ab sede* (209), we should take into account that this is the first colloquy between the Aeneadae and Italian natives.

[24] The opposite is the case with Carthage, where the similarity is what threatens to undermine the poem's insistence on Roman power and exceptionality, and specifically the Romans' distance from an Oriental Other.

[25] A fuller discussion of the problem of Corythus is forthcoming in *SIFC*.

read it offers a different way to be Roman in the world. The case of Corythus is the order of the poem.

III

Almost any passage in the *Aeneid* could be read for meaningful differentiations of this kind, and I expect and hope that the readings in this book will suggest others along the same lines. The present argument follows one particular thematic trail, starting from desire (what Virgil's Latin regularly expresses by *amor* or *cupido*). We begin this theme in chapter 1 with Virgil's most elaborate—and on close inspection most peculiar—descriptions of slain warriors: passages in Books 9–11 wherein he objectifies the bodies of Euryalus, Pallas, Camilla, and Lausus in distinctly erotic terms. Thematically the images in chapter 1 prove vital to our main topic, since the slain warriors in question come from different nations that will one day be absorbed into the Roman empire, while the dying-god imagery that suffuses them is mythologically bound to the Orient, whence the people of Aeneas have traveled toward their Italian destiny; moreover, these scenes showcase the sexual and gender questions that the poem frequently poses in connection with national identity. From a discussion of these death scenes as nodes of a loose network of passages tied together by verbal and thematic links and commenting on one another, we go on to discuss them as points of reception for Virgil's Latin and Greek background. These scenes have often been held to represent young death and all it means in the *Aeneid*; let us read desire as an operative trope in their representation of lost (national) promise, and as analogous (at least) to the sense of lack that drives the poem's representations of national identity. I wish not only to account for the way the given passages thematize youth, death, and desire in the poem, but to read them as giving us readers a standpoint in the narrative and a relationship to the characters, as well as to the narrative voice and its literary precursors (it should be remembered that both the synchronic and diachronic aspects of the text involve questions of national identity). We thus begin with a narratological study, in preparation for the book's basic concern with Roman identity in the *Aeneid* as a function of perspective.

The next two chapters, focusing on Turnus and Dido, explore the repercussions of the death images in the treatment of those two obstacles to Aeneas' divinely appointed mission. Thematically, Turnus and Dido too have to do with youth, death, and desire, and the figure of the dying god lurks behind them in unexpected ways. Our methods remain principally narratological and intertextual, and in these chapters help show how narrative viewpoint and literary appropriation are mutually involved with the ethnicity of those characters, especially as they serve as foils for an ethnic self (as "anti-Romans"). The narrative dynamics sketched out in chapter 1 prepare for chapter 2, where the Italians resisting Trojan settlement are seen to possess, oddly, the very Oriental traits and effeminate luxuriousness (*mollitia*) that are elsewhere attributed to the Trojans. Chapter 3, together with 4 and 5, traces the gradual separation of Aeneas' band from an Oriental identity through growing contrasts with Carthage and indeed Troy itself (often represented by female figures like Dido and Andromache) and tries to establish the different lines that the poem draws between the self and an Other and to show how those lines are constantly being erased and redrawn. These three chapters are much concerned with Virgil's revision of his Greek and Latin models to create new constructions of Rome's imperial mission. Chapter 6 follows Aeneas into the Underworld and traces how desire becomes a contested metaphor for the Roman imperialism with which Anchises inculcates Aeneas. The synthetic Trojan-Italian nation of Anchises' prophecy remains unstable on its own terms: Roman identity is still radically dependent on the perspective one takes on its composition. The last chapter concentrates on the role of Aeneas as a viewer and a medium for our viewpoint on these topics, and on the contradictions in his viewership that parallel the shifts in perspective we have been tracing in the poem's version of Roman identity, always better treated as a dialectic than as a definition.

This is a literary, not a historical or ethnographical study; we are thus less concerned with the sources of the various ethnic influences that Virgil gathers and arranges than with the meaningful structure that the language of his text gives the ethnically significant motifs that already crowd and complicate the material he has inherited. What his text does with an ethnic unity is our focus, rather than the criteria (like a common name, language, religious practice, and so on) under which it may appear as a unity outside his text; we are likewise less concerned with the constructions of ethnic identity, explicit or implicit, in other ancient texts (let alone with modern assessments of ancient ethnic distinctions). Moreover, the *Aeneid*'s creation of a multiple Roman identity out of other nationalities is at the fore of our discussion; the bestowal of Roman identity on subject peoples is not. This precision will vex some readers, I know, as will the related omission of anything to do with Mantuan Virgil's own stance toward the Roman; I have just felt inadequate to the book that such a widening of my focus would have entailed. Nevertheless, we shall occasionally compare constructions of nationhood in other Latin writers; the book is intended to complement recent work on national identity in Augustan literature and its debt to, and departure from, earlier versions. In particular I hope to supplement current work on how the *Aeneid* represents in literature a new Roman subject (I think particularly of Hardie 1986, Quint 1993, and Feeney's series of studies); it has more general affinities with Habinek's ideological readings of Latin literature, and with studies like Hardie 1993 on later Latin epic, which problematizes Romanness not only in terms borrowed from the *Aeneid*, but in agonistic response to the *Aeneid*.

Methodologically I hope for the book to operate at an intersection of different lines of recent criticism, especially in the Anglo-American tradition.

Since Fowler's 1991 article, Virgilian narratology needs rethinking in a less formalist direction; Feldherr (1995), for one, points to the ideological dimension of narratology in the *Aeneid* (and offers a similar reading of Livy in his 1998 book). Interpretation of viewpoint in the material evidence has long been moving in an ideological direction (see, for example, Fredrick 1995 on gender in Roman wall paintings). Always in the background are the visions of the poem offered by its great twentieth-century interpreters, particularly Otis and Putnam; Putnam has also paved the way for the study of an erotic gaze in the poem, particularly as connected with its larger themes. My style of intertextual interpretation has been influenced both by the detailed and layered readings of Thomas and by the semantic notion of intertextuality that informs the work of such critics as Conte and Hinds. Barchiesi in particular has pointed the way toward a reconciliation of synchronic and diachronic dimensions in Augustan poetry, in his insistence (following an especially Italian tradition) on the ideological potential of narrative viewpoint and in his sense of intertextuality as a dynamic process, better studied as a rhetoric than a grammar.[26]

A rhetorical notion, in fact, is at the heart of this methodological intersection. This book is also, very broadly, a study of the metaphoric economy of the *Aeneid*; that is, the system of exchanges in his repetitions of his own and his precursors' words and ideas, and the passing of personae between poet and reader that narrative viewpoint entails. Indeed, metaphor is the principal trope of the *Aeneid*: everything invites comparison and contrast with everything else, down endless chains in all directions. Not all comparisons are definitively interpretable, or even interpretable at all. The chains run on forever, and sometimes run out on us. But an interplay of sameness and difference is the engine of Virgilian meaning, and it is what makes the poem the synthesis and consummation that it is. One thinks of the consummational binding power of the personae the poem invokes: Aeneas is like Augustus is like Alexander . . . Or of its intertexts: the *Aeneid* is like the *Argonautica* is like the *Odyssey* . . . (to take a few large-scale examples). Comparisons bridge boundaries of text and reality, of myth and politics, and between texts. The poem gives us a standpoint that binds and unbinds, creates likenesses and unlikenesses, and it invites us to identify that standpoint with the Roman.

[26] See e.g. Barchiesi 1997, 2001, 2002.

Chapter One

EURYALUS

I

Among the dead of the last third of the *Aeneid*, in the foundational war Aeneas must fight against the natives of Latium in order to settle in the area (and in order for Rome eventually to rise there), four stand out for the elaboration of their deaths and the emotionally peculiar descriptions of their fallen bodies: Euryalus, Lausus, Pallas, and Camilla. These figures represent both sides of the war (Euryalus and Pallas on the Trojan side, Lausus and Camilla on the Italian) and several of the nations that will help comprise the future Roman race, or will fall subject to Roman dominion (and the difference is often a matter of perspective): Trojan, Etruscan, Greek, and Italian. Their importance to the poem's construction of national identity, however, goes deeper than this tabulation or potential synecdoche; the mode of their description provides us readers with a place in the narrative on more than one level—a relationship to the characters as well as to the narrative voice and its precursors. Each time Virgil lingers visually over the body of a fallen warrior (as opposed to the many brief "obituaries"[1] that follow warriors' deaths in the latter books of the poem) he invokes the *sermo amatorius*, the conventional language of love. The unexpectedly erotic view that the poem gives us on these four figures goes back to Hellenistic mythological poetry and helps cast each fallen warrior as an Adonis-figure: beautiful, loved, and slain. Each Virgilian reincarnation of Adonis differently embodies themes that are central to the *Aeneid*, and *as* Adonis-figures they complicate those themes: potential paradigms of *virtus* and of the Roman ideal of a male warrior are assimilated to a sexually ambiguous type of youth; prototypes of Roman citizens to a figure who embodies a both quintessentially Greek and quintessentially Oriental stereotype; Augustan martial epic to late Hellenistic narrative at its most fervid and non-heroic. Pierced and pinned already by enemy weaponry and again by the poet's gaze and ours, the fallen warriors of the *Aeneid* become sites of the poem's reflection on nationhood, sex, and power.

In stressing the coherence of these images and their erotic slant we are following later poets of epic, who conflate and telescope Virgil's four passages for

---

[1] The term used for such passages in the *Iliad* by Griffin 1980:104.

their own youthful slain warriors, using much the same tone.[2] The image can be understood historically as a revaluation of certain Homeric descriptions (that of Hector's body, for example), redirecting the force of the image from the realm of martial prowess to that of erotic beauty. A psychoanalytical approach might see this sort of description as a sublimation of eroticism, traditionally eschewed in epic, in terms of the violence native to epic. A more formalist analysis might stress the interplay between death and sex elsewhere in the *Aeneid* (in later chapters we will compare such episodes as the death of Dido) and suggest that erotic beauty cannot be acknowledged in traditional epic until death has reduced the person to an object. Here we do not aim for a general explanation. Our main concern is narratological; our central question is what kind of viewer the poem sets up in response to these images, and makes us over into. The gaze (an emotionally charged visual description, often assimilable to what and how a particular viewing character sees) implies a series of conceptual oppositions: male and female, maturity and youth, lover and beloved, self and other. But these oppositions are by no means repeated in the same patterns from view to view, nor do they yield a single, consistent message even within any one description of a view. The indeterminacy of this viewpoint, and its fundamentally semantic—specifically metaphorical—nature, is the object of this study. We shall first investigate this peculiar gaze in the cases of Euryalus, Pallas, and Camilla (Lausus, in whom the sensuality is more subdued, will receive treatment further on). Next we must establish the narratological nature of the gaze: the imagery constructs a flexible or capacious subject position—or rather identity, since I wish to emphasize the play of likeness and difference that the trope effects. Finally we relate the gaze and its constructions of identity and alterity to the construction of Roman nationality in the poem.

The first and most elaborate passage in this series is the one on Euryalus, who gives his name to this chapter as the prime representative of what we may provisionally call the "Euryalus-figure" and "Euryalus-scene"; I would emphasize, however, that none of the four figures literally stands as an avatar of some underlying type (as heuristically useful as that construction may be), but more as just one participant in an interplay among the broad themes of the poem. At *Aeneid* 9.431–37 Euryalus falls dying:

> viribus ensis adactus
> transadigit costas et candida pectora rumpit.
> volvitur Euryalus leto, pulchrosque per artus
> it cruor inque umeros cervix conlapsa recumbit:
> 435 purpureus veluti cum flos succisus aratro

[2] Statius *Theb.* 9.877–85; Valerius Flaccus *Arg.* 3.178–80; Silius *Pun.* 4.203–205, 7.631–33, 12.225–50. Cf. Reed 2004:32; Dewar on *Theb.* 9.883.

languescit moriens, lassove papavera collo
demisere caput pluvia cum forte gravantur.

Driven by force, the sword pierced his ribs and broke through his white chest. Euryalus collapsed in death, and the blood ran over his beautiful limbs, and his head toppled and came to rest on his shoulders, as when a crimson flower, cut by the plow, languishes as it dies; or as poppies with weary neck droop their head when by chance they are weighed down with rain.

One aspect of the eroticization here is well studied: the comparison of violence to sex.[3] Sword thrusts in particular lend themselves to this metaphor, and it is at least worth noting that Ausonius uses the first half of line 432 for the bridegroom's climactic thrust in the *Cento nuptialis* (line 127). Our passage, however, not only eroticizes the violence, but characterizes the dying Euryalus himself as physically attractive: involved in the sexuality of our passage is an odder sexuality, an unsettling erotic exuberance that lights upon the boy. His limbs are "beautiful" and his chest is "white" (or "gleaming": *candida*): adjectives used for loving, not killing, attach to his body at the very moment that it is stabbed and falls limp.[4] This is the death, we remember, of "Euryalus, outstanding in beauty and burgeoning youth" (5.295 *Euryalus forma insignis viridique iuventa*), "Euryalus, whom no other follower of Aeneas surpassed in beauty" (9.179–80 *Euryalus, quo pulchrior alter / non fuit Aeneadum*).[5]

The simple mention of physical beauty in the death of a young warrior, which has well-known antecedents in Greek epic, is not uncommon in the *Aeneid*.[6] Heuzé, noting that beauty mentioned in a death scene can have a powerful pathetic effect, observes that in the *Aeneid* all characters marked by beauty meet with tragic ends (with the significant exceptions of Rome's founding family, Aeneas, Ascanius, and Lavinia).[7] Yet most of those descriptions only make us lament the splendor of the rising young warrior; the description at 433–34 picks up conventionally erotic features latent in Euryalus' beauty. Johnson 1976:61 perceives here "something that smacks of the grotesque, of *Liebestod*." The sensual emphasis on Euryalus' body and its sleeplike (*conlapsa recumbit*) decline into death, which seeps into the first flower simile (*languescit moriens* is strongly redolent of the *sermo amatorius*),[8] likens his death to an orgasmic collapse and repose. The passivity that marks Euryalus as a victim

---

[3] On this trope in the *Aeneid* see Gillis 1983, Heuzé 1985:170–78, Fowler 1987, Mitchell 1992.

[4] Cf. Heuzé 1985:292. On the use of *candidus* as a term of physical acclamation (attested first in Plautus *Pseud.* 1262), see Pichon 1902:98. On the attractively "white" complexion of young men in Greek and Latin poetry (e.g. Virgil *Ecl.* 2.16, Horace *Carm.* 1.18.11) see Bonanno 1989.

[5] Cf. 5.344 (of Euryalus) *pulchro . . . corpore.*

[6] Cf. e.g. 9.335–36 (with Heuzé 1985:291–92), 583; 12.270–76.

[7] Heuzé 1985:290–95.

[8] See Pichon 1902:183 on *languescere*; 208 on *mori* (also Adams 1982:159). *Lasso* in the second simile continues this imagery; cf. Pichon 1902:184.

also serves a technique of display, spreading his beauty before us. We are dealing with the body of a fallen warrior as the site of sexual objectification.

Camilla's death also shows a refocusing of sexuality from the violence of the deed to the view of its aftermath. Arruns' spear-throw is a spectacle, witnessed by multitudes, described in stages, and culminating in a scene of perversely meaningful gore (11.799–804):

> ergo ut missa manu sonitum dedit hasta per auras,
> 800   convertere animos acris oculosque tulere
> cuncti ad reginam Volsci. nihil ipsa nec aurae
> nec sonitus memor aut venientis ab aethere teli,
> hasta sub exsertam donec perlata papillam
> haesit virgineumque alte bibit acta cruorem.

So when the spear, hurled by his hand, gave off a sound [as it passed] through the air, all the Volscians turned their eyes and sharp attention to their queen. She herself was unaware of either the [whistling] air or the sound or the weapon descending from the sky until the spear stuck beneath her exposed nipple[9] and, driven in deep, drank of her virginal blood.

The phases of the spear's trajectory, described with a kind of backtracking repetition (*sonitum . . . hasta . . . auras . . . aurae . . . sonitus . . . teli*), create a sense of slow motion that exacerbates the helplessness of the Volscians, whose view we are invited to share at lines 800–801 (Camilla's own viewpoint on the scene is emphatically negated for now). What they see is grotesque: clinging beneath the nipple and drinking her blood, the spear is like a vampire baby; moreover, we are reminded that the penetrated, bleeding "mother" is a virgin.[10] The sum of this imagery would make Camilla's death a defloration that results in a lethal spawn.

In contrast to this kinesis, the description that follows shifts our attention to a still, sensual beauty (11.816–19):

> illa manu moriens telum trahit, ossa sed inter
> ferreus ad costas alto stat vulnere mucro.
> labitur exsanguis, labuntur frigida leto
> lumina, purpureus quondam color ora reliquit.

---

[9] See Heuzé 1985:174 n. 357 and Fowler 1987:195 n. 38 on *papillam* = "nipple." The image is especially striking in contrast to 11.649, where the exposed part of the "Amazon" Camilla's torso is the more discreet *latus*, "side" (Heuzé 1985:332–34).

[10] See Fowler 1987:195–96 on *virgineum cruorem* and the defloration imagery latent here; inter alia, he notes that Ausonius uses 804 for the bride's defloration in the *Cento nuptialis* (compare Ausonius' use of the slaying of Euryalus, mentioned above). Heuzé 1985:176–77 sees a further sexual image in the wolf simile that describes Arruns' flight: *caudamque remulcens / subiecit pavitantem utero* (11.812–13).

Dying, she pulled out the weapon with her hand, but the metal point stayed in the deep wound in her ribs, between the bones. She sank down bloodless, her eyes sank cold in death, the former crimson color left her face [or lips].

Her feeble, futile effort quiesces toward a loss of consciousness; the repeated verb makes the descent gentle, as *conlapsa recumbit* does for Euryalus' death. But it is the "crimson color" in particular that concentrates the diffuse sensuality of the verses on Camilla's person. Gransden notes on 11.818 that *purpureus* denotes the glow of youth, citing the *lumen iuventae purpureum* bestowed on Aeneas in 1.590–91 and (in an indirect application) the *purpureus flos* to which Euryalus is compared at 9.435. This scene presents, in a sense, the inverse of Lavinia's famous blush that arouses the ardor of Turnus (12.64–70). We are made to see the signs of Camilla's young beauty just as they disappear.

Pallas, who is not given much of a description when he dies (10.482–89: Turnus' spear pierces his chest; he pulls it out, then keels over with a clatter of weaponry), exemplifies an even more radical refocusing from kinesis to quiescence. As the weeping Aeneas enters where women are beating their breasts and wailing for the dead prince, the sensuality comes quite in passing (11.39–41):

> ipse caput nivei fultum Pallantis et ora
> ut vidit levique patens in pectore vulnus
> cuspidis Ausoniae, lacrimis ita fatur obortis.

When [Aeneas] saw the bolstered head of snowy Pallas, and his face, and the wound from the Ausonian spear gaping in his smooth chest, he spoke thus in tears.

Putnam says of the passage, "Two words are gratuitous in this description—*niveus*, snowy, and *levis*, smooth—and both are highly sensual. What Aeneas takes note of is the adolescent, androgynous beauty of the youth. *Niveus* has nothing to do with the whiteness of death (Virgil would have used *pallidus*) and everything to do with physical allure. . . . Smoothness of skin is also a mark of youthful beauty."[11] In other words, we are dealing with well-established terms of sexual acclamation suited, as Putnam suggests, to young men as well as women.[12] One might add that mention of *ora*, Pallas' face,

---

[11] Putnam 1985:10–11, noting that "Virgil's only other use of *niveus* in connection with the human anatomy occurs in book 8 where Venus uses her 'snowy arms' (387 *niveis lacertis*) to fondle hesitant Vulcan in her soft embrace." Cf. Gransden 1991:73 on *levi*: "V. wants to stress P.'s adolescent beauty."

[12] On *levis* see Pichon 1902:187. On *niveus* see Pichon 1902:213–14, Lyne 1978:170. It is a term of physical acclamation as early as Catullus 61.9, 63.8, and 64.364; cf. already the pseudo-Ciceronian *Rhetorica ad Herennium* 4.44 *corpore niveum candorem . . . assequebatur* (exemplifying hyperbole).

reminds us of his youthful, beardless appearance, a requisite of the junior partner in a male-male relationship—in Greek terms, the *erômenos*, the "beloved."
Elsewhere we encounter the downy male faces of Euryalus (9.181) and Clytius
(10.324), *erômenoi* both.[13] The "smooth chest" of "snowy Pallas" reminds us of
Euryalus' *candida pectora*, and this connection reinforces the erotic slant of
both scenes.

Servius on 11.39 offers a refinement of Putnam's observation on *nivei*: "The
force of the epithet is wide open: it can refer to the whiteness of pristine
beauty, and to the pallor that comes with death, and to the coldness that is
characteristic of dead bodies."[14] (This is not the only time we see Servius refus-
ing to pin a single interpretation on a word or phrase.) He seems to register
the "wide openness" of the adjective (*late patet*), its semantic capaciousness,
hierarchically: the body's whiteness and coldness, the signs of death, literally
compared to the best-known properties of snow, are subsumed under an adjective that has most positive connotations, especially as juxtaposed with the
"smooth chest" (whose connotations Servius also recognizes, glossing *levi* in
40 as "beautiful, boyish, not yet bristly").[15] These fallen warriors' nakedness can
similarly imply both vulnerability and sensuality (one is reminded of the category that Clarke, in his typology of the nude, labels "pathos"): we can see (with
the grieving Aeneas) Pallas' smooth chest; we can see (with the Volscians)
Camilla's exposed nipple; Euryalus' gleaming white chest is open to view.
Partly explicable by the convention of heroic nudity of warriors in art, the
motif has affective potential that resonates strongly in these passages.

The glimmer of erotic appreciation at 11.39–41 does not go unreprised.
Like Euryalus, Pallas at 11.67–71 is compared to a plucked flower, here explicitly one that has not yet lost its beauty:

> hic iuvenem agresti sublimem stramine ponunt:
> qualem virgineo demessum pollice florem
> seu mollis violae seu languentis hyacinthi
> cui neque fulgor adhuc nec dum sua forma recessit,
> non iam mater alit tellus virisque ministrat.

Here they place the youth high on a rustic pallet, like the blossom of a
soft violet or languishing hyacinth culled by a young girl's thumbnail,
whose sheen and beauty have not yet passed away, though its mother the
earth no longer nourishes it and lends it strength.

---

[13] Compare also Evander in his vaguely paiderastic encounter with the older Anchises (8.160 *tum
mihi prima genas vestibat flore iuventus*).

[14] *Late patet hoc epitheton: referri enim potest et ad candorem pristinae pulchritudinis, et ad pallorem ex
morte venientem, et ad frigus quod proprium mortuorum est.* Donatus *ad loc.* also takes *nivei* as a sign
of high *pulchritudo*.

[15] *Pulchro, puerili, nondum saetoso.*

Gransden in his commentary speaks of "the body of Pallas, its erotic beauty not yet faded, lies like a tableau before the reader." Indeed: the reader's essential voyeurism is again rewarded with an image of passive sensuality, which *mollis* and *languentis* in the flower simile reinforce. The choice of flowers to which Pallas is compared—violet and hyacinth—recalls the myths of Attis and Hyacinthus and the flowers that grew from their blood when they died: through the simile Pallas is likened to doomed *erômenoi* of gods (Cybele and Apollo, respectively).[16] The "soft" violet's epithet redounds to Pallas himself. First there are the sensual connotations of *mollis*: physically a "soft" body, connoting voluptuously touchable youth, is attractive in a boy; ethically the adjective connotes amorousness and susceptibility to love.[17] The *persistence* of the flower's beauty suggests the opposite of the loss of Camilla's rosy hue. If we read Pallas' *ora* (most readily interpreted as "face" here) back against hers at 819 (whether "face" or "lips" there is indeterminate), we may speculate that it is the loss of color that Aeneas notices—verbally subordinated to the more positive whiteness of his "snowy" skin, but ominous.

In looking at Euryalus and Pallas, let alone Camilla, one is reminded of the viewpoint Fredrick discerns in Pompeian wall paintings of mythical women whose distress, often amatory, serves to affirm the male viewer's gender (not in a simple bipolar schema, but complicated for the Romans by considerations of age and social rank)—that is, to cast the viewer as a man of high estate.[18] Our characters are visually *available*; their erotic beauty "lies like a tableau before the reader," in Gransden's comment on Pallas, and the passivity that makes each character a victim blends with the sexual passivity reminiscent of the treatment of women and boys in erotic literature and art. One of the most remarkable aspects of these scenes is the contrast between their subjects' aggressiveness up until their deaths and the passivity that ensues. Upon dying, Euryalus and Pallas not only (predictably) lose whatever place the text gave them as subjects, but take on qualities that are schematically opposed to the Roman ideal of masculinity. The violence of Euryalus' death can be feminizing, in a tradition going back at least to the *Iliad*, in which Achilles, scoping

---

[16] On Attis and violets see Arnobius 5.7, Buecheler *CLE* 467.5; already hinted at in Ovid *Fasti* 5.227. Cf. Servius on Euryalus (9.433): "There is a special motive for the simile: he is evidently drawing a comparison between Euryalus and Hyacinthus, who was preeminent for his beauty and was changed into a flower after his death" (*habetur ratio comparationis: videtur enim Euryalo Hyacinthum comparare, qui pulcherrimus fuit et post mortem conversus in florem est*). The myth of Hyacinthus also emerges, oddly, in the hometown of Euryalus' slayer Volcens, Amyclae, homonymous with the Lacedaemonian town associated with Hyacinthus and the Hyacinthia.

[17] Cf. Pichon 1902:205–206. On the quality of *mollitia* in Roman sexual discourse see further Williams 1999:125–59 and his General Index s.v. *mollitia*.

[18] Fredrick 1995; see also the papers in Fredrick 2002. Y. Syed, *Vergil's* Aeneid *and the Roman Self* (Ann Arbor 2005), which also takes a narratological approach to the poem's formation of (male) Roman identity, came into my hands too late for me to take full account of it.

out the exposed part of Hector between his collarbones, drives his spear point "straight through his tender [*hapaloio*] throat" (22.327); noteworthy also are sensual epithets like *kalos* ("beautiful"), *leukos* ("white"), *terên* ("tender"), and *leirioeis* ("lilylike"), applied in the *Iliad* to the skin of warriors threatened by wounds: at the moment of penetration, a male warrior's latent femininity emerges, a trope for his vulnerability.[19] Through its epithalamic pedigree (Catullus 62.39–47, perhaps going back to Sappho's usage), Euryalus' first flower simile casts him in death as a bride; Pallas also receives bridal imagery in his scene.[20] Female qualities in a male can be alarming, implying as they do an abdication of the male sociopolitical role (compare the lover in Latin love elegy, or the transsexualized Attis of Catullus 63—whose hands at line 8 are *niveae*, "snowy," like Pallas' body).[21] In Euryalus and Pallas, the shadow of a feminine persona figuratively registers the loss of their adult male potential; the erotic light that falls on them in a sense confirms their now permanent status as boys, whose viewpoint was inconsequential and whose bodies were sexually possessable.[22]

Yet it is important to note that the penetration of these fallen warriors is not necessarily or automatically feminizing. War wounds that a soldier survives can be symbols of civic manliness, as Loraux has argued, construing the masculine body of Greek and Roman epic as "a body to be opened—but according to the rules."[23] Nor in Euryalus' case is his presumptive status as junior partner in a paiderastic relationship[24] to be held alone accountable for the characterization in 9.431–37. He can be called *vir*, "man," in opposition to both women and underage males: he and Nisus are *viri* together at 9.252, 376, 471.[25] It is noteworthy that the speakers in those passages represent two different sides of the war and one omniscient viewpoint: the reverend Trojan Aletes, the men's Rutulian assailant Volcens (who, to be sure, cannot see Euryalus clearly), and the epic narrator describing the abuse of their corpses.

---

[19] Loraux 1989:120–21, citing (336 n. 42) *Il.* 5.858, 11.352 and 573, 13.830, 14.406, 15.316, 21.398, 22.321. Three of the citations refer to Ajax, two to Hector, one to unnamed Greeks—and two, provocatively, to Diomedes' wounding of Ares.

[20] See n. 34 below.

[21] For the elegiac lover, Greene 2000 gives references to recent discussions; see Skinner 1997:142–43 on Catullus' Attis.

[22] Though in real life questions of social class would inevitably complicate the objectification of boys.

[23] Loraux 1989:118: "un corps à ouvrir, et dans les règles"; generally 108–23. Cf. Walters 1997:40: "a soldier's wounds are honorable, not dishonoring."

[24] See Makowski 1989:2–3, Horsfall 1995:170–71, Williams 1999:116–19. I approximate the Greek spelling (rather than Latinize with paed- or ped-) in order to suggest the Greek paradigm and Roman consciousness of it.

[25] Williams 1999:118. Elsewhere he is a boy, *puer* (5.295; 9.181, 217, 276); Petrini 1997:22 notes that this characterization is confined to the period before his mission.

Euryalus is not necessarily opposed to acceptable masculinity in life, then; only in the view on his death.

Camilla, the warrior maiden and the only woman in our group, is the paradox against which the gender complications of the others' cases may be studied with greater clarity. Her death wound—whose ghastly maternal imagery, symbolically deflowering her, exposes and parodies her sex—would seem to resolve her androgyny and restore her to a more traditionally female objectivity, according to the ancient treatment of sexual difference; her failure to kill Chloreus then underscores her regression to a traditional feminine persona.[26] Already her "womanly love" of Chloreus' fancy dress (11.782), which leads to Camilla's death, sets the stage for her reduction to femininity. Yet the text complicates this seemingly unsurprising result. In the first place, the *amor* for which she stalks Chloreus (and thus becomes the prey of Arruns) is not called a womanly love of fine clothes, but a "womanly love of booty and spoils" (*femineo praedae et spoliorum ardebat amore*). Even if *femineo* here is directed not at the object of this love, but at its degree and quality (as Servius interprets: *impatiens, irrationalis*),[27] the male despoilers of the poem are hardly exempt. One thinks, significantly, of two other objects of the present study, Euryalus and Turnus, whose avid stripping of enemy corpses indirectly kills them. Pallas' dream of stripping Turnus, still half alive, of his gore-soaked armor likewise leads to his death (10.462). Aeneas himself strips Mezentius and dedicates the *spolia* (11.5–8). Camilla's motive is either to dedicate Chloreus' arms to a deity or to wear them herself: neither would be out of place in a male warrior. Far from separating Camilla from her masculine role, the phrase *femineo amore* implicitly feminizes—or at least extends her androgyny to—the men. Likewise, the gaze that descends on her in lines 818–19 does not claim her body as a conquest distinct from our other fallen warriors, who are male. Her death, coming last in our series, does not so much reestablish her femaleness as confirm and retroactively exacerbate a tension of gender in all three scenes. It is again the amorous gaze, alighting on her face once her own "amorous" subjectivity has been cut off, that "feminizes" her according to the conventional schema.

II

The implied viewer of these scenes, then, is assimilable to a schematic adult male Roman citizen, and the view insists on alterity. In discussing the thematics of these passages we are in effect construing, even more than the dead or dying

---

[26] As recently as the simile at 11.721–24 Camilla had been compared to a (masculine) falcon, while her male victim was a (feminine) dove.

[27] His supporting example is 7.345 (on Amata's "womanly anxiety and anger") *femineae ardentem curaeque iraeque coquebant*.

figure, a viewer. There is a strong visual element in each description, often with the verb *videre* present and a viewer specified, but the identity of the explicit viewer differs in each case, and their relations with one another, and with the implicit viewer as we are characterizing him, are problematic.[28] Most deceptively clear-cut is the point of view in the Euryalus passage, which exegetes have frequently identified with that of Nisus, the horror-stricken lover who literally sees the slaying.[29] His perspective is first made clear verbally at 9.396 *videt Euryalum . . .* ("he sees Euryalus . . .") and is implicit in the "free indirect discourse" in 399–401 (*quid faciat?* etc.), vividly representing Nisus' own anguished internal debate at seeing Euryalus cornered; but it already begins insinuating itself around 386: "Nisus is elsewhere, and without thinking ahead had already gotten past the enemy" (*Nisus abit, iamque imprudens evaserat hostis*). The lines on the death of Euryalus betray nothing inconsistent with Nisus' sensibility. One could imagine, for example, that at the moment their relationship comes to its violent end, the bodily causes of his love flash out to the lover as if in a tragic etiology. Immediately afterward, Nisus falls dying on top of Euryalus, as if in a last embrace (9.444–45):

> tum super exanimum sese proiecit amicum
> confossus, placidaque ibi demum morte quievit.

Then, stabbed, he threw himself upon his lifeless friend and there at last found rest in placid death.

Even here we share Nisus' mind: the final phrase seems to reflect the satisfaction of his own desperate desires[30] (the text never smothers his subjectivity, to make him a figure like Euryalus). "At last" in 445 should be read with Nisus' words at 186–87, at the beginning of the episode: "my mind has long urged me to enter into a battle or some great enterprise, and is discontent with placid rest" (*aut pugnam aut aliquid iamdudum invadere magnum / mens agitat mihi, nec placida contenta quiete est*). The irritating languor that spurs him to the expedition,

---

[28] It is in the treatment of the view, incidentally, that Virgil stands apart from his successors Statius, Valerius Flaccus, and Silius, whose sensual death scenes (see n. 2 above) do not superimpose a specific character's viewpoint onto the one they provide us.

[29] Cf. Klingner 1967:564, especially recalling the mood of the two similes: "Der Erzähler sieht Euryalus mit den Augen des Liebenden." Otis 1964:388–89, in his chapter on Virgil's "subjective style," calls Nisus the "sympathetic narrator" of the episode and discerns Nisus' feelings in the similes (cf. Williams 1980:46, Lyne 1987:229–30).

[30] As Servius notes on *placidaque*: "the epithet is either proper to death, or is used because of the feelings of the one dying, who died together with his friend" (*aut proprium est mortis epitheton, aut ex affectu pereuntis dictum est, qui cum amico moriebatur*). Note Servius' refusal to decide between the subjective reading and the other (compare his similar note on 1.691 *placidam per membra quietem*). Cf. Bonfanti 1985:55.

the placid *quies* driven out of his mind by *ardor* and the "terrible desire" (*dira cupido*) that (he speculates in 184–85) has become his god, returns as the end of that very desire, in the form of death.

Narratologists, following Genette, have taught us to distinguish the narration in a text from the focalization, the words from the sentiments that they provoke or entail.[31] Assigning the viewpoint evident in a passage to a definite mind—the poet narrator's or, more interestingly, a character's—accounts for anomalous, gratuitous, or unexpectedly evaluative words (like *candida, pulchros,* and *languescit moriens*). Viewpoint thus becomes identifiable: Is the attitude expressed that of the narrator (as one might normally expect outside of direct speech)? Or is the narrative voice appropriating the attitude of one of the characters? The focalizer provides the answer: Fowler sums up the usual critical use of the focalizer as providing a "*lysis* of a familiar type to literary *problemata.*"[32] Our reading of *Aeneid* 9.431–37, too, is enriched by a definite perspective: one might say, to simplify, that Nisus' gaze adds point to an already almost unbearably poignant description. Focalization by Nisus is a provisional solution to the unsettling description of Euryalus, explaining the sexual objectification of the boy and the consequently heightened sense of loss upon his death.

But if the description at 9.431–37 represents Nisus' viewpoint and reaction, whose do the other passages represent? Putnam assumes that Aeneas focalizes the eroticism in the dead Pallas ("What Aeneas takes note of is . . ."); the verb of seeing at 11.40 (*vidit*), as with Nisus, will then signpost the focalization. No sooner has one accepted this, however, than further questions arise. Does Aeneas really feel sexually attracted to Pallas, dead or alive?[33] How does this attraction ring against their other relations in the poem? Putnam traces verbal links in the episode in Book 11 that tie it to Dido's love in Book 4, and in some sense reenact Dido's "marriage" to Aeneas as a funeral.[34] From this observation, together with the amorous view attached to Aeneas' gaze at 39–40, it is only a short step to the conclusion that Aeneas has a sexual love for Pallas, and that his battle rage in Book 10, after he learns of Pallas' death (not to mention his final avenging of Pallas at 12.948–49), comes from those feelings. As always, however, we are talking about a textual representation, not provable or

[31] See Genette 1980:185–94, 1988:64–78. On recent approaches to these issues in the *Aeneid*, see the introduction to Bonfanti 1985; Fowler 2000b:40–63 (originally published in 1990).

[32] Fowler 2000b:42. This critical use of the focalizer is especially associated with the work of Bal and, in Classics, that of de Jong.

[33] Cf. Williams 1999:118: "some scholars have even detected an erotic element in Virgil's depiction of of the relationship between Aeneas and Evander's son Pallas," with citations on p. 314 n. 90.

[34] Putnam 1985:12–13, noting inter alia that Pallas' bier (11.66 *toros*) uses the same word as Dido's marriage bed/funeral pyre (4.508, 650, 659, 691); cf. p. 82 below. The general comparison of marriage to death is old and traditional, often found, for example, in the grave inscriptions of those who died young.

falsifiable reality, and must consider perspective. For instance, it may be that if Pallas repeats the role of Dido, it is only that we are adopting *his* view of things, not Aeneas'—or even that we, *with* Aeneas, are assimilating Pallas' view. The metaphor Pallas-as-bride resonates against his devotion to or even crush on Aeneas at 10.160–62 ("and Pallas, joined to Aeneas' side . . .")— which repeats his father's youthful crush on Aeneas' father (8.155–68).[35] And the love that inheres in this imagery need not be literal, but can be a metaphor for a nonsexual relation; the verbal repetitions from Book 4 may link it to the themes of national mission and destiny that emerge from comparison (or indeed contrast) with Dido. The erotic language that emerges in 11.39–40 rings against those themes and enriches the metaphor of love in the representation of the dead Pallas, but does not entitle us to make a definitive judgment about Aeneas' feelings toward him, no matter who the text says is looking.

Another focalizer—or a group of them—is of course available in the Pallas scene, if we accept a metaphorical figure operating between characters: the women who surround the body in the lodge at 11.36–38, the "Trojan women with their hair undone in mourning in the customary way" (11.35 *maestum Iliades crinem de more solutae*):

> ut vero Aeneas foribus sese intulit altis
> ingentem gemitum tunsis ad sidera tollunt
> pectoribus, maestoque immugit regia luctu.

But when Aeneas entered the high doorway they raised a great wailing to the heavens, beating their breasts, and the royal dwelling bellowed with mournful lamentation.

Then comes Aeneas' own view of the body and his speech. So he passes through a crowd of mourning Trojan women; in response they raise their lament, and he perforce absorbs their viewpoint sympathetically, imaginatively, registering the snowy complexion and smooth chest as experience tells him his countrywomen might, women ready to sentimentalize such a brutal loss in terms of beauty and even eroticism. Their implicit treatment of Pallas as a fallen compatriot also emerges at 43–44, where Aeneas laments that Pallas will not share in his victory or live to see his new kingdom. Although this scenario might founder if pressed, as a fleeting hint of a perspective it resonates well against the characterization of these figures. It also reinforces Aeneas' role here as representative of his people, and reminds us of the bond between Evander's people and a nation that is still Trojan.[36] But were we to accept focalization (mediated or unmediated) by the attending women as the final word on the source of the gaze here, we would run into a problem that is even more acute

---

[35] Lloyd 1999.

[36] Cf. Babcock 1992:48–49 on these *Iliades* and their role in the transition from Trojan to Roman.

in the Camilla scene, where the source of the amorous gaze at 818–19 is in no way indicated, and the source of the explicit view shifts from one vaguely defined group to another. Her Volscian regiments (the explicit viewers at 800) are general and anonymous; her attacker has fled (806–15); and only her thinly characterized female companions flock around her in alarm (11.805). An Amazonized Alcmanic homoeroticism? Why not. Yet for all that this resonates meaningfully in the surrounding text, we might as well claim as focalizers the anonymous attendants who lift Pallas' corpse onto its bier in 11.67–71. No doubt the sensual description *could* represent their impression of the deceased, but the point is that such an interpretive decision either closes off our inquiry with an unprovable, unfalsifiable explanation or opens it up infinitely wide. The amorous beholder of the body of Pallas remains anonymous and incorporeal, and to identify it definitively with a single character or group of characters would exclude from our inquiry a rich lode of meaning in the *Aeneid*. We would do better to entertain a rhetoric of viewpoint, treating a gaze as a signifying system in which effects are always provisional and ready to change.

Even in the Euryalus passage there are practical reasons not to identify the viewing Nisus seamlessly with the source of the erotic gaze, despite its coincidence with his own feelings. In the poet's own apostrophe and blessing upon of the deaths of Nisus and Euryalus at 9.446–49, Otis, invoking "sympathetic narration," shrewdly sees the coincidence of poet's, reader's, and Nisus' emotions as smoothing over a dislocation of perspective, as the gaze widens its scope from Euryalus to take in both him and Nisus.[37] The very fact that it is in this nodus of viewpoints that Virgil's poetic voice reveals itself most plainly—frames itself as the author of the poem and distinguishes itself from Nisus or any embedded focalizer—should raise doubts about the wisdom of attributing a focalization to a definite character. It is disconcerting to find that the eyes of the focalizer can blink and become the eyes of another, gaining and losing associations in the process. It seems important to distinguish conceptually between the view signposted by (for example) a verb like *vidit*, indicating a literally gazing subject, and the emotional attitude we find in the text, whose provenience may be indeterminate—not to divorce the two, but to acknowledge how they both overlap and diverge. In all cases, the solution offered by a focalizer only leads to a new set of questions.[38]

---

[37] Otis 1963:389: "In the end the episode is assimilated to Roman history, to the ideology of Roman patriotism, but the connexion is poetically possible only because of the sympathy between Nisus, Vergil, and reader that has already been established." Cf. Fowler 2000b:45 on 9.401 *pulchram mortem*.

[38] Cf. Fowler 2000b:62: "the concept of focalization can be used either to solve problems or to create them."

Our indecision about the narrative source of Virgil's imagery should rest not just on our readings of the text itself and how well they solve interpretive problems, but on principle. The term "focalizer," transparently based on "narrator" and analogous to the latter term, irresistibly creates the impression that we are talking about an agent to be found and identified. But there exists no such agent; or if there does, he exists only as a creation of the authorial voice in one of its impersonations—which in turn is a reenactment on the part of the reader.[39] The search for a definite focalizer in a given passage presupposes a definitively recoverable authorial voice in control of its different possible perspectives and distributing them neatly among his characters. But Virgil's narrative is a tissue of metaphors, a horde of personae—including the narrating persona—vying for authority, inflecting one another's meanings in unexpected and unpredictable ways. The choice we are faced with is not just between an internal focalizer and a focalizer to be identified with the narrator;[40] there is no reason why a viewpoint has to originate in any identifiable part of the poem or why it should not contradict and subvert elements of the passage into which it irrupts. We are dealing with a floating identity associated with a particular view and a particular desire; we take on this identity as we read (perhaps adding our own inflections), and the slippage between it and the explicit viewer, Nisus or Aeneas or whomever, can be as interesting and meaningful as the overlap. We should also distinguish this method from those that discern different "voices" within the poem[41] (which, in common with focalization, tend to reduce to a decision between the narrator's—too readily, Virgil's—sentiments and others in the text). Whereas the "vocal" metaphor implies passive listening on the part of the reader, for our present purposes we would do well to prefer the metaphor of the "gaze" not only because it suits the thematics of our passages better, but also because it implies an active—even aggressive—*role*. It is first the poet's, and is his way of constructing the reader within his

---

[39] Compare the refinements of Genette (1988:64): "But the very symmetry between 'Who perceives?' [which he has just said is preferable to "who sees," as less narrow] and 'Who speaks?' is perhaps slightly factitious: the narrator's voice is indeed always conveyed as the voice of a person, even if anonymous, but the focal position, when there is one, is not always identified with a person. . . . So perhaps it would be better to ask, in a more neutral way, *where is the focus of perception?*—and this focus may or may not . . . be embodied in a character." Cf. Walker 1993:370–73 on the author as spectator within his narrative, e.g. 371: "To the many gazes . . . in Polybius' *History* should be added this fundamental gaze of the historian"; Feldherr 1998:4–19 discusses these matters as they concern Livy.

[40] The "deviation" in Fowler's (2000b) concept of "deviant focalization"—where focalizer and narrator are expected to coincide but do not—partly depends on this interpretive choice. Thomas 1998:300 n. 62 suggests "focalizational trespass" as a more useful term.

[41] Two such (deservedly influential) studies are Parry 1963 and Lyne 1987. This critical trope has mainly been used to oppose a doubtful or melancholy attitude within the poem to a triumphalist, pro-Augustan one.

poem—indeed, of casting the reader as a sort of disembodied character.[42] It is our eyelet into the text.

Ancient rhetoricians had the means to recognize the power of images like these as essentially subjective and sensory (especially visual), and implicated in the collaboration between author and audience. Quintilian cites the latter part of 11.40 (on Pallas' wound, *levique patens in pectore vulnus*) as an example of the device of *enargeia* (the Greek term is often translated as "vivid description"), which, he says, "seems not so much to describe as to display; emotions ensue no differently than if we were involved in the very events."[43] *Enargeia* (and equivalent terms) broadly denotes language that conveys a narrative point through the accumulation of attendant circumstances, bringing the scene as nearly into the presence of the audience as words can; it is closely related to ecphrasis and is often treated along with it or as a subspecies of it.[44] Zanker finds its first attestation as a critical term in Virgil's friend Philodemus. A text answering to this description must of course involve the "we" in the events, the *res*, that it describes, and when a viewer is specified by the context, he or she becomes metaphorical with the audiential "we."[45] The anonymous Hellenistic author of the treatise *Peri hermêneias* treats as *enargeia* the report, in the historian Ctesias, of Parysatis' reaction to Cyrus' death, "casting both the mother and the listener into anguish." One thinks of the Virgilian passages' affinities with a "Stabat Mater" motif and the way a concretely personified view (like the Virgin's in a crucifixion) draws us into a scene of loving grief, lending us the viewer's emotions.[46] Thus Quintilian's reading may be taken to supplement

---

[42] Cf. Otis's idea of shared sympathy between Virgil, Nisus, and reader (n. 37 above). With Genette 1988:73 (critiquing Bal), we would have to consider the "focalizing character" a focalizer strictly in a metaphorical sense, as being comparable (as perceiver of the action) with another, primary persona: "For me, there is no focalizing or focalized character: *focalized* can be applied only to the narrative itself, and if *focalizer* applied to anyone, it could only be the person who *focalizes the narrative*—that is, the narrator, or, if one wanted to go outside the conventions of fiction, the *author* himself, who delegates (or does not delegate) to the narrator his power of focalizing or not focalizing."

[43] Quintilian *Inst. or.* 6.2.32 . . . *non tam dicere videtur quam ostendere; et adfectus non aliter, quam si rebus ipsis intersimus, sequentur.* With 11.40 he cites 9.476 *excussi manibus radii revolutaque pensa* and 10.782 *et dulcis moriens reminiscitur Argos;* cf. his citations of Virgil for *enargeia* at 8.3.63, 70. For a Latin treatment of the trope before Virgil's time (under the name of *demonstratio*) see the pseudo-Ciceronian *Rhetorica ad Herennium* 4.68. Identical or related terms are *phantasia, evidentia, illustratio.* These ideas ultimately go back to Aristotle's mimesis theory.

[44] On *enargeia* generally, with the sources, see Zanker 1981. On the role of "vivid description" in constructing an emotional viewpoint for the forensic audience, see Vasaly 1993:104, Innocenti 1994. Hardie 2002:5–7 discusses the quality of presence aimed at by *enargeia* as it concerns Ovid.

[45] Webb 1999:13 is especially well attuned to the social (and hence ideological) basis of the trope. Cf. p. 18 on its semantic nature: "Ancient discussions of verbal representation—*enargeia, hypotyposis, ekphrasis*—thus side-step the problem of whether language can or should represent reality by assuming that words appeal instead to the mental impressions left by reality."

[46] Ctesias *FGrH* 688 F 24 = [Demetrius] *Eloc.* 216 καὶ τὴν μητέρα εἰς ἀγωνίαν ἐμβαλὼν καὶ τὸν ἀκούοντα. On the "Stabat Mater" motif see Gould 1990:68, 292.

Putnam's predication of Aeneas—the named viewer and, as the passage goes on to show, the one affected by the pitiful scene—as the appraiser of the smooth, creamy Pallas, since the use of *enargeia* implicitly attaches viewer to character; or rather, it enlarges the role of viewer to include the audience.[47] The alternative to focalization-as-solution here is to remember the status of focalization as a trope of *enargeia* and accept that the explicit viewer shares a gaze with an implied viewer: the desirous gaze supervenes on and coexists with the gaze of Aeneas, but is not strictly identical with it; and that we readers are being made to share that same gaze—in other words, that the narratology in these two passages cannot be reduced to a hunt for a source within the narrative.

Focalization should be understood not as identity between the narrative attitude and the focalizing character, but as a more indirect relationship: in a word, rhetorically. We are entitled to identify, assimilate, compare (one is driven to ever looser formulations) the attitude we readers are given on a scene with that of a particular character: yes, we might say of *Aeneid* 9.433–37, this sense of erotic appreciation is comparable to the sensibility of Nisus, as we know it.[48] But that is all. The relationship is essentially metaphorical, and partakes of all the slippage, the interplay of likeness and difference, that that entails. Thus focalization in the *Aeneid* participates in the general metaphorics of the poem and therefore necessarily involves intertextuality and ideology: to which we now turn.

III

Our proper concern is the intentions of the text, a retrospective trope for the meaning that we perceive the text to have gotten us to; yet in a strong sense the gaze is Virgil's, if only to make it ours. It is a link, a vantage point shared between writer and reader—and character too, wherever the focalizer coincides with a definite character. In a sense, our active collusion in Virgil's fiction makes us a kind of character, just as his involvement in the narrative that he is creating makes him, qua narrator, a kind of character.[49] And this chain of poetic identities also accommodates Virgil's precursors via the focalizations (along with other narrative turns) that he adapts from them. The intersection between the literary history and the internal dynamics of Virgil's text occurs in the places where we find the poet assuming, adapting, and passing on to us

[47] Cf. Walker 1993 on *enargeia* in the historiographers.

[48] Cf. Laird 1997 on the fixity of boundaries between characters (and other narrative personae) in the *Aeneid*.

[49] Laird 1997:287 notes that Servius' constant reference to Virgil as a *speaker* reflects his role in the poem as "a character who is always present, addressing his audience." Cf. Feeney 1991:57–98 (on the limited viewpoint of Apollonius' narrator).

(whether or not through a particular character) a focalizing role created by a precursor.

"Homer has a habit, in mocking moments," discerns Vermeule, "of treating enemies as lovers, fusing the effects of Eros and Thanatos."[50] We have taken note of a few such moments (pp. 22–23). Among Virgil's epic antecedents, the passages we are discussing most especially recall Iliadic descriptions of corpses, like those of the dead Patroclus or Hector, whose lingering beauty is considered proper to a young warrior,[51] and it may seem curious that parallels to the *Iliad* are not more evident here. When Hermes reassures Priam, "If you went there you would see how dewy-fresh [Hector] lies: the blood has been washed from him, and there is no decay,"[52] the focus is on the seemly integrity of the corpse (compare Thetis on Patroclus at *Iliad* 19.32–33). The Greeks marvel at the stature and appearance of the dead Hector, not desirously, but in amazement at the daunting foe whom Achilles had been able to subdue (*Iliad* 22.370). A youth (dead or, indeed, alive) is *kalos*, "beautiful," in early epic not by virtue of the sensual properties that arouse desire in those who look at him, but because of those physical properties that mark an able warrior in his prime.[53] In the *Aeneid*, as we have seen above, beauty may simply add pathos to a death; it can also add glamour to an entrance, as in the cases of Aventinus and Virbius, or of *pulcherrimus Astyr, Astyr*.[54] The "beautiful death" that Nisus weighs at 9.401 (and subsequently achieves) sublimates beauty into the fine behavior of the warrior, equating it with valor, courage, *virtus*, the Greek *andreia*—literally "manliness," the proper end of the male warrior.[55]

But in the cases of our Euryalus-figures beauty does more. Virgil is rendering explicit an eroticism that, following Classical Athenians, he saw in heroic pairs like Homer's Achilles and Patroclus.[56] Plato's Phaedrus, refashioning

---

[50] Vermeule 1979:157; see in general on love and death 151–77.

[51] See Vernant 1991, esp. 63–67. He suggests that "the youth and beauty of the fallen hero's body reflect the shining glory for which he sacrificed his life" (67); see also pp. 84–91, on *Il.* 22.71–73.

[52] *Il.* 24.418–20 θηοῖό κεν αὐτὸς ἐπελθών / οἷον ἐερσήεις κεῖται, περὶ δ' αἷμα νένιπται, / οὐδέ ποθι μιαρός. Cf. Hecuba at 24.757–59.

[53] Compare Priam's words to Hector at *Il.* 22.71–73. In Tyrtaeus' similar passage (fr. 10.27–30 West) the value of the term *kalos* is placed alongside and in partial contrast to the other entailments of youthful beauty, the admiration of grown men and the desire of women: by bringing out the erotic affinities of martial "beauty," Tyrtaeus throws its non-erotic value into relief. See Prato 1968:99–100.

[54] *Aen.* 7.657, 761; 10.180–81. The repetition of *Astyr* recalls *Il.* 2.671–75 on beautiful Nireus; his starry name, with the epithet *pulcherrimus*, distantly recalls the erotic and funereal epigrams on Aster transmitted under the name of Plato (*A.P.* 7.669–70). As for Virbius, although we do not hear anything about him after his entrance, he vaguely recalls our figures: his mother sent him to war; his father was the resurrected Hippolytus, the virginal youth whose death is best known from Euripides' tragedy.

[55] Loraux 1989:110; cf. Vernant 1991. On the phrase in *Aen.* 9.401 and its Greek and Latin antecedents see Alfonsi 1963.

[56] Cf. Makowski 1989:4–5, Hardie 1994:32, Reed 2004:36–38.

Achilles and Patroclus after his own ideal of *erôs*, is Virgil's precursor: Achilles, he says, chose not only to die for his lover Patroclus' sake, but even to add his own death to his[57]—the very choices made by Nisus for Euryalus at *Aeneid* 9.427 and 444. Consider how impoverished an intertextual reading of Virgilian against Homeric "beautiful" corpses must be: we have to supply so much from the *Aeneid* that is not in the *Iliad*, the earlier epic recedes so far into the field, that the Homeric images are little more than borrowed motifs whose semantics come from elsewhere in the *Aeneid* or the pre-Virgilian tradition or both. In all such bodies, alive or dead, sexuality is potential, as any connotation of a beautiful young body is potential. Of Hermes, Thetis, Priam, the Greek soldiery—the Iliadic characters who gaze upon or speak of the *kalos* bodies of dead warriors—none lets the latent erotic values of their beauty resonate. The difference, to be sure, lies in the eye of the beholder and is a function of narratology: Iliadic corpses are not focalized by a desirer.

Something like Virgil's trope can be traced in art: dying Niobids, for example, both provide the attractions of a beautiful body and elicit pity.[58] In Euripides' *Phoenician Women* 1159–62[59] and *Iphigenia at Aulis* 875, characters pityingly combine beauty and gore in images of a youth's "blond head" cracked open, "newly darkened beard" bloodied, "white skin" put to the sword, and so on. One possible parallel in early Greek epic is tantalizingly beyond our reach for lack of extant texts: Achilles falls in love with the Amazon queen Penthesilea by meeting her gaze at the moment he kills her in battle. Her epithet "beautiful," *eueidês*, at the opening of the *Aethiopid* ascribed to Arctinus (fr. 2B Bernabé) could have prepared for the motif (if it was not a Hellenistic addition to Arctinus' version of the myth: Proclus' summary of the *Aethiopid* does not include it).[60] Aeneas' own gaze upon the image of Penthesilea at 1.490–93, the immediate substitution of Dido for the Amazon queen as object of his and our view, the presence of the Amazon-like Camilla among our three objects of study (in the thick of battle at 11.648–49 she is called an Amazon outright, with special reference to her bared breast; note also the comparison at 659–63), and other details create a fine network in which the Greek story might resonate in the Latin poem.

A direct precedent for Virgil's imagery does not emerge earlier than the later Hellenistic period, in the *Epitaph on Adonis* attributed to Bion of Smyrna.[61]

---

[57] *Symposium* 179E–180A.

[58] Cf. Clarke 1956:298.

[59] See Mastronarde ad loc.

[60] There is a later treatment in Quintus of Smyrna 1.654–74.

[61] In one principal manuscript the poem is anonymous, in the other it is ascribed to Theocritus, but the ascription to Bion is virtually certain: Reed 1997:15. He seems to have been active in the decades around, perhaps shortly before, 100 B.C.E.

A passage at the beginning of this poem paradigmatically eroticizes Adonis, who is dying of a wound sustained while hunting boar (*Adonis* 7–11):

κεῖται καλὸς ῎Αδωνις ἐν ὤρεσι μηρὸν ὀδόντι
λευκῷ λευκὸν ὀδόντι τυπεῖς καὶ Κύπριν ἀνιῇ
λεπτὸν ἀποψύχων· τὸ δέ οἱ μέλαν εἴβεται αἷμα
χιονέας κατὰ σαρκός, ὑπ᾽ ὀφρύσι δ᾽ ὄμματα ναρκῇ,
καὶ τὸ ῥόδον φεύγει τῶ χείλεος.

Beautiful Adonis lies in the mountains, white thigh stricken by a white tusk, and gives grief to Aphrodite as he faintly breathes his last. And his dark blood runs over his snowy flesh, and his eyes grow numb beneath his brows, and the rose flees from his lip.

Here is the unsettling imagery we are looking for: a dying youth is sensually available, the description of his bloodied body combined with an erotic appraisal. Adonis' "white" thigh is a locus both of death and desire. His beauty (presented over and over in the poem by his traditional epithet *kalos*) intensifies the tragedy of the scene by making us feel—with his lover Aphrodite, who is called to witness in lines 3–5—what is being lost. Indeed, Bion is not only a precedent but a model for the view on Virgil's fallen warriors. To take the clearest example, for the death of Camilla, Virgil has almost translated his precursor: compare *Adonis* 10–11 "and his eyes grow numb beneath his brows, and the rose flees from his lip" with *Aeneid* 11.818–19 "her eyes sink cold in death, the former crimson color leaves her face [or lips]." The epithet of "snowy" Pallas recalls Adonis' "snowy flesh." Euryalus too belongs in this group: 9.433, "Euryalus collapsed in death, and the blood ran over his beautiful limbs," strongly recalls the blood running over Adonis' flesh in *Adonis* 9–10 "and his dark blood runs over his snowy flesh," especially since both passages are preceded by an account of the weapon (boar's tusk, Volcens' sword) plunging into the white body (μηρὸν . . . λευκόν, *candida pectora*) of the victim.[62]

The poem continues (*Adonis* 11–14):

ἀμφὶ δὲ τήνῳ
θνᾴσκει καὶ τὸ φίλαμα τὸ μήποτε Κύπρις ἀποίσει.
Κύπριδι μὲν τὸ φίλαμα καὶ οὐ ζώοντος ἀρέσκει,
ἀλλ᾽ οὐκ οἶδεν ῎Αδωνις ὅ νιν θνᾴσκοντα φίλασεν.

And on it [his lip] dies the kiss that Cypris will never carry away. To Cypris the kiss is pleasing even though he is not alive; but Adonis does not know that she has kissed him when he is dead.

---

[62] For a more detailed comparison of Virgil's passages with Bion's, see Reed 2004. Other Latin poets of the late Republic and early Empire also echo this poem, which was evidently well known (Reed 1997:60–61).

A precedent for the sentiment in 13 might be Aeschylus fr. 137 Radt (from the *Myrmidons*) "and yet they [kisses?] are not repulsive to me, for I love,"[63] spoken by Achilles over the dead Patroclus, but it is unknown whether that body itself was described in the exuberant terms we are discussing here. Adonis, on the other hand, with his rosy lips and white flesh set off by the dark blood, is a tableau of fleshliness, after which Aphrodite's desire for a kiss and her pleasure in it seem almost natural; in the verb ἀρέσκει ("is pleasing") lingers enough of his beauty to make her pleasure more than the assuagement of sorrow in memory that Achilles seems only to derive.[64] Her plea for a last kiss at lines 45–50, with its profusion of metaphors for Aphrodite's frantic passion, will retroject explicitly erotic love into 11–14 and heighten the sensual treatment of Adonis' body that lies behind that passage. The sensuality of the color fading from Camilla's face or lips—the very targets of a kiss—benefits from these lines.

Just before that plea, Aphrodite reaches the dying Adonis after a search through thorny mountain glens (*Adonis* 40–42):

ὡς ἴδεν, ὡς ἐνόησεν Ἀδώνιδος ἄσχετον ἕλκος,
ὡς ἴδε φοίνιον αἷμα μαραινομένῳ περὶ μηρῷ,
πάχεας ἀμπετάσασα κινύρετο, "μεῖνον Ἄδωνι."

When she saw, when she spied his unstaunchable wound, when she saw the gory blood on his languishing thigh, she spread her arms and keened, 'Wait, Adonis.'

Here is the narratological crux, the viewpoint of Aphrodite—implicit throughout the poem—made explicit. The passage on Pallas (11.39–41 "When [Aeneas] saw the bolstered head of snowy Pallas, and his face, and the wound from the Ausonian spear gaping in his smooth chest, he spoke thus in tears") closely follows the structure of *Adonis* 40–42: "when he/she saw" with the mortally wounded body as object, leading into tearful speech. Most obviously here, Virgil does not simply reach for Bion's sensual language, but for his language of gazing. He takes up the very architecture of viewpoint in Bion's poem and uses it to configure the view on his characters—but he changes the nature of the viewer. The descriptions of Adonis in the *Epitaph on Adonis* are constantly identifiable with Aphrodite's point of view; the narrator and minor characters (the mourning deities in lines 80–96) adopt her love and grief. Virgil's voluptuous modifiers adumbrate a more labile focalization. The authorial impersonations that are characters and those that are of precursors are on principle

---

[63] καὶ μήν, φιλῶ γάρ, ἀβδέλυκτ' ἐμοὶ τάδε.

[64] Cf. Aeschylus fr. 135 and 136 Radt: σέβας δὲ μηρῶν ἁγνὸν οὐκ ἐπῃδέσω, / ὦ δυσχάριστε τῶν πυκνῶν φιλημάτων ("You had no respect for [my?] pure reverence of [your?] thighs, ungrateful for [my?] many kisses") and μηρῶν τε τῶν σῶν εὐσεβὴς ὁμιλία ("and the reverent companionship of your thighs")—again, the eroticism is not focused on the corpse itself or on the present.

interchangeable, a continuum potentially encompassing all the characters and models in the poem and (intertextually) in any other poem; critical interest lies in the varied paths the substitutions take, where they are bent, where they are blocked. When Virgil impersonates Bion impersonating Aphrodite, he turns Aphrodite's gaze into something more fluid and capacious.

We thus find in the *Aeneid* a network of clear echoes of the *Epitaph on Adonis* and similar descriptions, and this network coincides neatly with the network of Euryalus-figures—for the sake of our intertextual reading we might now call them "Adonis-figures." Lausus, the son of the exiled Etruscan king Mezentius, is a fourth Adonis-figure, despite the less overt eroticism in his death scene. Like the other three, his body receives a detailed description (rather than a brief "obituary"). Like Euryalus, he was introduced with a remark on his supernal beauty: "whom no other surpassed in beauty except for the body of Laurentian Turnus" (7.649–50 *quo pulchrior alter non fuit excepto Laurentis corpore Turni*). His slayer Aeneas' reaction to his death shows the same Bion-derived structure as in the passage on Pallas (10.821–32):

> at vero ut vultum vidit morientis et ora,
> ora modis Anchisiades pallentia miris,
> ingemuit miserans graviter dextramque tetendit,
> et mentem patriae subiit pietatis imago. . . .
>   . . . terra sublevat ipsum
> sanguine turpantem comptos de more capillos.

But when the son of Anchises saw the countenance and the face of the dying [boy], the face wondrously pale, he groaned heavily in pity and stretched out his hand, and the image of his own devotion [*pietatis*] to his father came into his mind. . . . He lifted Lausus from the earth, his stylishly well-coifed hair sullied with blood.

Pallas' laying-out at 11.39–67 is an expanded doublet of this scene: in both, Aeneas beholds the deceased and utters his lament (which in each case begins with the apostrophe "pitiable boy," *miserande puer*), and the youth is lifted from the ground.[65] One recalls that at 10.433–36, in the thick of battle, Lausus and Pallas were compared for their youth, beauty, and imminent deaths at the hands of greater warriors.

In a description whose wording recalls the stabbing of Euryalus, Aeneas had "driven his powerful sword through the youth's midriff and buried it [in him] entirely" (815–16 *validum namque exigit ensem / per medium Aeneas iuvenem totumque recondit*), thrusting it through "the tunic that his mother had embroidered with supple gold" (10.818 *et tunicam molli mater quam neverat auro*). Once again, hints of an equation between the slaying of an unmarried youth

[65] Cf. Conte 1986:176.

and defloration enrich this scene and increase its pathos; Fowler finds particularly suggestive the image in *implevitque sinum sanguis* (819 "and blood filled the fold [of the tunic]"), with *sinum* overtly enlarging upon *tunicam* in 818 but making one think of its sense "lap,"[66] and in this connection the reference to Lausus' mother recalls the conventional scene of a bride's parting from her mother. The gaze that is common to Euryalus and Pallas reflects back onto Lausus an eroticism that otherwise is quite latent. The conventions of visual beauty are not so much as hinted at until the last line, "his stylishly well-coifed hair sullied with blood," where "the neat hair described by *comptus* is a mark of the attractive young man."[67] This dandyish feature, together with Lausus' gold-embroidered tunic and its reminiscence of his mother's care, evokes a touching boyish vanity. Wiltshire links Lausus' cloak to that woven for Euryalus by his mother (9.488) and involves them both in a complex of cloaks made by their mothers for doomed boys.[68]

Unlike the appealingly "gleaming white" Euryalus and "snowy" Pallas (let alone the rosy Camilla), Lausus' face is flatly pallid in death: his paleness sums up the difference in tone between this scene and the three similar ones. But the adjective *pallentia* has the double effect of forestalling and introducing sensuality in conjunction with the insistently corporeal *ora, ora*, which reiterates a sort of buzzword that we will also see in the passages on Pallas and Camilla, here (as with Pallas) focusing our attention on the boy's paiderastically attractive beardless aspect.[69] Lausus' fancy get-up also lends him a little of the sensuality of the others, when read in anticipation of the scene of Pallas' laying-out: at 11.72–75, directly after the flower similes, Aeneas shrouds the body with a robe that Dido had made, "interweaving the fabric with gold thread" (75 *tenui telas discreverat auro*). In the *molli auro* of Lausus' tunic ("supple gold," literally "soft gold"), the epithet is significant. The suggestion in *molli auro* that he himself is "soft," almost a mama's boy, is piquant enough in the scene of his suicidal valor, and takes on the incongruity of the other descriptions when we read it alongside the paiderastic "soft violet" to which Pallas is compared (11.69).

We have characterized the gaze on these victims as erotic and pitying, as imperious and masculine, and as occupying both personal and political levels

---

[66] Fowler 1987:194–95.

[67] Harrison 1991:269. See Harrison ibid., on *de more*, "stylishly." Virgil's model is Euphorbus' elaborate hair at *Il*. 17.51–52; again, viewpoint is made more pointed and relevant to an *Iliad*-derived image. But the wording of the Latin (literally "from the earth he lifts [Lausus] himself who sullies stylishly coiffed hair with blood") leaves open the possibility that it is *Aeneas*' well-coiffed hair that Lausus's corpse sullies; cf. Iarbas' derisive remark on Aeneas' perfumed hair at 4.216.

[68] Wiltshire 1989:54.

[69] The same enjambment is used at 6.495–96, where Aeneas sees the still grievously wounded figure of his brother-in-law Deiphobus in the Underworld; Deiphobus, killed as a recent bridegroom the night Troy was taken, resembles our figures in certain ways.

of the poem. The position of dominance over these four warriors that the gaze on them gives the reader creates an opposition not only in terms of gender (understood broadly), as discussed above. A national opposition is also implied, and it too involves a sense of dominance, even conquest (not necessarily metaphorical in this poem). Euryalus is a Trojan, Pallas an Arcadian Greek settled in Latium, Lausus an Etruscan, Camilla an Italian, specifically a Volscian from Privernum. The first two die fighting for Aeneas, the latter two against him, but all four belong to peoples that will be absorbed into the new nation that is eventually to become Rome. The retrospective sense of conquest is most obvious with regard to the Etruscan and Italian, Rome's earliest conquests; but Greeks too will fall under Roman sway. The case of Troy is more complicated: Trojan itself (as later chapters will discuss) is a nationality destined to be left behind by the rising race of Rome; moreover, Trojan can be grouped, in this poem as in fifth-century Greek literature, with "Oriental" peoples (like Anatolians, Syrians, Phoenicians, and Egyptians), over whom Rome will gain dominion. The shared objectification of four fallen warriors who come from different nations both symbolically unites those nations as constituents of a greater, and subjects them to an implicitly Roman eye. The gaze establishes difference. It delineates a subject position empty of nationality in itself, but defined by opposition to other nationalities: "we" are not Trojan, not Greek, not Etruscan, not Italian. This empty nationality we are invited to identify as Roman; the Roman thus takes its lineaments and purpose from what it is not. The Roman, above all, is the subject, not the object, of a domineering gaze.

Yet this interpretation of our cluster of scenes is schematic, indeed overschematic, proceeding from only a limited perspective. The text, after all, directs upon these four victims not triumphant scorn, but pity—and not just pity, but sympathy. (I am not speaking, of course, of the kind of definitive sympathy, authorizing a general interpretation of the poem, that rouses critics to wholesale agreement with, say, Dido on the one side, or Aeneas on the other, but rather of an always contingent narratological effect.) There is more to these fallen warriors than passivity and contrast with the Roman. They represent peoples who, in the settlement negotiated by Jupiter and Juno in Book 12 and in reality, will ultimately meld into the Roman nation; all are conceivable as proto-Romans, regardless of what side of Aeneas' war they stand on. Aeneas' eulogies of both Lausus and Pallas lament in them the qualities that the poem characteristically upholds as essentially Roman: Aeneas' own paradigmatic qualities, in fact. In both of them, Aeneas recognizes scions of races that will have a part in his settlement, though themselves tragically fated not to share in that future. He says as much over the dead Pallas (who, more obviously than Lausus, might have taken part in the settlement): "Did Fortuna enviously steal you from me, pitiable boy, that you might not see my realm?" (11.42–44 *tene . . . miserande puer . . . invidit Fortuna mihi, ne regna videres nostra*). He implies something of the same for Lausus whose corpse he also addresses as "pitiable boy" (10.825 *miserande puer*)—using, as over Pallas, the words he heard his father use to Marcellus in the Underworld when exalting him as a paradigmatic Roman.[70] To be sure, one is free to see Aeneas in both places as sugaring over with a tendentious melancholy the fact that his very foundational mission has killed Pallas and Lausus (Anchises' lament over Marcellus is open to such an interpretation)—that is, as sidestepping a latent paradox, de-ironizing the tragedy. But either way, the sympathy directed toward the Euryalus-figures at their deaths becomes sympathy for would-be Romans—and particularly for young people who will never have a chance to contribute to the great enterprise that the *Aeneid* foretells.

We noted above that in the case of Euryalus' death, the apparent source of the gaze slides from his lover Nisus to the narrator of the poem, who pronounces over both of them a blessing that links both young men indissolubly to the Roman future, and to the *Aeneid* (9.446–49):

> Fortunati ambo! si quid mea carmina possunt,
> nulla dies umquam memori vos eximet aevo,
> dum domus Aeneae Capitoli immobile saxum
> accolet imperiumque pater Romanus habebit.

Fortunate pair! If my song has any power, no day will ever remove you from the record of time, as long as the house of Aeneas abides on the immovable rock of the Capitol and the Roman Father [or "a Roman father"][71] keeps his throne.[72]

Speculation on Euryalus' place in the future order enters Ascanius' promise of their future companionship at 9.275–80 (where by contrast Ascanius treats Nisus as an old-time Iliadic hero, promising him lavish gifts) and, tragically, in his mother's lament at 490–91: "Where shall I go on to? Or what land holds your body and rent limbs now, and lacerated corpse?" (*quo sequar? aut quae nunc artus avulsaque membra / et funus lacerum tellus habet?*). He will be buried a stranger in a strange land—is this home? Even the Oriental identity that inheres in Euryalus' Trojanness (and also in Lausus' "Lydian" Etruscanness) is by no means strictly opposed to Romanness. We have already (p. 9) raised the assimilation that can emerge from the poem's opposition between Rome and "Tyrian" Carthage. Later chapters will explore the persistence of the Trojan within Roman identity as a link to an Oriental past that will prevent Rome's conquest of the East, and ultimately of Egypt, from being only a conquest, and

---

[70] Cf. p. 153 below.

[71] See Toll 1997:50 n. 55 on this phrase and its meaning for both poetry and national and familial survival.

[72] Cf. Williams 1999:118. Otis' emphasis on the place of Roman ideology in the nexus of viewpoint here (n. 37 above) is very germane to our concerns.

make it much more like an inheritance. The images here interpret the multinational nature of the war as a prediction of the nature of Rome.

Quite apart from the imagery that their death scenes share, modern critics have emphasized that Euryalus (along with Nisus), Lausus, Pallas, and Camilla participate in a group of unmarried, childless young warriors whose deaths involve the broad themes of the poem.[73] Euryalus' mother (9.473–502)[74] and Pallas' father (11.139–81) react at pathos-inspiring length to their sons' deaths; in light of Diana's account of her father's exile and narrow survival (11.539–66), Camilla's death too becomes emblematic of the lost young generation of a family. Lausus' devotion to his father (who returns it) leads to his death—a condition that expressly moves Aeneas.[75] In this emphasis we can see a tragic inversion of the poem's vision of generational progress and of national destiny as an inheritance, most clearly embodied in the descent from Dardanus to Anchises to Aeneas to Ascanius (the last two of whom survive to become Roman in some proleptic way, a definition of Romanness gradually inhering in their actions and self-awareness) and down through the generations ultimately to Augustus, in whom the culmination of the lineage coincides with the culmination of the destiny Jupiter promises for Rome. An initiatory paradigm is relevant: Euryalus, Lausus, and Pallas are in transition from boyhood to manhood, learning to become adult warriors. Pallas' emotional departure from home at Aeneas' side, Lausus' defense of his father, and Euryalus' eagerness to participate in Nisus' plan are all emblematic of a boy's adherence to an older model, an attempt to *become* that model.[76] The analogy with the transmission of national identity is patent.[77] Later chapters will compare our four figures to Turnus and Marcellus, doomed youths who even more critically embody the problem of national identity in the poem. What is particularly significant is the failure of these fallen warriors to continue national or family lines: in context the symbolic message is that the future has passed to a new race. I would

[73] See especially Heinze 1915:159; Hardie 1994:14-19, 25; Petrini 1997 passim.

[74] She is also prominent at 9.283–302; see Babcock 1992 on her and the other remaining Trojan women among Aeneas' followers, especially in connection with the transition from a Trojan identity. Note also Euryalus' father, *bellis adsuetus Opheltes*, introduced by Euryalus at 9.201 as a model to live up to. On parallels between Euryalus and Lausus in this regard, and how they influence the themes of the last third of the poem, see Egan 1980 (cf. Petrini 1997:23–24). Servius compares the lament over Pallas in 11.42 to that over Euryalus in 9.479: *nam [adlocutio] locis omnibus commovet miserationem, ab aetate, a tempore, a vulnere, a spe parentis* ("For [the address] in all particulars arouses pity, because of his age, the occasion, the wound, the hopes of his father").

[75] On this crucial aspect of Aeneas' reaction see Johnson 1976:72–74.

[76] Evander's recollections of admiring and emulating Anchises parallel both his son's emulation of Aeneas and Aeneas' own emulation of Anchises (cf. Lloyd 1999). Petrini 1997 *passim* discusses the relevance of initiation as a metaphor in the stories of our four characters and others; see also Hardie 1997:321.

[77] Hardie 1994:17 notes the connection of the formation of the adult male warrior and the definition of national identity in the *Aeneid*; cf. 25–26 on Ascanius as initiand.

connect this loss of the future with the loss, narratologically expressed, of consciousness and agency on the part of all four: subjectivity symbolically passes to a different self. The sorrow that suffuses the viewpoint on them could be interpreted (though by no means exclusively) as a reflex of adult male anxiety, predicated on potential identification. Warrior, adult, Roman citizen—all converge as the goal of human development, ontologic or phylogenetic, that lies at the heart of Virgil's epic, and our four warriors are negative examples of this development. Since that goal converges figuratively with the ultimate goal of Roman identity, their deaths become sites of reflection on just what it means to be Roman.

Silverman, drawing upon Lacanian psychoanalysis and Althusser's concept of ideological interpellation in the formation of subjectivity, analyzes the (erotic) cinematic gaze as a way of constructing the viewer as a subject within a fiction, analogous to the real-life constructions within which our egos are actually formed—or not just analogous to them, but identical to them in all important respects.[78] Aside from the congenial linkage in her theory between author, audience, and character as narrative personae, the ideological component of her analysis suggests for our scenes a way of drawing the reader—indeed, interpellating the reader—through a fantasmatics of desire into a particular, complicated Romanness. The gazing persona provisionally serves us as a convincing ego, its desirous nature the vehicle of a fiction of national identity.[79] An allegory of this process occurs in Anchises' words to Aeneas in Book 6: *tu regere imperio populos, Romane, memento* ("You, Roman, remember to rule the nations with imperial sway")—Aeneas, the overt addressee, is hailed directly into Anchises' version of Roman identity.

Adonis is a most apt persona on which to calque our figures, who would be easily comparable with him even without the echoes of Bion's version of the myth. Like him they are young, beautiful, slain. Adonis is passive, dominated by the mourning goddess; a boy, effeminized in certain respects, but characteristically treated with pity. He rarely speaks in extant versions of his myth (in Bion's version he is never even sentient). In sum, he is a paradigmatic dead lover, a supreme paragon of the figure in which Halperin, wondering about its recurrence in literature and art, is inclined to see a kind of extreme of the very qualities that incite desire: "What men value in sleeping, dying, or dead lovers is their turning aside from the subjects who desire them. . . . In turning away from us, the dead lover enacts the ruses of erotic desire itself, mimicking the characteristic unfindability of the erotic object, its simultaneous immanence in

---

[78] See esp. Silverman 1992:21–23. The reproduction of Mategna's St. Sebastian on the cover of her book nicely adapts Silverman's thesis to our topic.

[79] Cf. Feldherr 1995, who discusses how the athletic competitions in Book 5 mold their spectators—and the "spectators" who read—in the likeness of Roman citizens. His discussion of Mnestheus in particular (pp. 259–61) involves a metaphorics of persona.

and transcendance of its material medium, its tendency to recede from the lover in his every attempt to possess it."[80] Halperin's retreat from the pathetic aspect of the theme in favor of its potential for a paradoxical gratification speaks well to the sense of pleasure that Virgil's focalizer shows, alongside the horror and grief.

In the matter of national identity, too, Adonis is a most apt mythological model. In Greek mythology he was constantly derived from the East, either from Phoenicia or (later) the Phoenician areas of Cyprus.[81] The quality of "softness," *mollitia,* in the three boys' descriptions, in conjunction with the implicit Adonis-image, creates a sense of what Greek calls *habrosynê,* an Eastern, foreign voluptuousness, both coveted and under suspicion.[82] For the Romans he is at the same time Greek, derived from Greek culture (Virgil's source for these images is a Greek poet from Smyrna in Asia Minor); both Greek and Oriental can fall on the far side of the ethnic boundary from Roman and are susceptible to the same charges from a Roman viewpoint. We shall be particularly concerned with the way our four characters resonate against characters who pose questions of national origins and identity more insistently than they do: Turnus and Dido especially. They, too, are in different ways involved with Adonis.

Virgil's gaze is imperial; in it, desire becomes a figure for imperial subjection and subsumption—a gathering-in under a single national identity. We should keep the subsumption as much in mind as the subjection: the gaze that positions the reader in opposition to these fallen warriors has a capacity for openness and assimilation—it creates a foil against which to identify, rather than an absolute antitype. The subjectivity of the gazer is in fact receptive; the gaze changes the gazer, instituting a dialectic—analogous to the dialectic that is Jupiter's gift to the Romans, "empire without end" (1.279), which under its autocratic surface conceals a perpetual give-and-take between commander and commanded. The poem's readerly persona is already a kind of ktistic desirer: first, by the teleological, almost erotic nature of plot itself, which this poem sedulously exploits and binds to its story of national foundations,[83] and more specifically because desire is itself a figure in the *Aeneid* for national foundation.

---

[80] Halperin 2006:17, citing Girard's reading of Freud's essay on narcissism (Girard 1978:391–405). Cf. Haggerty 2004 on the way the poetry of grief tends to trope the apartness of death as *erôs.*

[81] Earliest in [Hesiod] *Cat.* fr. 139 M–W and Panyassis fr. 27 Bernabé, deriving him from Phoenicia; from Cyprus first in Antimachus fr. 102 West, Plato Comicus fr. 3 Kassel/Austin. In fact the Greek cult of Adonis derived from a Syro-Palestinian adaptation of the Mesopotamian ritual lament for Tammuz; the Greeks later identified various Near Eastern lamented gods with Adonis.

[82] On the ideology of *habrosynê* in Archaic and Classical Greece see Kurke 1992.

[83] See esp. Barthes 1973, Brooks 1984 and 1993; and Quint 1993:50–96 on the *Aeneid,* with special attention to the ideological aspects of its narratology. Cf. pp. 149–50 below.

In our four scenes this is most clear in Aeneas' speech over Pallas, in which the desire in the gaze is transfigured into hopes for a future nation. But the metaphor that emerges from these scenes will reemerge at key moments in other forms, inviting us to read Aeneas' Roman mission as a kind of love or desire. At 4.347 Aeneas equates Italy with *amor*, a substitute for—or sublimation of—his love affair with Dido (*hic amor, haec patria est*: "*this* is love, *this* is home"). At 6.889 he will leave the Underworld spurred on (literally "kindled") to his mission by "love of the fame that was to come" (*incenditque animum famae venientis amore*). Nor should we forget that Aeneas' mother is the goddess of love and that his ultimate object, *Roma*, is, by a well-known anagram, *amor*.[84] And since desire is fundamentally about trying to make up a lack, a difference, it is an apt figure for nationality in a poem in which a final imperial identity proves elusive.

[84] Skulsky 1985:449–50 (for a general treatment of the anagram see Stanley 1963, who connects its use to the early Roman reception of Hellenistic philosophy, citing Ennius in particular). See further p. 109 on the anagram, and pp. 149–50 on *amor* as a ktistic metaphor.

Chapter Two

TURNUS

I

It could be argued that the network of themes we have been tracing in our images naturally converges on Turnus—the one prominent fallen youth of the *Aeneid* who is *not* given a sensual description at his death—and that in some sense his death at the end of the poem makes each of our fallen warriors his prototype. Turnus too is a handsome young man whose aged father and failure to produce offspring are prominent in his story. The very fact of his age is noteworthy, since it is unspecified in earlier and contemporary surviving accounts: Virgil has elaborated Turnus' scant role as a (would-be) bridegroom into a fuller image of striving youth.[1] The abrupt ending of the epic is made all the more abrupt when we miss the sensual description that the passages on the comparably developed figures have conditioned us to expect. The moment of Camilla's death—*vitaque cum gemitu fugit indignata sub umbras* (11.831)—echoes in the last line of the last book of the poem (12.952), and sends the reader back not only to her death, but through it potentially to all the Adonis-images in the war.

Every motif of a stereotyped Adonis-scene can be related to Turnus, though fragmented and recomposed, scattered over his story and recombined with different motifs. In this regard he is not so much the center of our group as the climactic figure for whom they provide the language; their themes of sex, family, and nationhood, and the same narratological and intertextual strategies, spell out his special status as an antitype of the Roman. If we look away from the death of Turnus we find that a desirous gaze *is* directed at him, but that the moment is displaced, so to speak, to a spot earlier in Book 12. At 12.216–21 Turnus and Aeneas declare formal oaths in preparation for their decisive single combat:

> at vero Rutulis impar ea pugna videri
> iamdudum et vario misceri pectora motu,
> tum magis ut propius cernunt non viribus aequos.
> adiuvat incessu tacito progressus et aram

[1] Cato *Orig.* fr. 9–11 Peter, Dionysius of Halicarnassus *A.R.* 1.64.2–3, Livy 1.2.1, Justin 43.1.11. Cf. Thomas 1998:275 on how Virgil rescues from "an increasingly sophisticated and national consciousness" a more defensible Turnus. In this regard his youth is a correlative to his greater political complexity and pitiability.

220   suppliciter venerans demisso lumine Turnus
       pubentesque genae et iuvenali in corpore pallor.

But the fight seemed unfair to the Rutulians, and by now their hearts were stirring with conflicting emotions—even more so when they saw from close by that the combatants were unequal in strength.[2] [This impression] was abetted by Turnus, as he came forward with silent tread and in suppliant fashion paid worship at the altar with downcast eyes, and by his downy cheeks and the pallor on his youthful body.

What do these physical characteristics—silent tread, downcast eyes, downy cheeks, youthful body, pallor—mean for Turnus? When we last saw him he was happily arming for this morning's combat, fired by the prospect of marriage to the blushing Lavinia, scorning Aeneas as an Oriental effeminate, and vaunting like a bellowing bull (70–106); when we next see him he will be seething again with the renewed battle (325 *fervidus ardet*). Here, as he fulfills a lesser role in the rites over which Aeneas and Latinus preside, he is mysteriously subdued. Heinze's insight that Turnus' silence and downward gaze betray his flagging spirit as the moment of decision approaches[3] (for which his pallor might be taken as an even surer sign) may be too unnuanced: reverence, deference, and trepidation are all possible causes for these physical signs, perhaps mingled and filtered through one another. His own sentiments in this externally described scene remain unexpressed. What is really at issue here is the comparability of this gaze with that of Turnus' men, whom *videri* and *cernunt* at 216–18 mark as the explicit viewers (of a youth whose lowered eyes occlude his own visual agency). The gaze revaluates his youth, which at 12.19 indicates (to Latinus) his hotheadedness, in need of mature counsel. Since we last saw Turnus, we and his sister Juturna have been made privy to Juno's awareness that the Latins are doomed and Turnus is in imminent danger (134–60). "But now I see this youth rushing to meet a fate he is no match for," Juno advises Juturna (149 *nunc iuvenem imparibus video concurrere fatis*). As the Rutulians awaken to this awareness, line 221 vividly brings to the reader's eye, as to theirs, the extreme youthfulness of their prince, matched against a battle-hardened man.[4]

What exactly do they see? Turnus was "most beautiful," *pulcherrimus*, at his first mention in the poem (7.55), but the present description is different in the now familiar way. "Downy cheeks" and "youthful body" are flagrant signals of

---

[2] With Mynors I print Schrader's conjecture *viribus aequos* in 218 for MS *viribus aequis* (which implies a lacuna or at least a very harsh ellipsis); the sense in either case is that Turnus is not Aeneas' equal in strength.

[3] Heinze 1915:212 ". . . es ist ein fein beobachteter Zug, daß gerade nach dieser fieberhaften Erregung ihm im Angesicht der Entscheidung der Mut entsinkt."

[4] Cf. Sabbadini 1889:45. Their fears are realized at 12.905: "his knees collapsed, his blood froze solid" (*genua labant, gelidus concrevit frigore sanguis*).

the *sermo amatorius*: the last line of the passage is thus composed of conventional erotic language, except for the negative *pallor*, which replaces youthful
candor and signals that something is wrong.[5] Macrobius notes the sense of
pathos (*pathos misericordiae*) that comes with Turnus' youth in this line.[6] The
most striking term is *pubentesque genae*, denoting as it does the conventional
acme of paiderastic beauty.[7] That reading is preferable, on balance, to the variant *tabentesque genae*, "wasted cheeks," read by Donatus and picked up by a few
ninth-century manuscripts.[8] Either word appears first in the *Aeneid* and only
once elswhere in this poem (*tabentes* at 1.173, and *pubentes*, of downy plants,
at 4.514). The root of the verb *tabeo*, "to waste away" (from disease or the like),
is *tabes*, referring at its strongest to a draining, liquefying putrescence, or more
mildly to a consumption or sickly dwindling. At 1.173 the verb reflects the
uncleanness of seawater (*et sale tabentes artus in litore ponunt*, "they lay their
limbs, dripping with salt, on the beach"). Here it could theoretically suggest
"dripping with tears or anxious perspiration," but the participle alone would
carry that sense with difficulty. Moreover, a reading that gives Turnus "wasted"
or "dripping cheeks" is suspect here because the rest of the passage makes his
age and relative prowess the problem. At the very least, *tabentes* would imply
some blatant debility, an objective source for the men's concern that is otherwise unknown to the text and untraceable in Turnus's own actions (*pallor* more
delicately registers a trepidation that may be unconscious on his part, but over-
estimated by his anxious men).[9] By contrast, what is exceptional about *pubentesque* is what is exceptional about *iuvenali corpore*, whose potential
connotation of young strength (as at 5.475) gives way, in this contrast with
Aeneas, to an uneasy combination of weakness and youthful allure.

The basis for the Rutulians' concern finds no parallel in the most obvious
model for this scene, the death of Hector in *Iliad* 22, where the apprehensive
speeches of his father and mother are not motivated by any such view of
Hector. There is some precedent for the view at *Iliad* 22.124–25, where Hector
himself imagines Achilles killing him "naked, like a woman" (γυμνὸν ἐόντα

[5] Cf. the dying Lausus' "face wondrously pale" (10.822 *ora, ora modis . . . pallentia miris*) and,
by contrast, Putnam's remark on Pallas' *niveus* body (p. 20 above). On the amatory overtones of
iuvenalis, "youthful," see Pichon 1966:179–80.

[6] Macrobius *Sat.* 4.3.1, 4; cf. Sabbadini 1889:45, Fowler 1919:64–65, Stok 1989:39 (citing the
seventeenth-century humanist de la Cerda).

[7] Williams 1999:19; cf. p. 21 above. Pandarus' beardless cheeks add pathos to his gruesome death
at 9.751: he is younger than his young slayer Turnus.

[8] For references see Stok 1989:29–30.

[9] Stok, who offers the most detailed discussion of the passage, wants the draining or reduction that
tabentes entails to refer not to Turnus' cheeks, but to the blood within them: "drained of blood,"
whence the pallor (1989:48–49). This would be a very strained metonymy, and the quotations he
brings to bear do not offer a parallel; they rather refer verbs in *tab-* to long-term wasting (of the
body, limbs, etc.) from illness, lovesickness, or the like—for which there is no time or evidence at
Aen. 12.221.

αὔτως ὥς τε γυναῖκα); at least, related ideas about sex and gender underlie both passages. But the scene before the altar directs the Hector model elsewhere. The situation here echoes 1.474–78, one of the scenes of the Trojan War that moved Aeneas in Juno's temple in Carthage:

> parte alia fugiens amissis Troilus armis
> infelix puer atque impar congressus Achilli,
> fertur equis curruque haeret resupinus inani,
> lora tenens tamen; huic cervixque comaeque trahuntur
> per terram, et versa pulvis inscribitur hasta.

In another section Troilus, his weapons abandoned, an unlucky boy and an unequal opponent for Achilles, is carried along in flight by his horses and clings to the empty chariot upside down, still holding the reins. His head and hair are dragged along the ground and the dust is scrawled by his inverted spear.

Except for the death and ransoming of Hector (1.483–87), every scene in this series of pictures—the plundering of Rhesus' sleeping camp, the women's supplication in the temple of Minerva, the heroics of an Amazon warrior—is answered by one in the Italian war later in the *Aeneid*, delineating the "second Trojan War" that the Sibyl foretells (6.83–97) and pointing up its repetition and, ultimately, reversal of the original.[10] Her "new Achilles" (6.89)—who seems to predict Turnus, if we interpret *Latio iam partus* as "already born in Latium"—will unexpectedly emerge in the very person of Aeneas (we can equally well take *Latio* as a dative of disadvantage: "to the detriment of Latium"); he will kill Hector in the person of Turnus, whose death scene verbally echoes Hector's in the *Iliad*.[11] In Juno's temple, however, Hector pointedly does *not* prefigure Turnus, whom the *Aeneid* will not show ransomed by his aged father (a suggestion Turnus offers at the moment of his defeat). It is rather Hector's younger brother Troilus who prefigures the Rutulian prince here: a lesser, tenderer Hector, an "unlucky boy" preeminent for his beauty as is Turnus (though the ecphrasis does not include this point) and rash enough to join battle with Achilles despite his lesser powers.[12] It is one small irony of Aeneas' own transformation into a new Achilles and his reversal of the Trojan

---

[10] On this reversal see Anderson 1957, Quint 1993:50–96. Gransden 1984 offers a detailed analysis of Virgil's "visionary misreading" (p. 4) of the *Iliad*.

[11] This inversion is underlined by the wording of Neptune's recollection of an Iliadic fight at 5.808–10, "I snatched Aeneas up in a sheltering cloud when he joined battle with the mighty son of Peleus [Achilles], with neither equal gods nor equal strength" (*Pelidae tunc ego forti / congressum Aenean nec dis nec viribus aequis / nube cava eripui*). Prophecies of the sending of Achilles to Troy, i.e. to destroy Troy, are a prominent theme of Latin poetry: see Catullus 64.338–60, Virgil *Ecl.* 4.36.

[12] On the ways Troilus here foreshadows the doomed youths of the poem, including Turnus, Pallas, and Lausus, see Clay 1988:203–205.

War that the pity with which he views the scene of Troilus (and that he attributes to the Carthaginians who created it) will not carry over to his dealings with Troilus' Italian counterpart.

The focalization at 12.221 transfigures a view that has already been imputed to the Rutulians: some of them were originally drawn to Turnus' company precisely because of his beauty and youth (7.473–74):

> hunc decus egregium formae movet atque iuventae,
> hunc atavi reges, hunc claris dextera factis.

> One man is stirred by the extraordinary glory of his beauty and youth; another by his royal ancestors; another by his right hand, for its illustrious deeds.

But as with the examples we collected in the previous chapter, the erotic slant to the description in Book 12 seems to have its source elsewhere than in the actual viewers. Are these same recruits now looking at Turnus sexually? The possibility does not resonate. The "extraordinary glory of his beauty and youth" in Book 7 has erotic potential, but is limited by its context to other, more civic values for beauty. Thomas compares 7.473–74 with the old accolades in the epitaph of L. Cornelius Scipio Barbatus, "whose beauty was altogether a match for his valor" (*quoius forma virtutei parisuma fuit*).[13] The wording of 7.473 *decus egregium formae* ("extraordinary glory of his beauty") recalls Pallas and Lausus at 10.435, *egregii forma*, as well as Marcellus at 6.861, *egregium forma iuvenem et fulgentibus armis* ("a youth extraordinary for his beauty and flashing armor"), whom we shall look at in a later chapter. These phrases, and Turnus' "outstanding physique" (*praestanti corpore*) at 7.783, all recall the beauty of a Homeric warrior. What we have again in *pubentes genae* and *iuvenali corpore* is an addition to the actual gaze, an extra nuance that extracts the erotic potential of Turnus' beauty and links him to our Adonis figures.

The seed of both his beauties, martial and nubile, is sown in his introduction to us as *pulcherrimus*, "most beautiful" (7.54–57):

> multi etiam magno e Latio totaque petebant
> Ausonia; petit ante alios pulcherrimus omnis
> Turnus, avis atavisque potens, quem regia coniunx
> adiungi generum miro properabat amore.

> And many men from great Latium and all Italy were seeking [Lavinia's hand in marriage]; most beautiful beyond them all, Turnus sought her, he who held power from his grandsires and great-grandsires. The queen, with wondrous love, was eager to have him joined to her as son-in-law.

[13] Thomas 1998:283. This Scipio died in 298; the epitaph (*CLE* 7) was composed around 200 (Courtney 1995:216–20).

His ancestral power lends his beauty warlike splendor, but the context makes it nubile, sensual. Both connotations are no doubt mixed in the eyes of the focalizer, which cleaves, surprisingly, to the figure of Queen Amata, not Lavinia herself (whose viewpoint never plainly governs the narrative). The erotic potential of *pulcherrimus* here is not fully expressed, but this passage anticipates the one in Book 12, even influences how we read it, by casting Turnus as the object of appreciation of an amatory, possessive kind. If we were to attach the focalization there to the viewpoint of the Rutulian soldiery, we could speculate that the very signs of Turnus' impending failure in the eyes of his men represent him as an erotically desirable youth—or rather, what could be signs of desirability become warnings of a *puer delicatus* unfit to fight. By now the erotic imagery of 12.221 suggests a whole complex of ideas, and functions as if Turnus' Adonis-moment were displaced from his actual death to a premonition thereof; it has become metonymic for the grief and remorse that it has accompanied. This description is a foreshadowing: Turnus is going to die.[14] The Rutulians watching him fear it, and the amorous eye superimposed on theirs—the eye that suddenly sees in the Rutulian prince Euryalus, Lausus, Pallas, Camilla, and Adonis behind them all—knows and deplores it.

There is a more direct way in which Turnus becomes an Adonis-figure, not just through a focalization recalling earlier echoes of the *Epitaph on Adonis* and its themes, but through a closer similarity to Bion's poem. Alerted by Jupiter's omen that fate requires her brother's death, Juturna laments that she has been made a goddess and therefore cannot follow him to the Underworld (12.872–84):

> "Quid nunc te tua, Turne, potest germana iuvare?
> aut quid iam durae superat mihi? qua tibi lucem
> arte morer? talin possum me opponere monstro?
> 875 iam iam linquo acies. ne me terrete timentem,
> obscenae volucres: alarum verbera nosco
> letalemque sonum, nec fallunt iussa superba
> magnanimi Iovis. haec pro virginitate reponit?
> quo vitam dedit aeternam? cur mortis adempta est
> 880 condicio? possem tantos finire dolores
> nunc certe, et misero fratri comes ire sub umbras!
> immortalis ego? at[15] quicquam mihi dulce meorum
> te sine, frater, erit? o quae satis ima dehiscat
> terra mihi, Manisque deam demittat ad imos?"

"How can your sister help you now, Turnus? Or what remains for my endurance? By what art am I to keep the light from passing for you? Can

---

[14] The introduction of Turnus also anticipates this ominousness: it continues, ". . . but portents of the gods, accompanied by terrors of different kinds, stand in the way [of the marriage]" (7.58 *sed variis portenta deum terroribus obstant*).

[15] J. J. O'Hara conjectures *at* for MS *et* (*RhM* 136 [1993] 371–73).

I set myself against such a portent? So be it; I hereby leave the battle. I tremble—do not try to frighten me, obscene birds. I recognize the beating of your wings and the deathly sound, and am not ignorant of the proud commands of high-hearted Jupiter. Is this his compensation for my maidenhood? To what purpose did he give me eternal life? Why was I deprived of the provision of death? Would that I could put an end to such great sorrow for sure and go as my miserable brother's companion down to the shades! I immortal? But will anything in my life be sweet without you, brother? Oh, what land will gape open sufficiently for me and send me down, a goddess, to the furthest ghosts below?"

Then she veils herself and disappears from the poem into her river.

The motif of regret, in deep and endless suffering, of one's own immortality is used sparingly in ancient literature. We first hear it in the mouth of Prometheus in Attic tragedy.[16] Commentators have long compared Juturna's wish to cast off her immortality and accompany her brother into death with Aphrodite's lament that she is immortal and so cannot accompany Adonis (*Adonis* 51–53):

> "φεύγεις μακρόν, Ἄδωνι, καὶ ἔρχεαι εἰς Ἀχέροντα
> πὰρ στυγνὸν βασιλῆα καὶ ἄγριον· ἁ δὲ τάλαινα
> ζώω καὶ θεός ἐμμι καὶ οὐ δύναμαί σε διώκειν."

"You flee far away, Adonis, and go to Acheron, to a dreadful and savage king. Wretched me! I live on, and am a god, and cannot follow you."[17]

The similarity between the passages is not just that both goddesses lament that they are immortal; in addition to the common "Stabat Mater" treatment of Aphrodite and Juturna, both their wishes are motivated by the impending death of a loved one, and both are couched in the same terms: the loss of his companionship and the inability to follow him to the land of the dead.[18] Juturna expresses her regret more explicitly and lengthily than Aphrodite, but the length itself of her soliloquy recalls the twenty-line duration of Aphrodite's lament for Adonis.

There are no close verbal similarities (though 884 *immortalis ego*, with *deam* at 886, does approach ζώω καὶ θεός ἐμμι); the differences are telling. Aphrodite's

---

[16] [?Aeschylus] *P.V.* 752–54 and fr. 193.22–26 Radt. See Barchiesi 1978:118–19, who draws Philodemus' and Longinus' analyses of divine suffering into the discussion, and Obbink's thorough comparison between Philodemus and Virgil (see Obbink 2002:101 on the hint present in *Il.* 5.873). Related is the idea that even the eternity of a god's life is worthless without pleasure (e.g. in Simonides *PMG* 584).

[17] Heyne on 12.878, Eichhoff 1825:396, Barchiesi 1978:118 n. 27, Boella 1979:321–28. Boella and Obbink address the Epicurean affinities of the motif.

[18] Thus also, Juturna recalls Nisus' wish not to be separated from Euryalus, both in the theme and in the literary model. On the "Stabat Mater" motif see p. 30 above.

use of "flee" and "pursue" recalls their use in amatory contexts for the flight and pursuit of beloved and lover.[19] The conceit is anticipated by her odd formulation, "wait, Adonis, so that I may catch up with you for the last time," as if she already thought of him as running away from her (43 μεῖνον Ἄδωνι, πανύστατον ὥς σε κιχείω; the next lines expand this request into her increasingly fervid wish for a last kiss). The juxtaposition of φεύγειν and διώκειν raises their use in traditional formulae of (unrequited) love. Aphrodite has just lost the happy security of unity, and with loss comes the yearning that characterizes the bittersweet kind of love; but she must renounce even that. But her wish has other motivations. Obviously, it expresses her misery that she cannot be with Adonis; in our surprise at the wish of an immortal to die we are reminded that the glamour of immortality is only the glamour of eternal happiness. Finally, the sudden declaration of her divinity (especially after the poet has so effectively humanized her grief at lines 19–27) reminds us from what a great height love has dropped her into the flux of mortal life. Aphrodite's words telescope into a few rapid thoughts a typical sequence of feelings about such a loss as hers: perfect security, loss, pursuit and hope of regaining, and resignation, with a feeling of general hopelessness and mistrust in the ability of anything beautiful to be constant (cf. 55, 61).

When Virgil replaces an element of a borrowed phrase or image with one that invokes special associations in his own poem, the original element is seldom lost, but turns up somewhere else in Virgil's text with a new function.[20] We do not have far to look in Book 12 for correlatives to Bion's "flight and pursuit": reenacting the flight of the Hector he has now become, Turnus is running from the pursuing Aeneas, and is twice the subject of *fugio*.[21] These instances make ironic his rhetorical question to Juturna at 645, "Will this land see Turnus fleeing?" The Greek verb pairing that Bion uses metaphorically is indeed used literally of the flight and pursuit of Hector and Achilles at *Iliad* 22.158 "a good man fled, but a far better man pursued him" (πρόσθε μὲν ἐσθλὸς ἔφευγε, δίωκε δέ μιν μέγ᾽ ἀμείνων). But Bion's verb emerges most notably in a later echo of Juturna's wish that she might "go as my miserable brother's companion down to the shades." Repeating her phrase with a verb closer to the Bion's, but retaining "down to the shades" for "to Acheron. . ." the last line of the poem says that Turnus's life, with a groan, *fugit indignata sub umbras*.[22] As noted above, the verbal coincidence with Camilla's demise, of course, strengthens Turnus's connection with Adonis.

---

[19] Cf. Theognis 1299, Sappho fr. 1.21 Voigt, Theocritus 6.17 and 11.75, Callimachus *A.P.* 12.102.5–6.

[20] See e.g. the exemplary readings in Wills 1998, who speaks of Virgil's "allusive economy."

[21] See lines 733, 758; and note *fuga* at 733, 742.

[22] A Near Eastern idiom may lie behind Bion's usage; Job 14:2 *homo conteritur et fugit quasi umbra* in the Vulgate (LXX ἀπέδρα δὲ ὥσπερ σκιά), however molded to Jerome's memory of Virgil, accurately reflects the Hebrew verb (*brḥ*).

Nor does Virgil's economy of allusion permit Bion's phrase "to Acheron, to a dreadful and savage king" (which Virgil already used in the *Georgics*)[23] to vanish without a trace. At 12.849 *saevique in limine regis* ("on the threshold of the savage king"), used of the seat of the Fury that Jupiter sends to dismay Turnus (the one that frightens Juturna away), has long attracted exegesis. Servius Auctus explains *saevi* as an epithet of circumstance, to be paraphrased "when he is savage" (*cum saevit*), explained by 851–52 ("[both Furies appear at the threshold] if ever the king of the gods wages horrific death and pestilence or terrifies cities that deserve it"). Perhaps; but a divine "savage king" occurring a few dozen lines before Juturna's impersonation of Bion's Aphrodite also invites comparison with Bion's Hades.[24] Virgil retains as more appropriate to his theme the epithet he had eschewed in the *Georgics*, now eschewing the other: the allusion likens Jupiter to his more characteristically savage brother and reinforces the frightening image of him that emerges as the poem weaves its theodicy to a climax (compare his *saeva numina*, "savage divine will," at 11.901). The whole image of his deployment of the two Furies recalls two Greek images of his justice: Hesiod, *Works and Days* 238–47, which lists the terrors that Zeus may send against a city even for the sins of a single inhabitant[25]; and *Iliad* 24.527–33 (in a place roughly corresponding to this spot in the *Aeneid*), Achilles' account of the two urns on the threshold of Zeus, one full of blessings, the other of curses, stored up by the king of gods for distribution in human lives. Virgil does not give Jupiter anything corresponding to Zeus's jar of blessings, or to the beneficent justice dealt by Zeus in the preceding passage in Hesiod. Here, all chastening savagery as he speeds forth his infernal messenger, he adequately takes the place of the dread god of the Underworld, whom Juturna leaves unmentioned. It is his enmity alone that Turnus himself avows to fear at 895, responding to an Aeneas who speaks from a "savage breast" (*saevo pectore*) and threatens combat with "savage weapons" (*saevis armis*): Jupiter's proxy.

So Turnus becomes an Adonis-figure, not only through his sudden ecphrastic assimilation to Euryalus, Pallas, and the rest, but by a reminiscence of Bion's telling of the myth, and by the grief of a loving goddess expressed in an unheard lament. Virgil appears to have invented the kinship between Turnus and the water goddess Juturna[26] and to have been the first to make Turnus

---

[23] *Georg.* 4.469 *Manisque adiit regemque tremendum* ("[Orpheus] went to the ghosts and the dreadful king"). *Tremendus*, literally "to be shuddered at," is very close in meaning to Bion's στυγνός, which is derived from the same root as στυγέω, "to shudder (at)."

[24] Dis (= Hades) has the same epithet, also in the genitive, at 7.568. On Obbink's reading of 878 *magnanimi* (which I have translated "high-hearted"), this idea enters Juturna's speech directly; he connects it to the poem's theology of anger and emotions in general (2002:106). Cf. Wigodsky 1972:124.

[25] Traina also finds a model in *Il.* 16.385–92 (a simile), where Zeus sends destructive weather to the unrighteous.

[26] It occurs elsewhere only later; cf. Ovid *Fasti* 1.463 and 707–708.

explicitly a young man, with the effect that Juturna seems naturally his protector. The caring, maternal sister is a recurrent persona in the *Aeneid*, always presented as a "Stabat Mater" figure, weeping over her motherless sibling and attracting our viewpoint on the tragedy. Now finally we see in such a figure a goddess weeping for a young male, more closely approximating the role of Aphrodite over Adonis than did Dido's sister Anna and Camilla's *soror* Acca. Virgil's wording underlines the similarities between these characters. The line that introduces Juturna's lament, 12.871 *unguibus ora soror foedans et pectora pugnis*, repeats a line about Anna at the death of Dido (4.673).[27] We can see the part her lament plays in Virgil's textual economy: after Aeneas' laments over the dead bodies of Pallas and even of his slain enemy Lausus, we half expect him to lament over Turnus. But in the same way that the erotic gaze is displaced onto Turnus' living body and given to his men, the lament is displaced to a point before he dies[28] and given to his sister, in a way that suggests Aeneas' loss of sympathy at this point—or rather leaves us permanently in suspense about it. The end of the poem does not find him murmuring over Turnus' pale countenance, as over Lausus at 10.825 and Pallas at 11.42, "*Miserande puer. . . .*"

Let us not seek a definitive message about Turnus in these intertextual and intratextual connections, waiting to be decoded. Rather we have traced a way of looking at him, a suggestive way that brings out a new side of him, and this new side resonates within the poem and picks up important associations. Adonis, the passive, voiceless minion of the great goddess, provides a shortcut between the Rutulian prince's personae, from Turnus the raging tiger to Turnus the little brother, Turnus the wan youth trembling in the grip of fate. Scholars debate endlessly whether we are meant to feel sorry for Turnus or not. The real interest in this question is the perspective from which one approaches it; the *Aeneid* offers cues to construct both standpoints.[29] By some criteria present in the poem, he is contemptible; by others, equally compelling in their own way, he is a sympathetic victim. Nor can we dismiss his passivity, as he approaches the altar, as a mark of scorn. The explicit viewers do not react to it with scorn. He also has it in common with that exemplary future would-be Roman, the doomed Marcellus, whose sad "eyes in his downcast face" (6.862 *deiecto lumina vultu*) prefigure Turnus' "downcast eyes" (12.220 *demisso lumine*).

Turnus' very death likens him to our Adonis-type, of which we can now surely count him as the most significant avatar. The last three lines in the

---

[27] Note also 12.873 ~ 4.681; 12.881 ~ 4.677–78 (cf. [Ovid] *Consolatio ad Liviam* 298). Barchiesi 1978:104–105 cites these parallels; cf. Obbink 2002:91–92.

[28] See Barchiesi 1978 on the way Juturna's lament opposes an "epic code" (Conte's term) within the poem. Barchiesi 1994:112 is also relevant: "Il lamento di Giuturna . . . è un commento anticipato sulla fine del poema, vista con occhi simpatici verso lo sconfitto."

[29] A point well expressed and taken advantage of by Thomas 1998:273–74, who discusses this question with exemplary subtlety and judiciousness.

poem, which include the reminiscence of Camilla's death, offer dense variations on themes that interest us. Catching sight of the sword belt that Turnus
stripped from Pallas at 10.495–500, Aeneas declares his revenge; then
(950–52):

> hoc dicens ferrum adverso sub pectore condit
> fervidus; ast illi solvuntur frigore membra
> vitaque cum gemitu fugit indignata sub umbras.

Saying this, he buries his sword beneath [Turnus'] upturned chest,
seething. His limbs go slack with cold, and his life with a groan flees in
indignation to the shades below.

Turnus and Aeneas definitively switch roles in these lines: not only is Aeneas
"seething," *fervidus*[30]—Turnus' adjective when, after the oath, he returns to his
old fiery self (12.325 *subita spe fervidus ardet*)—but the note on Turnus' slacken-
ing limbs likens him to Aeneas as he was the very first time we saw him, in the
storm at 1.92: "forthwith Aeneas' limbs go slack with cold" (*extemplo Aeneae
solvuntur frigore membra*).[31] That is the most perilous moment in the poem for
Aeneas' mission, the low point he toils his way up from toward his goal. At the
poem's end the tables have fully turned, and it is his enemy who, among other
losses, misses his chance to father a nation (Putnam concludes his 1965 study
of the poem with a reading of this exchange as "one of Virgil's most bitter and
cogent ironies"). This thematic point is brought home by the grim pun in *condit*: the goal of Aeneas' suffering is to found the Roman nation (1.33 *tantae
molis erat Romanam condere gentem*); now that foundation is realized with the
sinking of his sword into Turnus' exposed breast.[32]

The immediate cause of Turnus' slaying, as Aeneas declares, is revenge for
his slaying of Pallas; he dies by a sort of economy of youthful death.[33] The
sword belt, with the slaughter of the newly married sons of Aegyptus by their
brides, the daughters of Danaus, inauspiciously engraved in gold on it, points
up the terms of this economy: intimations not just of premature demise, but of
unsuccessful procreation and failed nation building (set in a nation-defining
tale of Greek-Oriental exchanges, best known from Aeschylus' *Suppliants*) are
there for Aeneas to read as bitter commentary on the death of Pallas, and (for
us) to read on Turnus as well. Now as Turnus left a gaping wound in Pallas'

---

[30] Cf. his *fervida dicta*, in Turnus' expression (12.894–95). Aeneas is also *fervidus* at 10.788 and
12.748.

[31] Compare also 1.93 *tendens ad sidera palmas* with 12.936 *tendere palmas*. Wigodsky 1965:200
considers the shift signaled by these repetitions to be part—indeed the climax—of the general
reversal of roles, with the Trojans becoming like the victorious Greeks of the Trojan War; cf. Quint
1993:79–80 (and p. 47 above).

[32] Cf. Henderson 2000:6 (with 23 n. 9), 12. On the dual sense of *condere* in the poem, see James
1995.

[33] Compare Evander's words at 11.177–79.

chest—11.40 *levique patens in pectore vulnus*—he receives one in the same place (indeed, all our Adonis-figures die of wounds in their torsos). How easy it would have been to give him a snowy or smooth chest, like that of Pallas, and write in 12.950 *ferrum niveo sub pectore condit* or *levi sub pectore condit*. But the amorous gaze, which worked its effect on Turnus back at the altar, has deserted us. In the fulfillment of Aeneas' mission, the erotics and the ideology of the poem, desire and destiny, seem to have separated for good.

II

The death of Turnus, because he loses the chance to found a nation with Lavinia, more significantly than any of the others' deaths symbolizes the eradication of the familial stock. Lineage, inheritance, is of course the very dynamics of Aeneas' mission, the conduit of the heritage of Troy through Aeneas down to Augustan Rome; and the whole war between the Rutulians and the Trojans—the second half of the poem—is basically over reproductive rights, the privilege (in hindsight) of engendering a nation.[34] This contest is specifically fought between Aeneas and Turnus, who in the great simile at 715–24, where they are likened to two bulls fighting for the right to "rule over the woodland" and lead the herd (and thus to breed with the cows), are *Tros Aeneas et Daunius heros* (723), "Trojan Aeneas and the Daunian hero." The epithets underline how lineage hangs on this battle for the right to breed with Lavinia. (The national mission, whose price is evidently the death of brave, beautiful young warriors and particularly of *sons*, is from a certain standpoint what keeps human society part of the animal world with its brutishness and misery.) The treatment of Turnus' sword—his father's sword, forged by Vulcan himself—recapitulates this grand linkage of ancestry and posterity: he leaves it behind in his haste and trepidation, and the one he takes in its place shatters against Aeneas (12.90–91, 728–41). Symbolically and literally he proves himself unable to continue the family line.[35]

Daunus himself never appears in the narrative, and his character is never clear. He emerges as a vaguely pitiable figure, an old man far removed from the action and vitality of war, a beneficiary of our memories of decrepit fathers in the *Iliad* like Peleus and Priam. At 12.43–45 Latinus invokes him in urging Turnus to preserve his own life by ceasing from the fight:

> "miserere parentis
> longaevi, quem nunc maestum patria Ardea longe
> dividit."

[34] Cf. Gillis 1983:92.

[35] Cf. Hardie 1994:19: "If . . . Turnus in comparison with the two Trojan couples [Nisus and Euryalus, Pandarus and Bitias] seems a very adult warrior, eventually he too conforms to the pattern of the youthful fighter killed before he can realize his full potential as *paterfamilias*, dying before marriage to be mourned by his old father."

"Pity your aged father, whom now your homeland Ardea keeps far distant from you in his sadness."

Here are Priam's first words to Achilles at *Iliad* 24.486–87:

"μνῆσαι πατρὸς σοῖο θεοῖς ἐπιείκελ' Ἀχιλλεῦ,
τηλίκου ὥς περ ἐγών, ὀλοῷ ἐπὶ γήραος οὐδῷ."

"Remember your father, godlike Achilles, who is as old as I am, upon the baneful threshold of age."

Threatened with death, Turnus makes a similar plea to Aeneas (934): *Dauni miserere senectae*, "Pity the old age of Daunus," cannily—though in the event futilely—appealing to Aeneas' feelings about Anchises. Parentage is one way in which Turnus parallels Aeneas and is in a sense an anti-Aeneas: both have a mortal father and divine mother (Turnus' mother is the nymph Venilia, who appears only in a mention at 10.76 and is apparently even more neglectful than Venus).

The double catastrophe of family and nation is part of all of our slain warriors' stories. While all of them, however, belong to nations that Rome will conquer, the opposition that the gaze establishes between the gazer and the Adonis-figure crystallizes curiously in the case of Latin Turnus. First let us consider 8.659–61, the description of the Gauls, creeping up to attack the Capitoline by night, on Aeneas' Shield:

aurea caesaries ollis atque aurea vestis,
virgatis lucent sagulis, tum lactea colla
auro innectuntur.

Golden was their hair and golden their clothing; they gleamed in striped cloaks, and their creamy throats were bound with gold.

Notably conjoined are polyptoton of gold (as with Dido at 4.138–39 and Chloreus at 11.774), erotically charged "creamy" throats and flowing hair, and exotic attire. It is hard to define the boundary between the medium of the image and its referents; is their hair gold-colored or depicted in gold? Or both, like the torques around their white (surely ivory?) throats? The situation—sleeping Romans attacked—makes one think of the expedition of Nisus and Euryalus against the Rutulians in Book 9—but the standpoint is reversed here, where the slumberers are to be identified with the ethnic self, and the attackers are the foreign, even barbarian, objects of a covetous gaze. The "striped" (*virgatis*) cloaks, already suggestive of a Chloreus-like prize, are all the more so if we accept the cross-language pun that Servius finds here: "[The poet] aptly alludes to the Gaulish language, in which the word for purple-dye is *virga*; and so [he writes] *virgatis*, as if to say 'dyed with *virga*,' that is, empurpled."[36]

---

[36] Servius on 8.660: *et bene adlusit ad Gallicam linguam, per quam virga purpura dicitur. "virgatis" ergo, ac si diceret virga tinctis, id est purpuratis.* Cf. p. 90 n. 48.

Purple-dye and gold, as we shall observe in the next chapters, are hallmarks especially of Oriental luxury. Overall, this is an ecphrasis of conquerable Otherness, troped luxuriously, sensually—and at the same time it is, piquantly, a portrayal of conquerors of Rome, one that conceptually, defensively, makes them desirable, possessable (there is a prolepsis here, in that the Gauls were eventually conquered by the Romans).

The sensual description of Turnus in Book 12 does not lend itself to this kind of ethnological analysis. The explicit viewers in whom the gaze would seem to cohere there are Rutulians like himself, and no details arise to contradict their expected identification with him in this regard. The differentiation of Turnus from a national self, however, is pervasive elsewhere in terms very much like those in which the stealthy Gauls are couched. A few places in the text radically problematize his nationality, pushing it as far from Rome as possible. At 9.30–32 he leads his men into battle:

> ceu septem surgens sedatis amnibus altus
> per tacitum Ganges aut pingui flumine Nilus
> cum refluit campis et iam se condidit alveo.

. . . like the silently rising Ganges, fed[37] by his seven sedate streams, or the Nile with his rich flood when he flows back from the plains and has now buried himself within his stream bed.

The Italian armies keep coming and coming. The rivers to which they are compared are those of India and Egypt, Oriental rivers, flowing through lands far beyond the line of Roman ethnic identification, but to which Augustan imperial ambitions claimed title. The Nile—here represented in its rich, covetable fertility—reminds us of its symbolic place in Augustus' conquest of Egypt as prophesied by Anchises (6.800) and on the Shield of Aeneas (8.711–13, some fifty lines ago). The seven tributaries of the Ganges and its rising flood assimilate it to the Nile as conquered river, recalling the Nile's seven mouths in Anchises' prophesy (*septemgemini Nili*) and the *magnum corpus* that Vulcan gave the Nile on the shield (in any case the Nile flood is an unmistakable comparandum). They are distinctly unaggressive rivers here, complicating the image of the Rutulian advance. That the Nile is even in retreat likens the Rutulians' eventual defeat to the defeated Nile on Aeneas' shield.

The simile picks up apt connotations against the *Aeneid*'s use of rivers in a schema of national identity. As "shores" (*litora, orae*) measure the stages and vicissitudes of the Aeneadae's journey, so too rivers are prominent in the symbolism of the poem, often mapping out national transitions: as a conspicuous topographical feature a river stands for its country and can serve, if not as a natural boundary, at least as a mark of transition from one stage in a journey

---

[37] *Altus* is so rendered by R. D. Williams ad loc.

to another.[38] Turnus and his people, according to this schema, are momentarily Easterners, "Others" by both Roman and Greek definitions, and ripely conquerable.[39] The same schema is subliminally at work at 9.730, where a simile compares Turnus to a huge tiger: not only is the tiger an Indian beast, but Latin uses the same word for both tiger and the river Tigris in Parthia—that perennial object of Augustan imperialist bluster. We may compare the simile at the beginning of Book 12 that compares him to a lion in the Punic fields (another geographical synecdoche). Similes thus associate Turnus with four emblematically Eastern lands that Augustan Rome claimed: Carthage, Egypt, Parthia, and India (even if only the first two were really under Roman power). The Greek-derived schema that lumps these peoples together as "Oriental" in opposition to "us" is abetted by the Roman imperialist experience (to some degree following the model provided by Alexander). Turnus' ethnic characterization in these spots, consonantly with his model Adonis elsewhere, hints (despite the direct comparison with big cats in 9.730 and 12.4) at a stereotypically passive, voluptuous—"rich" and "sedate"?—Oriental persona behind the fierce Italian warrior.

This conceptual severing of Turnus from the poem's "Italy" would seem to chime with the idea that the war is Turnus' fault and that other Latins, even other Rutulians, are rightly happy to have Aeneas among them, even to serve him (this is Drances' position: see especially 11.130–31). The idea cuts Turnus off from the future Roman polity even as it unites Trojans with Italians. At 11.57–58 Aeneas treats "Italians" (or "Ausonians") as part of such a national unity, tendentiously ending his lament over Pallas: "Woe is me, what a bulwark you are losing, Ausonia, and you, Iulus!" (*ei mihi quantum / praesidium, Ausonia, et quantum tu perdis, Iule!*). Yet symbolically, at least, the Oriental qualities ascribed to Turnus are not his alone (and his men's) among the Italians of the poem. One can add the tiger-skin cloak that Camilla, according to her patron goddess Diana, has habitually worn (11.577). Whence did she acquire this rarity? Are there tigers in Italy? No, according to Virgil in his praise of Italy at *Georgics* 2.151-52: "raging tigers and the fierce race of lions are absent" (*at rabidae tigres absunt et saeva leonum / semina*).[40] Camilla's attire has nothing to do with her life as a forest-dwelling huntress, but rather envisions a trade route stretching from the Italian woodlands to the furthest East and back, the

---

[38] Baby Camilla is hurled across the swollen Amasenus, a journey that coincides with her exile and dedication to Diana: 11.561–63. More examples of this symbolic use of rivers will figure in chapter 4.

[39] Compare the far-fetched names whose connotations cast Italian warriors as Oriental (pp. 5–6 above). On the night episode in Book 9, Lennox 1977:337 speculates that the drunkenness of the Rutulians is "a sign of the *mollitia* of these 'barbarians' (they are likened to a *molle pecus* at 341) and of their vulnerability."

[40] Besides here and in the Turnus simile at 9.730, tigers occur elsewhere in the *Aeneid* in contexts that involve national definition: on 4.367 see p. 99 n. 69, on 6.805 see pp. 158–9. At 10.166 *Tigris* is the name of an Etruscan ship.

satisfaction of far-reaching desires. Their taste for Eastern luxury goods in general folds the Italians into an Oriental identity: the poem's encoding of royal wealth and power as Oriental holds true in Latium as elsewhere. The venerable portraits of Latin kings, eponymous ancestors, and tutelary gods housed in the sacred palace of Picus are carved from "ancient cedar," an imported Eastern wood (7.178).[41] The cosmopolitan wealth of Latinus is also attested by his queen's "purple" outer clothing, which she profligately rends in suicide (12.601). A similar ambiguity underlies 11.777, where Chloreus' embroidered greaves receive the epithet *barbara*: we are looking at him from a Greek-derived ethnic viewpoint and seeing him as an Oriental; but the viewpoint coincides with, and is not definitively separable from, that of his would-be attacker, Camilla. Pressing this coincidence, we find her both distancing herself from the "barbarism" of Chloreus' apparel (which overall is flamboyantly Oriental in its richness, color, and design) and at the same time desiring it, possibly to dedicate it to Diana, but possibly to wear it herself (779–80). Her desirous gaze (*femineo amore*) involves both assimilation and difference. Joining the catalogue of Italian troops, Camilla has exchanged her tiger skin for the equally Oriental purple and gold (7.812–17; compare the Rutulian warriors preparing for battle at 9.163, "youths purple of plume and coruscating with gold"), which she wears with a Lycian quiver; the ethnic connotations of her attire—which astounds the matrons of Latium—dissolve an opposition between her and Chloreus.

Alongside Camilla's Oriental traits we should consider 11.654, where she shoots in flight. This is the mark of an Amazon warrior (particularly of the "Libyan Amazons," according to Dionysius Scytobrachion); it is also, more notoriously (especially in Augustan poetry), the defining mark of the Mede or Parthian.[42] The detail not only brackets Amazons with "Oriental," "barbarian," in defining contrast with Greeks, but in the Virgilian text adds to the Oriental dimension of Camilla's persona and unites it with her Amazonian one, which likewise potentially casts her as a foil for the nonbarbarian male self (similarly, the costume she intends to take from Chloreus is characteristic of both Orientals and Amazons in the Greek iconographic tradition).[43] Again, this contrasts with her emphatically Italian origin and, here, with her companions, the connotations of whose names—Tarpeia, Tulla, and Larina (655–56)—together bracket Italian and Roman together as a cultural unity.[44]

[41] Cf. the cedar and cypress given for Italian houses by the Caucasus at *Georg.* 2.443.
[42] Dionysius Scytobrachion *FGrH* 32 F 7 = Diodorus Siculus 3.54.3; see Arrigone 1982:38 n. 59. For the Parthian practice see e.g. *Georg.* 3.31; Horace *Carm.* 1.19.11–12, 2.13.17–18.
[43] Amazons assimilated to *barbaroi* in the Greek tradition: Hall 1989:52–54, 202, 215 ("the most supremely 'other' of Herodotus' tribes"). Iconography of Chloreus' attire: Arrigoni 1982:51.
[44] Tarpeia is homonymous with the legendary betrayer of Rome to Titus Tatius; Tulla recalls the third Roman king, Tullus Hostilius (the conqueror of Alba Longa), and the *gens* of the Tullii. Larina recalls the Italian city Larinum, though it is also the name of a spring in Attica: Pliny 4.24.

The catalogue of Italians with which Book 7 ends is most obviously modeled on the catalogue of Greeks in Book 2 of the *Iliad*; this intertext casts
Trojans as Trojans and their new enemy, the Italians, as their erstwhile enemy,
the Greeks, in conformity with the Sibyl's prediction that in Italy Aeneas will
have to fight the Trojan War all over again (6.88–94). Yet Courtney finds that
another important model for the catalogue of Italians is Herodotus' catalogue
of the allies of Xerxes, perhaps filtered through the like catalogue in Choerilus'
epic on the Persian Wars, a notable Orientalist text from the later fifth century.[45] The warrior-maiden Camilla would fill the place of the warrior-queen
Artemisia. This intertext casts Italians as Orientals and Trojans as Greeks—
Greco-Romans, to anticipate a boundary of national identification that the
mission of Aeneas desiderates. The Oriental image of the Italians works to
erase, by contrast, the originary Orientalness of Aeneas' Trojans (or at least
neutralize it)—and not just to group the Aeneadae's current opponents with
Carthage, Egypt, and other nations defeated or defeatable by Roman arms, but
to remind us that the Aeneadae (descendants of Dardanus, who, according to
the Trojan Penates at 3.167 and Latinus at 7.206, emerged from Italy) have a
greater claim to this land than some of the natives.[46] We are offered the suggestion that ethnic roles have reversed. From no perspective do Italians and
Trojans appear on the same side.

   To the early philosopher Thales of Miletus was ascribed gratitude to
Fortune that he was born a human being and not a beast, male and not female,
a Hellene and not a barbarian.[47] Correlation between various self-defining differentiations is part of this discourse, and alongside the surprises in Turnus'
ethnic characterization, the poem holds some surprises for us about his gender. Yes, he is an emphatically masculine hero, exhorting his troops, slaying
Trojans right and left, and generally showing the correct solicitude for his people that his masculine role demands. He is repeatedly described as "huge,"
ingens, a word whose muscular connotations are aroused when after a day of
fierce battling he leaps, fully armed, into the Tiber and—albeit with some help
from the river—swims across (9.815–18).[48] His reaction to Lavinia's blush
bespeaks a barely repressed manly ardor (12.70–71). In his first words in the
poem he ruthlessly distinguishes himself as a young male against the old and
the female (7.440–44). Yet at several points in the poem Turnus curiously
approaches a recognizable female type, the distressed mythological heroine,

---

[45] Courtney 1988:5–7. Fragments of Choerilus' catalogue are to be found at *SH* frr. 318–20.

[46] This is Cairns's interpretation of similes given to Aeneas and Turnus, including that at 12.4–8
(the lion in Punic fields), in a discussion of the way the poem tends to make Turnus less Italian
and the Dardanid Aeneas more (1989:109–14).

[47] Diogenes Laertius 1.33 = Hermippus fr. 12 Müller. The thought is especially useful as coming
from the reputedly Phoenician Thales.

[48] It will be remembered that Pallas and Lausus, both "feminized" in death, are described as physically *ingens* (10.485, 842).

a woman either dangerously in love (with a kinsman or other forbidden object) or dangerously loved (typically by a god) or both. Cinna's Smyrna, Calvus' Io, Catullus' Ariadne are three examples from Latin poetry of the generation before Virgil; Apollonius' Medea is a prominent Greek example, with Euripidean heroines in the background.[49] Like the Adonis-figures of the previous chapter, an active masculine figure at moments becomes passive, "feminized" by means of imagery, connotation, and poetic allusion: and this characterization can be connected with themes of nationhood and foundation.

In this persona Turnus recalls Phoenician Dido, whom he parallels and resembles in other ways too; we may start with the commonplace that Turnus functions in the second half of the poem as Dido did in the first, as a doomed Juno-inspired hindrance to the fated outcome of Aeneas' mission. As at Turnus' first appearance he is *pulcherrimus*, "most beautiful" (7.55), at Dido's she is *pulcherrima* (1.496); on this comparison his superlative beauty is already imbued with a sense of foreboding, even apart from the portents of the gods that threaten Amata's marital designs.[50] Moreover, it may be on account of the Dido-parallel that at moments when Turnus' homeland and ancestry are particularly prominent, poetic allusion or a similar device makes his persona suddenly feminine, liquefying borders of both gender and nationality (some of the heroines mentioned above also carry ethnic otherness about them: Medea is an obvious such case, Io a more complicated one).

The phrase *placida quies* in 4.4–5 *haerent infixi pectore vultus / verbaque nec placidam membris dat cura quietem* ("his visage and words stick fast in [Dido's] heart, and anguish grants her body no placid rest") is traceable through a whole line of distraught heroines. It appears in the *Argonautae* of Virgil's older contemporary Varro of Atax (fr. 8 Morel = 10 Courtney):

> desierant latrare canes urbesque silebant;
> omnia noctis erant placida composta quiete.

Dogs had ceased their barking and the city was silent; all things were composed in the placid rest of night.[51]

This appears to correspond to, indeed rather closely translate, the lines of Apollonius' *Argonautica* that introduce Medea's unquiet passion, prototypical for later poetic description of sleepless heroines and their anguished, dilemma-filled soliloquies: ". . . nor was the barking of dogs heard any longer in the city; there was no noisy clamor, but silence held sway over the black darkness. Yet

---

[49] It should go without saying there is no single "lovelorn heroine" on which all examples depend.
[50] Cf. Gransden 1984:45.
[51] Virgil imitates this phrase even more closely, though metaphorically, at 1.249 (Venus on Antenor) *nunc placida compostus pace quiescit*. Similar phrases: Lucretius 1.463, *Aen.* 5.836 (cf. Wigodsky 1972:99 n. 495, 104).

sweet sleep did not take hold of Medea."[52] Dido, who is sleepless also at 4.80–85, where night finds her able to think only of Aeneas, follows in this tradition; the reminiscence helps articulate her role as a Medea-figure in particular (compare her use of magic later in the book). In "placid rest" (which suggests a combination of Apollonius' σιγή and γλυκερὸς ὕπνος), Varro may be reinforcing the connection with this type of heroine, particularly those of Latin miniature epic of his generation. It occurs in the nurse scene of the late, anonymous *Ciris*, line 343 *placidam tenebris captare quietem* ("[The nurse begins] to grasp placid rest in the darkness")—presumably the sleeping heroine's placid rest, although the phrase seems ill suited to the sense of its passage and reminds us how the *Ciris* is often a collage of earlier Latin poetry. Lyne fingers Cinna's lost miniature epic *Smyrna* as the source; there it will have described the restlessness brought on by Smyrna's illicit and miserable passion for her own father. If Cinna had Apollonius' Medea in mind (a probability), Varro will have used Cinna's line in his own adaptation of Cinna's model.[53]

The collocation recurs, not always with suggestions of the distressed heroine. At 5.836, as the sailors (except Palinurus) fall asleep, *placida laxabant membra quiete*. Palinurus ends his speech by asking for a final resting place in similar terms (6.371 *sedibus ut saltem placidis in morte quiescam*), and Deiphobus describes himself, in his last moments of life, as overcome by a "deep rest similar to placid death" (6.522 *alta quies placidaeque simillima mortis*). We recall the fitting of the phrase to Nisus' death (9.445 *placidaque ibi demum morte quievit*). But among these instances 7.408–14 stand out. The Fury Allecto, fresh from whipping Queen Amata into an anti-Trojan frenzy, sets her sights on Turnus:

> protinus hinc fuscis tristis dea tollitur alis
> audacis Rutuli ad muros, quam dicitur urbem
> 410   Acrisioneis Danae fundasse colonis,
> praecipiti delata Noto. locus Ardea quondam
> dictus avis, et nunc magnum manet Ardea nomen,
> sed fortuna fuit. tectis hic Turnus in altis
> iam mediam nigra carpebat nocte quietem.

Carried upon a headlong south wind, the dread goddess rose forthwith on somber wings to the walls of the bold Rutulian, the city that Danae is said to have founded with colonists from her homeland. The place was

---

[52] Apollonius of Rhodes *Arg.* 3.749–51 οὐδὲ κυνῶν ὑλακὴ ἔτ' ἀνὰ πτόλιν, οὐ θρόος ἦεν / ἠχήεις· σιγὴ δὲ μελαινομένην ἔχεν ὄρφνην. / ἀλλὰ μάλ' οὐ Μήδειαν ἐπὶ γλυκερὸς λάβεν ὕπνος. *Arg.* 4.1058–61, specifying night's enchantment or lulling (κατευκήλησε) of the whole earth, may have contributed to Varro's second line. Another, probably Hellenistic version of Medea's sleeplessness has recently been recovered in *Oxyrhynchus Papyri* 69 (2005) no. 4712.

[53] Lyne 1978:42–44. Ovid gives such a scene to his Myrrha (= Smyrna) in *Met.* 10.368–81. If Cinna's Smyrna is indeed the original heroine who bore the phrase in Latin, it is worth remembering that her illicit love led to the birth of Adonis.

once called Ardea by our ancestors, and even now the great name of Ardea remains, but its fortune is over and done. Here in his lofty dwelling Turnus was culling the mid-course of his slumber in the black night.

Remembrance of Varro and the "neoteric" model is betrayed by *nigra carpebat nocte*, which echoes Varro's *noctis quiete* and *tenebris captare* in the *Ciris* (assuming that that phrase is borrowed from one of Varro's contemporaries).[54] The link is reinforced by Allecto's rebuke (in the guise of the aged priestess Calybe) to Turnus at 427 *placida cum nocte iaceres*, "since you lay [asleep] in the placid night." This is not the only time that a virginal thoughtlessness alights on Turnus: note the implicit equivalence at 11.68, where his victim Pallas is compared to a flower snipped by a maiden's thumbnail. Awakened by the false Calybe, Turnus is like a male warrior version of a mythological heroine—a princess in a tower, like Danae herself—*un*troubled by love, an anomaly that Allecto will soon take care of.[55] His sleep and innocence are to be disrupted and replaced by a passion as self-destructive as Dido's. It is significant that at the end of his story, the terrifying simile at 12.908–12[56] begins with the same image of a carefree sleeper, eyes weighed down by slumber in the night (908–909 *languida . . . nocte quies*), only to expand into the nightmare of someone—indeed of *us* (910 *videmur*, "we dream that we . . .")—unable to run or cry out, to whom Turnus in his last effort is likened.

It is suggestive that of all the ktistic notes sounded in the *Aeneid*—a poem in which it seems every city has its history and its foundation, each commenting ultimately on Rome—Turnus' is the only city founded by an erotic heroine from Greek mythology. This story is unattested before Virgil, and the later authors who mention it briefly[57] may well be following the *Aeneid*; yet since *dicitur* has the sound of what Ross terms an "Alexandrian footnote," a type of learned allusion that disguises a particular precursor's myth as general tradition, an invention of Virgil's own seems uncertain, and Timaeus has been suggested as his source.[58] In either event, Virgil has chosen the story over another one, attested a century before his time, that makes a son of Odysseus and Circe the founder of Ardea[59] (unsuitable for his timeline?). Moreover, he

---

[54] "To cull sleep" (*carpere somnum* or *soporem*) is a favorite expression of Virgil's: cf. *Georg.* 3.435; *Aen.* 4.522, 555.

[55] Compare Vulcan's *placidum soporem* (8.405–406), induced by Venus. The simile that describes his waking to work (407–15) compares him to a woman. On the thumbnail image (which borrows from epithalamia: see Calvus fr. 4 Morel and Catullus 62.43), cf. Mitchell 1992:230, who emphasises the killing of "virgins" (i.e. unmarried youths) by "virgins" as a given in war, in connection with violence as a thematic displacement of sexuality. Our present emphasis is rather on the femininity inherent in the image.

[56] See Johnson 1976:96–99.

[57] Pliny *N.H.* 3.56, followed by Solinus 2.5 and Scholia on Statius *Theb.* 2.220.

[58] Rehm 1932:28. "Alexandrian footnote": Ross 1975:78, referring to Norden on *Aen.* 6.14 *ut fama est*.

[59] Xenagoras *FGrH* 240 F 29; so too Stephanus of Byzantium s.v. Ἀρδέα.

has simultaneously suppressed a story, retailed by Servius Auctus at 8.345–46, that would have made Danae and two sons of hers the colonists (by brute force) of Rome, replacing it in part with the version that quietly showcases Evander's extraordinary hospitality.[60] The foundational work of love-ravaged heroines is confined to the anti-Romes of the epic, Carthage and Ardea. We are reminded of Moschus' Europa, whose dream, in which the continents of Europe and Asia fight over her (*Europa* 1–15), gives Turnus' nocturnal vision of Allecto overtones of an anti-ktisis by contrast; we may even more pointedly contrast Ennius' Ilia, whose frightened retelling of her prophetic dream (of the conception of Romulus, at *Annales* 34–50 Skutsch) owes much to this type of heroine. It is from Ennius' Ilia, indeed, that the ktistic use of the heroine-motif derives for Roman literature. Moreover, as another consequence of Danae's role here, the soldiery of Ardea at 7.794 is *Argiva pubes* ("Argive youth"), with "Argive" in the Homeric, general sense of "Greek"; this reinforces the message of 672 *Argiva iuventa* (on troops from Tivoli) that the Italian war is a kind of replay of the Trojan, in ethnic oppositions as in other particulars.

Sed fortuna fuit: at Turnus' first appearance we hear an intimation of his failure. Ardea will not become the great city and center of empire, the homeland of the Lavinian race. The dread (*tristis*) goddess rising on somber (*fuscis*) wings is disturbingly like black (*atra*) Night who flew with mournful (*tristis*) shadow around Marcellus' head a few hundred lines before, a harbinger of early death and failure to continue the dynastic line, making ominous the "black [*nigra*] night" in which Turnus slumbers so placidly. And yet *avis* are "our" ancestors, pointing to the mixed ancestry of the Romans. Turnus is a Roman ancestor *manqué*, like the fallen warriors in the last chapter, whose peoples are destined to share in the Roman nation.

As a distressed heroine lies awake, tossing and turning over in her mind whatever amatory dilemma possesses her, she may express it in a soliloquy, as Medea's wakefulness introduces her soliloquy in Apollonius and presumably also in Varro. Elsewhere the plaintive soliloquy is independent of the sleep-lessness motif; Catullus' Ariadne piquantly delivers her soliloquy after waking from untroubled sleep (64.132–201), as does Bion's Aphrodite, roused by the speaker with the news that Adonis is dead (*Adonis* 3–4). Juturna follows this line in the valediction discussed above. Dido's instance of the topos comes at 4.522–52: first the observation that night covers all things, then the revelation that the Phoenician queen cannot sleep for desperate love of Aeneas, then her soliloquy. The metaphor in lines 531–32, "her anguish redoubles, and love, flooding back again, fluctuates on a great surge of anger" (*ingeminant curae*

---

[60] Virgil may have chosen the name "Daunus" for Turnus' father (see A. Russi in *EV* 1.1003 on the originality of Virgil's nomenclature) for its similarity to "Danae"; it also resonates ironically against the myth of Danaus on the sword belt.

rursusque resurgens / saevit amor magnoque irarum fluctuat aestu),[61] distracts and amplifies Catullus 64.62, on Ariadne: "she flucuates on great waves of anguish" (*magnis curarum fluctuat undis*).

This brings us to *Aeneid* 10.685–88. Juno has rescued Turnus from battle (as she proposed to do at 615–16 *quin et pugnae subducere Turnum / et Dauno possem incolumem servare parenti*, "that I might remove Turnus from the battle and keep him unharmed for his father Daunus") by luring him onto a ship in pursuit of a decoy, phantom Aeneas and then cutting him adrift. In the preceding lines, upon realizing his situation, Turnus launches into a soliloquy consisting mainly of questions nominally addressed to Jupiter—"Where am I going? What should I do? What will my men think of me?"—and ends in a prayer to the winds that they might take pity and dash him into the shoals. He contemplates either stabbing himself or swimming back to shore; but:

> ter conatus utramque viam, ter maxima Iuno
> continuit iuvenemque animi miserata repressit.
> labitur alta secans fluctuque aestuque secundo
> et patris antiquam Dauni defertur ad urbem.

Thrice he tried either route; thrice great Juno checked the young man and held him back, pitying him in her heart. He glides away, cutting the deep with the surge and swell speeding him on, and is carried down[62] to the ancient city of his father Daunus.

Here we see the best in Turnus, his equal concern for his self-respect and for his men. At 674 he refers to them as *palantis*, "straying," like sheep: he is the good shepherd, an old metaphor for a good king, at war and otherwise (compare, for example, Agamemnon as the "shepherd of the people [*laôn*]" at *Iliad* 2.243). It will be noted that even as Turnus replicates Aeneas' anguish, in his equivalent speech, that he will die miserably at sea instead of heroically in battle (1.94–101, Aeneas' first appearance in the poem), Turnus is less self-absorbed here than Aeneas, who speaks and feels as if he were alone—like Odysseus in the Homeric model (*Odyssey* 5.299–312). Yet this image of masculine responsibility contains another. Turnus' speech, especially the rhetorical questions and the self-destructive urges, the thoughts occurring and moving into new passages, thematically and structurally recalls the soliloquy of a distraught epic heroine; any of those mentioned above might serve as an example.[63]

---

[61] Line 4.564 *variosque irarum concitat aestus*, Mercury's assessment of Dido's situation, will bitterly revaluate 532.

[62] The verb, *defertur*, is the same used of Allecto's approach to Daunus' city at 7.411 (*delata*).

[63] Cf. Harrison on 10.668–79: "[Turnus' speech] shows some resemblance to the complaint-monologues of disturbed or abandoned heroines such as Medea or Ariadne, a literary colour which tends to present Turnus as vulnerable and sympathetic. Turnus' sister Juturna is given a similar pathetic complaint at 12.872–84."

Moschus' Europa, who herself is being carried over the sea, wonders why and whither; her questions too are addressed to Zeus, albeit unwittingly (*Europa* 135–52).[64] Both Turnus and Europa, it will now be recalled, carry detailed representations of the myth of Io, Europa on her golden basket (*Europa* 37–62) and Turnus on his golden shield (*Aeneid* 7.789–92); the latter representation is given great semantic prominence as a "huge narrative," an *argumentum ingens*.

Harrison discerns in 673 "[my men,] whom—the shame!—I have left one and all to an unspeakable death" (*quosne*[65]—*nefas!*—*omnis infanda in morte reliqui*) a reworking of Ariadne's self-reproach at Catullus 64.180–81: "Or am I to look for help from my father? Whom I myself left behind in pursuit of a young man splattered with brotherly slaughter?" (*an patris auxilium sperem? quemne ipsa reliqui / respersum iuvenem fraterna caede secuta?*).[66] The crime of the fratricidal princess, heiress to gaudy Hellenistic recenterings of epic, underlies the self-accusation of the epic hero. Turnus inverts the situation of Ariadne, watching the departing Theseus from the shore—and so also inverts the situation of Dido (a bit earlier, at 648, he asks the phantom Aeneas Dido's question: *quo fugis, Aenea*, "Where are you fleeing to?"). Compare his despairing *quid ago?* ("What shall I do?") in 10.675 with Dido's *en quid ago?* in the soliloquy that occurs when she finds herself unable to "cull placid sleep" like other tired bodies on this night (4.522–23). Ovid will use *quo feror*, "Where am I being taken?" (like Turnus at 670), for lovelorn heroines (Byblis and Myrrha) at *Metamorphoses* 9.509 and 10.320. In the lines immediately following Turnus' soliloquy he "flucutates now this way, now that way in his mind" (*animo nunc huc, nunc fluctuat illuc*), at one, perhaps, with his maritime surroundings,[67] but also echoing the ambivalence of the Apollonian Medea and her successors. In the episode just quoted from Book 4, Dido's love for Aeneas likewise rages and fluctuates on a great surge—*aestu*—of anger. Turnus wonders whether to commit suicide, again like a typical heroine, or, like Ciris, to dive into the sea (this even casts a faint feminizing light back onto his escape by swimming the Tiber at the end of Book 9, where his masculine size and strength were emphasized).[68]

---

[64] Compare Horace *Carm.* 3.27.37 (Europa) *unde quo veni?* and the rest of her monologue, surely influenced by Moschus' version.

[65] In *quosne* (otherwise *quosque* or *quosve*) Harrison follows Asper *apud* Servius Auctus, seeing it as part of the echo of Catullus.

[66] The emphasis on Ariadne's "brotherly slaughter" (her aid in slaying the Minotaur) assimilates her to Apollonius' Medea, who helps Jason kill her brother. Dido's reuse of the phrase "brotherly slaughter" (*Aen.* 4.21 *fraterna caede*) for the murder of her husband by her brother provocatively draws her into the same complex of personae.

[67] Note 683 *fluctibus* and 687 *fluctu*, both used literally of the waves of the sea.

[68] A bird metamorphosis (like that of a Ciris, Procne, or Alcyone) is insinuated by the taunting Aeneas at 12.891–93 "turn yourself into every shape . . . aspire to reach the steep stars on wings" (*verte omnis tete in facies . . . opta ardua pennis / astra sequi*).

Nor are the associations of this soliloquy isolated in the discourse that surrounds Turnus. At 12.666–68, the turning point of the last battle and for him the ethical crux, he appears for a second just like Myrrha, Medea, or Ciris:

> Turnus et obtutu tacito stetit; aestuat ingens
> uno in corde pudor mixtoque insania luctu
> et furiis agitatus amor et conscia virtus.

Turnus stood with silent stare. An immense shame surged in one and the same heart with madness mixed with grief, and love goaded by rage, and keen awareness of his own valor.

In the person of Turnus these lines are revalued from their first use, at 10.870–73, of Mezentius' battle rage. So too is the distressed heroine pulled in different directions by these same emotions, torn between *amor* and *virtus* (equally "valor" or "virtue": here he anticipates the heroines of Ovid's *Metamorphoses*); Turnus' situation transfigures them into the moral perils of the battlefield (lines 666–67 are repeated from the situation of Mezentius at 10.870–71), and finally, by one of the tropes we have seen *amor* performing in this poem, fuses his heroine-persona with his whole story. When he speaks, it is to tell Juturna that he must go to meet Aeneas, even if it means his death (676–80)—just so do the lovelorn heroines finally choose to go to their man at the risk of death.

At the end of his soliloquy in Book 10 Turnus becomes like a child, rescued from danger and helplessly returned to the parental nest. The viewpoint these lines invite us to take suggests that of Juno, satisfied that for the time being the ancient order of Italy is undisturbed. Her explicit goal in the deception was after all "to remove Turnus from battle and keep him safe for his father Daunus" (615–16). The close connection in 688 of Turnus' father to the "ancient city" (where the epithet has undertones of security and tradition) sends us back to the wider theme of fatherhood and ancestry; nor does the verse do so in vain, or only for an instant. On the contrary, fatherhood resonates for us in Turnus' response to his plight. *Ter conatus utramque viam*: "Thrice he tried both ways." Compare the wording of 6.700, where Aeneas meets his father's ghost in the Underworld: *ter conatus ibi collo dare bracchia circum, / ter frustra comprensa manus effugit imago* ("Thrice he tried there to throw his arms around his neck; thrice the vision eluded his arms, embraced in vain"). The echo resonates both against Turnus' recent pursuit of a phantom[69] and against the way his homeward voyage is described as a trip down (*defertur*) to his father's city. The verbal echo points up a contrast, reminding us of the crushing losses that Aeneas has endured; that he has no father and no ancestral home to return to. The two triple attempts are different in motivation.

---

[69] See the discussion by Thomas 1998:278–80 (not covering this episode) of Achilles and Aeneas in *Il.* 20.

Aeneas acts instinctively on filial love; Turnus, on his need for glory in battle. The failure of his own attempts at escape ultimately bring him back to his father and the ancient city, back to the place where we saw him in the dark of night, when he first appeared to us under the guise of an epic heroine.

The ship's easy motion in 687 *labitur* recalls Aeneas' voyage up the Tiber in 8.91 *labitur uncta vadis abies* ("the anointed pinewood vessel glides upon the waves"); both openings come from two unusually fluid (because wholly dactylic) lines preserved from Ennius' fragmentary *Annales*, 376 Skutsch *labitur uncta carina, volat super impetus undas* ("the anointed hull glides, its momentum flies over the waves") and 505 Skutsch *labitur uncta carina per aequora cana velocis* ("the anointed hull of the swift vessel glides over the whitened sea"). It is noteworthy that whereas 10.687 uses the opening verb of Ennius' lines, their noun phrase, with a different verb, is used (at line end) of the Trojan fleet, soon to depart from Carthage, at 4.398: *natat uncta carina* ("the anointed hull floats"). In this passage the viewpoint of Dido, through the description of the Trojans' activities and the ensuing ant simile, increasingly predominates. Turnus' homeward voyage, enmeshed in descriptions of Aeneas' fatal journeys away from a false homeland and upriver to the destined one, sets Ardea pathetically against Rome and contrasts the doomed line of Daunus with the chosen line of Anchises. Thomas notes the intertext with Catullus' Argo (64.6–7), which calls to mind the ktistic element in the *Argonautica*.[70] It would be interesting to know what nation-making voyages Ennius' verses described.

Turnus' assimilation to both heroine and helpless child in this episode is typical. In Juturna's soliloquy in Book 12 the "Stabat Mater" motif, which relies on a partial assimilation of the mourner to the mourned (insofar as our sympathies need to make the substitution), takes strength from these occasional, but meaningfully placed, treatments of her brother as a literary heroine of her type; and here it is significant that along with Turnus' youth and kinship with the water goddess, Virgil seems to have been the first to give her a tragic-erotic history, the myth that she gained her divinity in compensation for being raped by Jupiter. In the *Epitaph on Adonis* too, where Aphrodite provides a focus for our sympathy that the inert boy cannot accommodate, Bion takes every opportunity to assimilate the grieving Aphrodite to her mortal beloved: the wound in her heart answers his savage wound (lines 16–17); she is so cut by thorns and disfigured by the violence of her own grief that her beauty suffers death along with him (29–30); as his blood gives miraculous birth to a rose, so her equally profuse tears become the anemone (64–66). She even regrets, as we have seen, that she cannot follow him into death. It is in Juturna's echo of that regret that she most closely approaches her brother as a distressed heroine. At 12.883–84 she sums up her anguish: *o quae satis ima*

---

[70] Thomas 1999:29–30 (first published in 1982).

dehiscat / terra mihi, Manisque deam demittat ad imos? ("Oh, what land will gape open sufficiently for me and send me down, a goddess, to the ghosts below?"), repeating the very words of Turnus in his suicidal frenzy: *aut quae satis ima dehiscat / terra mihi* (10.675–76 "Or what land will gape open sufficiently for me?"). Here she also shares with him the precedent of Dido, fearing for her honor: 4.24 *sed mihi vel tellus optem prius ima dehiscat.* The pivot of the identification between sister and brother, so fundamental to the intertext with Bion and so crucial for the transferral of our sympthies to Turnus through Juturna, is precisely the transformation of his outraged sense of responsibility and honor into her grief, through a descent to the Underworld that collapses together his premature death wish, Aphrodite's and Juturna's impossible death wish, and Adonis' death.

Finally, the heroine motif that disturbs Turnus' gender also exacerbates our doubts (as discussed above) about his robustly asserted Italian ethnicity. The *argumentum ingens* on Turnus' shield comes into full prominence here: in carrying an implement adorned with the story of Io he is like Moschus' Europa with her decorated basket, and so like a Phoenician, identifiable from this perspective with Dido. But Turnus is indeed *descended* from Io, which relates him by blood to Dido, whose descent from Belus (1.621) places her, too, in the genealogical tradition established by the Pseudo-Hesiodic *Catalogue of Women*, among the progeny of Inachus along with Io, Europa, and Danae. These are pointed innovations by Virgil. The way this descent first comes up in the poem is notable: Amata, vainly persuading Latinus that Turnus fits the requirement that Lavinia's bridegroom be a foreigner, reserves as her clinching argument that "if one were to go back to the first origins of Turnus' house, his ancestors [lit. "fathers"] are Inachus and Acrisius" (7.371–72 *et Turno, si prima domus repetatur origo, / Inachus Acrisiusque patres*)—conjoining the fathers of Io and Danae, she unwittingly damns Turnus to a common ancestry with two distressed heroines.[71] What is most interesting is that the context makes this lineage that of the nation that Turnus would found with Lavinia—an Inachid anti-Rome, the narrowly avoided foil to the people who will come forth from the union between her and Aeneas. One is also reminded that in this schema Adonis too was an Inachid, the grandson of Belus' brother Agenor ([Hesiod] fr. 139 Merkelbach/West). This question cuts to the heart of the poem and the justification for Aeneas' settlement itself, and involves a paradox. If Turnus' family origin is not Italian, he has less of a claim to Italian land than his opponent, whose ancestor Dardanus sprang from Italy.[72] On the other hand, if he is Italian, he is not qualified to marry Lavinia, according to the oracle given to Latinus (7.96–101). The ethnic characterization also underlines the reversal of the Trojan War that the Italian war will effect: Trojans will beat Greeks this time.

---

[71] Cf. Hannah 2004.

[72] See pp. 10–12 for the problems in Aeneas' own family origin and its relation to his settlement.

The perspective given us by Turnus' genealogy draws a boundary between
~~the Greco-Oriental world on his side—in ethnopoetic terms, this combination~~
makes him the clearest Adonis-figure in the poem—and the Italian world
which is owed to Aeneas and to which his own *prima origo* can be traced.
While in terms of the Trojan War (which are still the active terms of understanding for Aeneas and the other characters) Turnus is opposed to Aeneas as
Greek to Trojan, he also takes on the burden of the Oriental, as he does in the
simile that likens him to the Ganges and the Nile. Unlike Moschus, who
depicted Io the cow on Europa's basket being driven to the Nile (lines 44–54),
Virgil has Io the cow[73] in the company of her keeper Argus and her father, the
river Inachus (7.789–92):

> at levem clipeum sublatis cornibus Io
> auro insignibat, iam saetis obsita, iam bos,
> argumentum ingens, et custos virginis Argus,
> caelataque amnem fundens pater Inachus urna.

But Io, in gold, with her horns upraised—now covered in hair, a cow
now—decorated the polished shield (a huge narrative), as did the
maiden's keeper, Argus, and her father Inachus pouring his flood from a
carven urn.

Caelata, "carven," denotes a sort of anti-ecphrasis, a frustrated *mise-en-abyme*:
we are not permitted to look closer and trace the carvings.[74] Inachus here
replaces the Nile, which is prominent—with its seven mouths—in Moschus'
ecphrasis. Yet the Nile will reappear, succouring Io's descendant Cleopatra, on
Aeneas' own golden shield; and despite these suppressions and substitutions,
Io's sojourn in Egypt resonates in the *Aeneid* too. In Hellenistic times she was
identified with Isis, the Egyptian goddess whom Cleopatra, brandishing the
sistrum, personifies on Aeneas' Shield; that portrayal is not just an ethnic slur,
but a Roman interpretation of the centuries-old identification of Ptolemaic
queens with Isis, as the sistrum's epithet "ancestral" indicates (8.695 *patrio
sistro*). "With her horns upraised" in particular recalls a common depiction of
Isis—one that would group her with the half-beast monster gods that support
Cleopatra against Rome on Aeneas' shield (8.698). Turnus' shield will figure in
a telling substitution: the end of the war finds him bearing a different representation of a mythological encounter between Greece and the East, the
sword belt stolen from Pallas with the daughters of Danaus and sons of
Aegyptus carved upon it, a prophetic symbol of curtailed lineage, whereas the
Io story always represents some kind of descent. Symbolically, he exchanges

---

[73] Compare the wording of Moschus *Eur.* 42 εἰσέτι πόρτις ἐοῦσα with *Aen.* 7.790 *iam saetis
obsita, iam bos.*
[74] We are given a somewhat closer look at the Inachid descendants carved (*caelata* again) on Dido's
golden plates at 1.640–41.

ancestorship for its lack, always in the same genealogical terms: the Aegyptids too were descended from Inachus.

Thus the play with Turnus' gender involves his status as a non-founder, a son doomed to end his father's line, an anti-Aeneas who is easy to imagine as a narrowly avoided ancestor—involves themes, that is, that we have come to understand as tropes of youth, death, and desire as they are embodied by the Adonis figures of this poem. Gender ambiguity also flickers over Turnus at 12.216–21, when he approaches the altar *demisso lumine*, "with downcast eyes." Have we not seen this somewhere else recently? At 11.479 Lavinia, "the cause of such great misfortune" (*causa mali tanti*), approaches the temple of Minerva with a group of propitiating matrons, *oculos deiecta decoros*—"with her comely [or modest] eyes lowered."[75] In the instant when Turnus momentarily appears most like our fallen warriors, he also becomes like his betrothed, the object of the great struggle. When we find at 12.216–21 the appreciation of his body that the end of the poem subliminally sends us looking for, it is part of a replay of the supplication of his would-be bride. He is introduced here as a virginal suppliant as modestly reverential as Lavinia (*incessu tacito*, etc.); his physical attractiveness, evoked in the following line, becomes part of that reminiscence. Let us try a refinement of our narratological analysis of the passage: the Rutulians who are the explicit viewers here momentarily take on the viewpoint of Aeneas, imagining him as seeing Turnus as young and callow. And this callowness of youth carries with it the attributes of an erotic object—not literally, but metaphorically, as if war were sex and martial defeat sexual conquest.[76] The latent erotic element in Turnus' youth and beauty surfaces to register the Rutulians' unease.

Nothing in the context locks in this interpretation of 216–21 as the only one possible. At most we can say that that is how Turnus' men in their apprehension might imagine that the enemy sees their commander; and the assimilation to Lavinia, whether or not it too is part of the Rutulians' view, reinforces this impression. The superimposition of personae eroticizes the coming combat[77] and makes of Turnus' and Lavinia's bodies two kinds of prize for Aeneas. The omen at 244–56, engineered by Juturna, and particularly Tolumnius' interpretation of it, picks up and complicates this view. An eagle swoops down upon a swan, only to be chased off by other shore birds. The augur Tolumnius (who must have been among the Rutulians standing by at 216–21) interprets the swan seized by the eagle (250 *rapit*) as their own "seized" king (265 *regem*

---

[75] Cf. Davies 1997:105–106 on the lowered gaze as a sign of female modesty in bridal portraits on second-century sarcophagi.

[76] A parallel is Goliath's view of David at 1 Samuel 17:42: "And when the Philistine looked about and saw David, he disdained him, for he was but a youth, and ruddy, with beautiful eyes" (the words on David's beauty may originally be an interpolation from 16:12, though present in both Masoretic and Greek texts).

[77] The kinetic sexual component of Turnus' slaying is discussed by Mitchell 1992:233–34.

raptum). Turnus becomes like Lavinia, who from an Italian viewpoint (represented by Amata) is a stolen bride, as well as like many another raped heroine: Ennius' Ilia stands out among examples, or the Sabine women on Aeneas' Shield (8.635 *raptas*). The allegory of Juturna's omen reduces Turnus to a passive state, analogous to that of a ravished maiden, in need of armed masculine protection. This is very much in line with Juturna's view of Turnus, as at 229–30, where her suggestion (like Juno's action in Book 10) infantilizes Turnus, makes him less of a hero than a victim: "Are you not ashamed, Rutulians, to put one life at risk in exhange for the whole army?"

At Turnus' Adonis-moment, then, Adoniac eroticism comes into its full force, inextricable from the various struggles of the poem. The assimilation to Lavinia on which this force depends may in some sense flow from his similarity to a Hellenistic epic heroine. Yet the relationship between those two comparanda of Turnus is metonymic; their effects cannot simply be exchanged, explained as the operation of the same thematics in different terms. In our comparisons to the Adonis myth, to put it another way, he sometimes emerges as like Aphrodite; sometimes as like Adonis. The combination of the two personae has an almost generic justification, as we noted above in connecting Bion's *Adonis* with Juturna's lament as instances of the "Stabat Mater," but in Turnus's case it has an additional, more immediate motivation, which the next chapter will explore in greater detail: the split is no doubt an effect of the epic heroine who most immediately stands behind Turnus' entrance in beauty and his shipboard soliloquy, Dido, who is simultaneously gazer and object. Dido's ghost is still haunting the text.

Chapter Three

DIDO

One of the sharpest ethnic boundaries drawn in the *Aeneid* lies between the Romans, heirs of Aeneas, and the Carthaginians, heirs of Dido. The earliest lines of the epic—the beginning of the narrative, directly after the proem and invocation—introduce the opposition of Rome to Carthage (1.12–14 *urbs antiqua fuit, Tyrii tenuere coloni, / Karthago, Italiam contra Tiberinaque longe / ostia*), a geographical opposition, but foreshadowing the mortal struggle. With exuberant polyptoton Dido picks up this double sense in her curse at 4.628–29: *litora litoribus contraria, fluctibus undas, / imprecor, arma armis* ("I pray for shore to be set against shore, sea against sea, weapons against weapons!"). Here is ethnic allegory, taking in the Punic Wars (mentioned only twice in the poem, and obliquely, at 1.19–22 and 10.11–13) and making them a subtext; behind the early lines of the poem, and behind Dido's words and actions, lies a whole series of implicit references to the Punic Wars, proleptic, ironic, and etiological.[1] Dread at the future destruction of her beloved Carthage, along with hatred toward the Trojans, is what motivates Juno and the first episodes of the poem—indeed, the narrator ascribes the travails of the Aeneadae, and the plot of the poem, to Juno's reaction to the Roman threat to Carthage. Yet the poem negotiates this opposition rather than fixes it: it draws the boundary and erases and redraws it, often through verbal and thematic allusion to earlier poetic treatments. Their sojourn in Carthage emerges as a pivot of the Aeneadae's movement away from Trojan identity. Fundamentally, the *Aeneid* makes the Romans an originally Oriental people who have left that national identity behind in ruined Troy, and traces the early, incomplete stages of this divestment; it makes the Carthaginians—Phoenician colonists from Tyre—persistently Oriental. In the beginning, then, the boundary between the Aeneadae and Dido's people is weak and permeable. It grows stronger as the Carthaginians offer the Romans an ethnic foil that both defines Roman identity by antithesis and yet remains part of Roman origins. Basic to this sense of a foil is the strongly represented consciousness of Dido herself, which draws us to her viewpoint and prevents us from seeing her and her people as simply alien.

---

[1] Horsfall 1990:128–31 reviews the passages. On the "otherness" of Carthage as embodied in Dido see Hexter 1992.

I

Let us first connect Dido thematically to the Adonis-figures discussed in the last two chapters, who also effect an ethnic antithesis. Her Tyrian origins foreshadow the Oriental provenience of the Adonis-model embedded in our passages and help establish its connotations in this poem; her viewpoint, moreover, is so much a part of her tragic love story that we might expect to find some residue of it elsewhere in the images that combine love and death. We should think now (and in the two succeeding chapters as well) of the ways in which a decision about focalization entails an ideological perspective, staying particularly alert to the various truth claims identifiable with various viewpoints and the way they vie for the reader's sympathies without cancelling one another out.[2] Finally, and most concretely, the figure of the dying god is relevant to Dido's story. The Adonis that lies behind Euryalus, Lausus, Pallas, Camilla, and Turnus is one of several dying gods, scattered through the subtext of the *Aeneid*, whose Oriental affiliations and tragic stories complicate the ethnic contrasts along which the action unfolds. At different times, in addition to Adonis, the text reminds us of Osiris, Attis, Hyacinthus, Pygmalion, and Ba'al (the last two draw Dido into the network), involving each time in some way the ancestry and national identity of the Romans.

At the head of the list of slayers and slain that opens the last battle of the Italian war (12.458), Osiris is named as a Rutulian warrior slain by a Trojan, Thymbraeus.[3] The name of the Egyptian dying god not only lends a sense of inevitability to the Italian's death,[4] but also, in opposition to Thymbraeus, makes him on an allegorical level a representative Oriental, and makes the battle foreshadow Octavian's triumph over Egypt. The combat between these two symbolically separates Trojan-Italian (that is, Roman) national identity from Oriental (Egyptian), making the former the conqueror, the latter the conquered. That the mythological connotations of Osiris—including syncretism with Adonis from at least the time of Ptolemy II Philadelphus—lend him a certain sympathy complicates our otherwise pro-Roman view of the combat. The miniature episode makes us look ahead to a final separation of Roman from Oriental under Octavian, which of course simultaneously meant the absorption of the last morsel of the eastern Mediterranean world into the Roman empire—anything but a separation.

Atys is one of three boys leading the show troops of boy horsemen in Book 5 (in the "Troy" exercise); the other two are a homonymous grandson of Priam and Ascanius, whose special friend Atys is (569 *parvus Atys pueroque puer dilectus Iulo*). He is thus symbolically placed among representatives of both the old country and the future, personifications, in a sense, of the transition from

---

[2] Cf. Conte 1986:156–62.

[3] Discussed in Reed 1998.

[4] Similar mythological connotations attach to the names of victims at 9.573–74 (Caeneus and Itys); cf. Hyacinthus at Apollonius *Arg.* 1.1044.

Trojan to Roman that this book, with its frequent mini-etiologies and references to Roman families and customs, registers more explicitly than any other in the poem. Atys himself is named as the ancestor of the Atii family (568 *Atys, genus unde Atii duxere Latini*). His name, of course, has an Anatolian ring to it and so is appropriate to a Trojan—but the very reason it does so is singularly inauspicious to the reader, who will remember Atys as the son of Croesus of Lydia who was killed by a boar.[5] He also inevitably calls to mind Attis, the beloved of the Anatolian great goddess Cybele, of whose story the one told by Herodotus is a thin rationalization: in one version he is killed by a boar while hunting (like Adonis, whose hunting myth is probably modeled after his).[6] His name is spelled "Atys" in an epigram by Dioscorides that was included in the *Garland* of Meleager.[7] In chapter 1 we saw Attis joined with Hyacinthus and Adonis in the subtext of Pallas' flower simile (violets were said to have grown from his blood). The pathetic anaphora in Trojan Atys' two lines (*alter Atys . . . parvus Atys . . .*), together with the elegiac note of boyish friendship expressively underscored by interlocked polyptoton (*Atys pueroque puer dilectus Iulo*), resonates against the death either of Lydian prince or of Lydian god. Young Atys' name makes the transition from Trojan to Roman especially vivid, as the transition from the emotional excesses of the Orient; and this Atys is the ancestor not just of any Roman clan, but of the clan of Augustus' own mother, Atia.[8] His friendship with Iulus prefigures the alliance between the houses that occurred when Julius Caesar's sister Julia married M. Atius Balbus (making Augustus possible); their friendship is a kind of proleptic marriage (not an unusual figure in this poem). Woven into this stately, noble ceremony passed down to the Romans by their Trojan ancestors is a hint of a wild, violent ceremony that is also part of the Anatolian heritage of Rome. Is the boy's name telling us that this is the kind of thing the Trojans must leave in the past in order to become proper Romans? Or is it telling us that an "Oriental" excess is forever embedded in Roman identity?

Cinyras, the legendary king of Cyprus and father of Adonis in a widespread myth, may also obliquely enter the *Aeneid*. At 10.185–86 certain manuscripts of respectable antiquity, together with Tiberius Donatus' commentary, name "Cinyrus" (in various spellings)[9] as an object of the narrator's apostrophe:

> Non ego te, Ligurum ductor fortissime bello,
> transierim, Cinyre, et paucis comitate Cupavo.

---

[5] Herodotus 1.34–45; cf. 1.94 on Atys, an early king of Lydia involved with the Lydian colonization of Etruria.

[6] Frazer 1914:1.286, Burkert 1979:108 with 196 n. 5. In another myth, followed in Catullus 63, he castrates himself. For other names in Virgil associated with Oriental cults (e.g. Sybaris, Thaemon) see Saunders 1940:543.

[7] Dioscorides *A.P.* 6.220.3.

[8] An Atys is king of Alba at Livy 1.3.8.

[9] Mynors in his Oxford text reports: "Cinyr(a)e, Cynir(a)e, Cinire (*quae idem valent*) MVω." *Cunerae* P (corrected to *Cinerae*), *Cumarre* R seem to reflect the same reading as Servius Auctus.

> Let me not pass you by, Cinyras, leader of the Ligurians, mighty in war, and you, Cupavo, with your small number of companions.

Servius Auctus reads *Cunare*, which as commentators note recalls Mount Cunarus in Picenum and would accord with Virgil's practice of giving his Italian warriors geographical names, not always from their own locales (in this case, far from Liguria).[10] No special associations of the mountain resonate in this warrior's brief appearance. It is arguable that those of Cinyras do, and that the reading *Cinyre* (or is this a corruption of *Cinyra* itself, as Sabbadini 1889:34 suggests?) meaningfully brings in the tale of Adonis' parentage by Cinyras and his incestuous daughter, who was metamorphosed into the myrrh tree.[11] The Ligurian leader goes to battle along with Cupavo,[12] son of Cycnus, who bears swan feathers on his head in token of his father. *Crimen, Amor, vestrum*, the poet explains at 187, where the plural *vestrum* is rightly accounted for by Nettleship as referring to the cooperation of both gods of love: "You, Love, are to blame—you and your mother."[13] The imputation is explained by the story that follows (187–93): Cycnus loved Phaethon, and after his death mourned so bitterly that he changed into a swan.[14] If Cinyrus is the name in 186, the myth of Cycnus resonates for both Cupavo and his companion in Virgil's apostrophe. *Crimen, Amor, vestrum* has meaning for both, as is the general idea of a father's love leading to a metamorphosis. Mourning is implicit in Cinyrus' name through wordplay with the Greek adjective *kinyros*, "plaintive," and the verb *kinyromai*, "lament, wail."[15] Once again a Roman ancestor—or at least an ally fighting at Aeneas' side—would cast a lurid, lugubrious Oriental shadow. Roman imperialism over the lands of Adonis also echoes strongly in the name via recent political events: Strabo 16.2.18 reports a Cinyras, last king of Byblos, beheaded by Pompey.[16]

---

[10] Cf. Saunders 1940, Zaffagno 1973.

[11] In extant texts Cinyras is first named as the father of Myrrha (also called Smyrna) in Ovid *Met.* 10 (perhaps following Cinna's *Smyrna*), but Theodorus *SH* 749 (Hellenistic or earlier) may have preceded; and Cinyras is named as father of Adonis since around 400 B.C.E. (Plato Comicus fr. 3. Kassel/Austin, Antimachus fr. 102 West). The incest myth of Adonis's birth is first attested, with Theias as the father, in Panyassis fr. 27 Bernabé = [Apollodorus] *Bibl.* 3.14.3.

[12] I pass over constructions of the line, starting with that of Tiberius Donatus, that make Cinyrus (or whatever the reading is) an epithet of Cupavo, or otherwise reduce the apostrophe in 185–86 to a single warrior; see E. S. Gaggero in *EV* I.958 s.vv. "Cunaro" and "Cupavone."

[13] Nettleship in Conington ad loc., comparing for the grammar 1.140 *vestras, Eure, domos* (i.e. "of all you winds").

[14] The myth was treated by Phanocles (fr. 6 Powell) in the early Hellenistic period (cf. Hollis 1992:276–77); other versions in Ovid *Met.* 2.367–80, Pausanias 1.30.3, anon. in Westermann 1839:347–48. A similar swan passage in the *Aeneid*: 7.699–702.

[15] See Ahl 1985:33.

[16] Frazer 1914:1.27–28; H. von Geisau in *RE* Suppl. 6 (1935) 164.

Cinyrus' claim to a place in this complex is fortified by a parallel in the catalogue of Italian warriors, where the narrator apostrophizes Oebalus in similar terms (7.734–36):

> Nec tu carminibus nostris indictus abibis,
> Oebale, quem generasse Telon Sebethide nympha
> fertur, Teleboum Capreas cum regna teneret.

Nor will you depart from my song unmentioned, Oebalus—you whom Telon is said to have begotten on the nymph Sebethis, when he held sway over Capreae of the Teleboans.

Oebalus was the name of the father of Hyacinthus (to whose homonymous flower, the "languishing hyacinth," Pallas is compared at 11.69) in a version of the myth mentioned by Hyginus;[17] here he is apparently a counterpart to the namesake of Adonis' father, fighting on the opposite side. Dying gods, woven into the texture of the *Aeneid* by Virgil's name play, seem invariably to lend Greco-Oriental notes to Roman origins—and not negatively or disapprovingly. Note that all are Greek mythological figures—even Osiris had a place in Greek religion by now—but typically have some Near Eastern associations in Greek mythology (and such cults were in any case a conspicuous feature of Eastern Mediterranean civilization). Deployed on either side of the Trojan-Italian war, these figures recall the Adoniac overtones of the deaths of Euryalus, Lausus, Pallas, and Camilla.

Osiris, Atys, Cinyrus, and Oebalus are isolated personages, mentioned only once each and taking part only in their own brief passages. Two other characters who recall dying gods play larger roles in the *Aeneid* and bring us to Dido. Her brother Pygmalion has a name derived from a Phoenician deity Pumai, an Adonis-type attested at Carthage, Sardinia, and especially parts of Cyprus; Hesychius has a note on a phonetic variant: "Pygmaion: Adonis among the Cypriots."[18] The mythological Cypriot Pygmalion whose statue came to life, first heard of in the paradoxography of Philostephanus (third century B.C.E.) and best known from Ovid's *Metamorphoses*, has the same derivation; figures more closely linked to the Phoenician origins of the name are an apparently historical king of Cyprus and a plainly legendary one who was the maternal grandfather of Adonis in one myth of his birth.[19] Virgil takes his Pygmalion

---

[17] Hyginus *Fab.* 271.1. In Ovid *Met.* 10.196 (cf. 13.396) and *Ibis* 586 it is an open question whether Oebalides means "son of Oebalus" or "Spartan." Elsewhere Oebalus comes later than Hyacinthus in the Spartan dynasty (e.g. [Hesiod] *Cat.* fr. 199.8 Merkelbach/West). The Hyacinthus myth also enters the *Aeneid* at 10.564; see p. 22 n. 16 above.

[18] Benz 1972:391–92, Müller 1988. Hellanicus *FGrH* 4 F 57 says that Pygmalion founded Carpasia in Cyprus.

[19] Neanthes of Cyzicus *FGrH* 84 F 32, Diodorus Siculus 19.79.4; [Apollodorus] *Bibl.* 3.14.3. Ovid *Met.* 10.297–99 makes the sculptor Pygmalion Adonis' great- (and great-great-) grandfather.

from the historian Timaeus, who told of Pygmalion's murder of Dido's husband Sychaeus and Dido's flight and founding of Carthage; Menander of
Ephesus finds the story in the city archives of Tyre.[20] Sychaeus himself also
recalls Adonis, if a version of the late-attested myth that has him killed by
Pygmalion while hunting boar was current in Virgil's time.[21]

Thus Dido's Tyrian background is subliminally marked by dying gods. They
are part of the web of eastern Mediterranean deities who stand behind her
people: her father is named Belus (1.621), an old adaptation into Greek
mythology of the Phoenician divine title Ba'al, which was applied to city gods
of the lamented type.[22] A representative ancestor of the Oriental races in
Greek mythology since the ethnographical genealogies of the Hesiodic
Catalogue of Women,[23] Belus seems to have this role at *Aeneid* 2.82, where
Sinon refers to *Belidae Palamedis*, a learned allusion to Palamedes' descent from
Belus through his son Danaus, who settled in Greece. At 1.729–30 *Belus et
omnes a Belo* seems to make him a remote ancestor or dynastic founder of
Dido's Tyrian line. Venus' designation of Carthage at 1.338 as "the city of
Agenor" engages with the same genealogy, which makes Dido a distant rela-
tive of Turnus (and Adonis) and sets up within the poem a mythological system for understanding national identity and destiny.[24] Dido herself sometimes
goes by the name Elissa, from the Phoenician god El (or more generally from
the word *'ēl*, "god").[25] According to Servius on 1.343, in naming Sychaeus
Virgil has altered an original Sicarbas; the latter Hellenizes the name
Sikarba'al, "Ba'al remembers," attested in Punic inscriptions[26] (it may be noteworthy that the new name Sychaeus, while suppressing the Semitic deity, pun-
ningly insinuates the tragic boar-hunting myth that he and Adonis share
through the new initial syllable *sy-*, the stem of Greek *sys*, "boar"; compare Latin
sus). The alterations transfer reminiscence of Ba'al from Dido's husband to her
father, whose name (according to Servius loc. cit.) was traditionally something
like Methres;[27] the change of paternity has something to do with Virgil's (possibly

---

[20] Timaeus *FGrH* 566 F 82, Menander of Ephesus *FGrH* 783 F 1 = Josephus *Ap.* 1.125.

[21] Preserved in John Malalas *Chron.* 6.19 (p. 126.66 Thurn); Malalas here may be following an
account preserved in a lost section of Servius (whom he cites).

[22] See Smith 1994:69–73 on the Bronze-Age Ba'al of Ugarit.

[23] [Hesiod] fr. 137.2 Merkelbach/West; see West 1985:77–78. Belus is the great-uncle of Adonis
in Pseudo-Hesiod's scheme.

[24] See Mackie 1993, Hannah 2004:144–48. On Turnus' genealogy see p. 69 above.

[25] Theiosso (with Gk. *theio-*, "divine"), the name under which Timaeus writes of her (n. 20 above),
is presumably calqued on the Phoenician name.

[26] *CIS* 1218, 1354.2, 2871.4; cf. Benz 1972:211, 305–306. Compare Heb. Zechariah. The historical background to Dido's story is full of names—conceivably understood by Virgil from learned
sources—that advertise the devotion of the Punic people to such gods: Hamilcar (*'bd-mlqrt*, "ser-
vant of Melqart"), Hasdrubal (*'zr-b'l*, "Ba'al has helped"), Hannibal (*'dn-b'l*, "Ba'al is my lord"). See
Brown 2000:119–29.

[27] The manuscripts disagree between Methres, Methes, Mettes, and Metthes; Menander of
Ephesus *FGrH* 783 F 1 = Josephus *Ap.* 1.125 names a perhaps related Mettenus or Mattenus as
Pygmalion's predecessor as king, and presumably his and Dido's father (this is the genealogy that

Naevius-derived) redating of Dido, but rings as well against his ethnic, cultic, and mythological constructions. It also reassigns Dido and Pygmalion from a specific, "historical" genealogy to a symbolically Phoenician one.

Dido stands in a complicated relationship to the Adonis-figures we looked at in chapter 1, since her relation to a dying god works less by metaphor than metonymy; and also since in her death scene she is both gazing lamenter and gazed-upon lamented, so persistent is her consciousness. One intertextual reading will illustrate this latter point. Dido has both figurative and literal wounds: 4.66–67 "meanwhile a fire eats away at her soft marrow and a silent wound lives beneath her breast" and 4.689 "the wound driven beneath her breast wheezes," both ending *sub pectore vulnus*.[28] This variation has a parallel in Bion's *Adonis* 16–17:

> ἄγριον ἄγριον ἕλκος ἔχει κατὰ μηρὸν Ἄδωνις,
> μεῖζον δ' ἁ Κυθέρεια φέρει ποτικάρδιον ἕλκος.

Adonis has a savage, savage wound on his thigh, but Cytherea carries a greater wound in her heart.

As against Bion's trope, Dido combines the wounds of the slain youth and the mourning lover. Apart from Dido, only Juturna's "Stabat Mater" scene comes close to uniting those personae (we should look back to the Greek model there, Bion's close assimilation between Aphrodite and Adonis). The verbal and thematic parallels between Dido's suicide and Juturna's lament in Book 12[29] may be the clearest suggestion that Dido's gaze can function as a powerful model or even source for a lamenting gaze; the close identity of mourner and mourned in Juturna's "Stabat Mater" scene can be read as a function of the duality of Dido's persona.

Our perspective on her death largely coincides with her own, consonantly with the sympathy that Virgil famously directs toward her character.[30] A rich, languorous sensuality suffuses her death scene, centered, perhaps, in the phrase at 4.659 *os impressa toro*, which interjects its gauzy, impressionistic pathos in the middle of her speech, just as she says "I shall die without vengeance, but let me die," and then stabs herself. "Pressing her face against the bed"?

---

relates Dido to Jezebel, through Ithobalus, Mettenus' paternal grandfather, who is Jezebel's father, "Ethbaal king of the Zidonians," at 1 Kings 16:31). Honeyman 1947:79, however, traces "Methres" to a Phoenician priestly title. Stocks 1936:37–38 interestingly traces the name given by Justin 18.4.3, "Mutto," to a Phoenician god like Mût, connected with the death of Ba'al. Our information on Naevius' version is tantalizingly reticent: "Naevius says whose daughters Dido and Anna were" (n. 63 below).

[28] On her assimilation here to Pallas at 11.40 *in pectore vulnus* (cf. below) see Reed 2004:31–32.
[29] Barchiesi 1978:104–106, Obbink 2002:91–92.
[30] Sanderlin 1969:82: "Most of the Fourth *Aeneid* is narrated from Dido's point of view." On his reading, however, the more one feels how extreme were Dido's love and devotion, the sharper appears the sacrifice that Aeneas made in leaving her; the effects of our sympathy with her are transferred to him.

"Pressing her lips against the pillow"? *Os* is not only ambiguous as between "face" and "lips, mouth," but, as an accusative of respect, is part of the greater problem that the phrase poses. The passive participle *impressa* has a middle or intransitive sense, and the translator is forced uncomfortably to decide between an active and a passive form: "pressing (herself with respect to her face or lips)" or "being pressed." *Toro* refers to the bed, or to any part of it, perhaps the bolster, or heaped-up coverlets; the word basically means a rounded bulging or swelling, and can be used erotically for the sensuous contours of a muscular physique. The phrase focuses the tender, pitying view on Dido's undeserved death that also emerges from her own speech (starting at 649 *dulces exuviae, dum fata deusque sinebat . . .* "O sweet remnants [of Aeneas], so long as fate and the god permitted . . ."), in moving counterpoint to the pride she also expresses.

Verbal and thematic similarities that bring our warriors' deaths into a metaphorical relationship with hers tend to displace emanations of her persona from the dying person onto the gazer. As Volcens descends upon Euryalus in Book 9, enraged by the deaths dealt his companions, the following words return us to Nisus' viewpoint (424–430):

>   tum vero exterritus, amens,
> 425   conclamat Nisus nec se celare tenebris
>   amplius aut tantum potuit perferre dolorem:
>   "me, me, adsum qui feci, in me convertite ferrum,
>   o Rutuli! mea fraus omnis, nihil iste nec ausus
>   nec potuit; caelum hoc et conscia sidera testor;
> 430   tantum infelicem nimium dilexit amicum."

Then, terrified, distraught, Nisus cried out, and could no longer conceal himself in the darkness or endure such anguish: "Here I am, the one who did it! Me, turn your swords on me, Rutulians! Mine is all the offense; he neither dared nor was capable of any. I swear by heaven and the knowing stars: he only loved his unhappy friend too well."

One recalls Dido deciding upon suicide (4.450–51):

> tum vero infelix fatis exterrita Dido
> mortem orat; taedet caeli convexa tueri.

Then unhappy Dido, terrified by fate, prays for death, grows weary of gazing upon the vaults of heaven.

Tum vero marks the transition to each passage. Dido's two modifiers, *infelix* (characteristic of her) and *exterrita*, are divided between the narrative description of Nisus and his self-description.[31] Nisus' oath in its turn echoes the

---

[31] Nisus' other epithet in 424, *amens* ("distraught, out of his mind"), will become especially characteristic of Turnus (7.460; 10.681; 12.622, 742, 776).

magic rite that Dido performs as a pretext for her preparations for suicide: *testatur moritura deos et conscia fati / sidera* (4.519–20 "Doomed to die, she calls to witness the gods and the stars that know fate"). These are the poem's only "knowing stars," *conscia sidera*; in Dido's case they reprise the *conscius aether* that witnessed her "marriage" to Aeneas at 4.167, and in Nisus' they recall his recent prayer to the Moon. In Nisus' words resonate ideas from Dido's earlier passage that are not expressed by verbal repetition: "she prays for death" (*mortem orat*) and "doomed to die" (*moritura*) are of course relevant to Nisus' self-exposure; memory of Dido's passages bring out the suicidal tendency of his outburst. Only Dido's fates—those that terrify her at 450 and the one that the stars know at 520—are hers alone.

Finally, the eroticism that bursts out upon the death of Nisus evokes Dido's love (9.444–45):

> tum super exanimum sese proiecit amicum
> confossus, placidaque ibi demum morte quievit.

Then, stabbed, he threw himself on top of his lifeless friend and there at last found rest in placid death.

"Placid rest" is what the lovelorn Dido sought in vain: "her anguish gives no placid rest to her body" (4.5 *nec placidam membris dat cura quietem*). In joining Euryalus in death, Nisus achieves what unsatisfied love had stolen from Dido.[32] The image brings us into what Vermeule, discussing Archaic Greek poetry and art, calls "the contiguous spheres of sleep, erotic change, and death."[33] But Dido too, of course, at last found her *quies* in death, and Nisus' scene itself (with the quasi-suicide, the sexual overtones of the stabbing, the sense of grim satisfaction) recalls the climax of Book 4. Verbal echoes cast Nisus as Dido, and insinuate Dido's special consciousness, divided now between viewer and slain, into the first of our Adonis-scenes (but whereas Dido dies to cure herself of love for Aeneas, Nisus dies in order to stay united with Euryalus). This process already begins at the outset of the Nisus and Euryalus episode: at 9.186–87 Nisus complains that

> "aut pugnam aut aliquid iamdudum invadere magnum
> mens agitat mihi, nec placida contenta quiete est."

"My mind for some time now has been driving me to undertake a fight or some great deed, and is not content with placid rest."

Now, we trust, he is content. In rejecting what Dido sought, he finds it anyway.

[32] For a similar scene see 4.522–32; see pp. 61–63 above for more on the phrase *placida quies*.

[33] Vermeule 1979:154. The identification of death and *quies* is potentially deconstructed by 6.522 *alta quies placidaeque simillima mortis* (the dead Deiphobus speaking of his last sleep: "deep rest, most similar to placid death"): *simillima* defers identity.

In the very last mention of Dido in the *Aeneid*, five books after her last appearance, her consciousness is still strong enough to insinuate itself in *laeta laborum*, "happy in the work" (11.73). We heard first about this work at 4.263–64: Mercury comes upon Aeneas overseeing work on Carthage, wearing the purple-dyed cloak "that wealthy Dido had made as a gift," embroidering it with gold thread (*dives quae munera Dido / fecerat, et tenui telas discreverat auro*). This embroidery echoes faintly in Lausus' mother's gold embroidery at 10.818 and its connotations. Now it transpires that Dido had made two such cloaks (11.72–75):

> tum geminas vestis auroque ostroque rigentis
> extulit Aeneas, quas illi laeta laborum
> ipsa suis quondam manibus Sidonia Dido
> fecerat et tenui telas discreverat auro.

Then Aeneas brought forth the twin garments, stiff with gold and purple-dye, that Sidonian Dido, happy in the work, had once made for him herself with her own hands, interweaving the fabric with gold thread.

Here she is not called "wealthy," but "Phoenician," which amounts to the same thing in one of the ethnic codes of her story. The gold and purple-dye recall that wealth—the wealth of purple-rich Tyre and the gold stolen from Pygmalion—and *quondam* points us back to that winter when Aeneas enjoyed it with her. But this scene is not happy; it is part of the funeral of Pallas, and goes on (76–77):

> harum unam iuveni supremum maestus honorem
> induit arsurasque comas obnubit amictu.

Sorrowfully he enrobes the youth in one of them as a final tribute and with this veil covered his hair that was soon to burn.

What does he do with the other? Presumably that is his own, the one he was wearing in Book 4 and will continue to use; he honors Pallas with the spare, and both wear the Orientalness that Dido still can impose on the embryonic nation. Yet Dido surely did not weave him an extra cloak in case of a fancy funeral; she wove two—twins—so that they could both wear them together on twin thrones in Carthage (one thinks of her hunting attire at 4.139, a purple-dyed garment with a golden clasp). Putnam has observed that Pallas is in some respects a double for Dido and a figurative "spouse" of Aeneas; he notes the overtones of the traditional bridal veil in 11.77 *obnubit amictu*.[34] Pallas' "hair that was soon to burn" on the pyre unites a remembrance (together with the other allusions) of Dido's pyre with a melancholy echo of the miraculously flaming hair of Ascanius and Lavinia (2.679–91, 7.71–80), which is prophetic

---

[34] See p. 26 above.

of a divinely approved national foundation. In the quick, faint focalization of *laeta laborum* is the queen of Carthage herself, somehow both viewer and corpse. Here most clearly the ghost of Dido returns to reenact her happiness, and her tragedy.

By *laeta laborum* in 11.73, the focalization of the scene has drifted away from Aeneas (who was identified as the explicit viewer at 40 *vidit*), as it always seems to desert him; it is replaced for a moment by Dido's. The trope could represent his memory of her, in which he momentarily identifies with her and conjures back her emotions. Through his overt viewpoint she repossesses the gaze. Would it be going too far to speculate that the eroticism in our scenes of violent death, the initial object of our inquiry, is a residue of her narratological haunting? In any case, the narrative finds it difficult to suppress her initial desire that her and Aeneas' people become one. Her intratextual presence insists upon the ethnic tension that already inheres in our passages and on their peculiarly amorous sensibility.

Verbal links thus typically liken the viewing characters in our scenes to Dido; where in the case of Camilla there is no clearly designated viewer, the victim herself takes on the Didonian viewing persona. Camilla's similarities to Dido constitute a special case. The last words of the former, *hactenus . . . potui* (11.823 "up until now I have prevailed"), have the same sense of proud summation as Dido's perfect-tense enumeration of her achievements (4.653–56). Camilla gradually releases herself from her body (11.829 *paulatim exsolvit se corpore*), as Iris had finally come to release Dido (4.703 *teque isto corpore solvo*; cf. 652). When she dies a great shout goes up to the stars (11.832–33), as the heavens had rung with great cries upon the death of Dido (4.668). Both bodies completely lose their warmth (4.704–705 *omnis . . . dilapsus calor*; 11.828–29 *tum frigida toto . . . corpore*, in an echo of 818). A memorable line describes the way each character's life (*vita*) departs to the winds (Dido, 4.705 *in ventos*) or shades (Camilla, in the line she will share with Turnus, 11.831 *sub umbras*); Dido had in fact specified her own destination as the shades (4.660 *sub umbras*).[35] Most pointedly (since gratuitously), Camilla is given as a final audience a "sister," a hitherto unmentioned member of her brigade, one Acca (homonymous with the foster mother of Romulus and Remus), to whom her apostrophe *hactenus, Acca soror, potui . . .* eerily echoes Dido's *Anna soror . . .* (4.9) and whose presence helps gather and direct our sympathies in the same way that Anna's does at the death of Dido. Anna wishes to receive Dido's dying breath in a last kiss (4.684–85); the introduction of Acca with the phrase "then breathing her last to Acca . . . she speaks" (11.820–21 *tum sic exspirans*

---

[35] Cornelius Severus will attach to Hannibal the phrase Virgil uses for the defeated obstacles to Aeneas' mission: *nostraeque cadens ferus Hannibal irae / membra tamen Stygias tulit inviolata sub umbras* (fr. 13.24–25 Courtney), in a catalogue of Eastern enemies of Rome, and in connection with Mark Antony.

Accam . . . adloquitur) hints at the same, without realizing it. Finally, let it be remembered that Camilla had gone to war not in her customary tiger skin, but in an equally Oriental purple-dyed cloak and golden hair clasp: dressed, in other words, like Dido (7.814–15; compare 4.139). She carries a Lycian quiver and a spear of myrtle wood: rich, amorous, Oriental habiliment (see 5.72 for the special connections of myrtle with Venus).[36]

Camilla is the only one of our fallen warriors who regains consciousness after her mortal wound and the scene that depicts it. Objectified in the terms we became familiar with in chapter 1, she alone revives to subjectivity. Her death is correspondingly only weakly focalized by other characters; Acca eventually arrives to focus our sorrow (as Nisus and Aeneas do more strongly in the other scenes), but the gaze returns to Camilla's cold eyes for one moment more—just as Dido raises her eyes one last time to seek the light (4.688–92). I would connect Camilla's persistent consciousness with her assimilation to Dido, who is both subject and object of her death description. It is as if among the four warriors, Camilla's sex—or her androgyny, similar to that of the *virago* Dido, the female *dux*?[37]—imparted to her some of the queen's powerful consciousness that will not be kept down.

II

If the Adonis-figures implicitly problematize Roman identity, Dido does so explicitly by attracting sympathy to a Carthaginian—and not just sympathy: a potential identification of the Aeneadae with the Carthaginians is built into their first encounter and waveringly persists, always predicated upon the more glaring opposition between the two. The line of division grows sharper as the epic wears on. At Dido's last appearance in the Mourning Fields of the Underworld, when her ghost tears itself away from him without responding (6.450–74), we have reached a point where her identification between Aeneas' people and her own has been shown for fantasy. It is at this point (460) that an echo of Catullus' *Lock of Berenice* assimilates her to a Ptolemaic queen, a magnificent being, but one on the opposite side of the ethnic boundary for the descendants of Aeneas.[38] Cleopatra herself, the last Ptolemaic queen, when she appears on the shield of Aeneas in opposition to Augustus (8.696–713) will represent a crystallization of the ethnic "Other" that is still fluid in the early part of the poem, and that Dido only ambivalently represents.

---

[36] Cf. p. 59 above.

[37] Cf. 1.364. *Virago*, "manly woman," was one (complimentary) etymology of Dido's name, given by Servius on 1.340; see Hexter 1992:348–50.

[38] *Aen.* 6.460 *invitus, regina, tuo de litore cessi* - Catullus 66.39 *invita, o regina, tuo de vertice cessi*. See Wills 1998 for a comprehensive recent discussion.

In the ethnographic terms that Virgil inherited, Trojan Aeneas was originally an Oriental like Dido. His Oriental nature is particularly strong during the sojourn among the Tyrians. In his first views of Carthage, Aeneas, in slack-jawed awe of Dido and her wealth, has something of the proto-Roman encountering in his native simplicity the ancient splendors of the East, an identity he has achieved, in terms of the epic narrative, through seven long years of wandering and deprivation (*Dardanidae duri*—"hardened," "enduring," the opposite of *molles*—is how Apollo addresses his people at 3.94). In Carthage, with Dido, he reverts to a softened Easterner, reclaiming the ease with which he once lived with opulence, and stereotypical East-West distinctions, derived from a Greek ethnographical tradition that took shape after the Persian Wars (particularly in the influential Athenian literature),[39] can always work against the protagonists of the *Aeneid* from a certain angle available to their opponents. The contempt of the rugged Iarbas is ethnographically complicated (4.215–17):

> "et nunc ille Paris cum semiviro comitatu,
> Maeonia mentum mitra crinemque madentem
> subnexus, rapto potitur."

"And now that Paris with his half-male coterie, his chin and perfumed hair tied up in a Maeonian *mitra*, is in possession of what he has seized."

The comparison of Aeneas to Paris (also raised at 7.361–64 and 11.484) is immediately broadened to catch not just the implications of wife stealing, but of a uxorious effeminacy signaled by scented hair and even womanly attire. The characteristically feminine *mitra* was a piece of decorative fabric worn under the chin and over the head. Varro felt the word as Greek;[40] here Greek and Oriental are assimilated, likening Iarbas' viewpoint to that of an ultra-Roman and suggesting the progress Aeneas has yet to make toward Romanness.

Has Iarbas or his agents seen Aeneas dressed like this? For his ethnic progress seems to be arrested in Carthage. Line 4.142 *infert se socium Aeneas atque agmina iungit* ("Aeneas comes in as an ally and joins his ranks with theirs"), in the royal hunt, is a little hint of his merging with Dido's people. When Mercury finds him misguidedly overseeing the building of Carthaginian citadel,[41] his attire suggests an even more wholehearted commitment (4.260–64):

> Aenean fundantem arces ac tecta novantem
> conspicit: atque illi stellatus iaspide fulva

---

[39] Hall 1989. The stereotype of Easterners (both Greek and non-Greek) as luxurious is already visible in Archaic Greek writing; cf. e.g. Asius fr. 13 Bernabé on the Samians, Xenophanes fr. 3 West on Lydian influence on the Ionians.

[40] Varro *L.L.* 5.130. The feminine *mitra* even seems to assimilate Aeneas to Dido, especially since one is worn by Dido's model Ariadne (Catullus 64.63).

[41] This is what initially troubles Jupiter in this episode (4.235): *quid struit*, "Why is he building?" (as the context clarifies, not just "what is he doing, intending," as at e.g. 8.15).

ensis erat Tyrioque ardebat murice laena
demissa ex umeris, dives quae munera Dido
fecerat, et tenui telas discreverat auro.

He sees Aeneas laying foundations for the citadel and making new
buildings; and he had a sword starred with tawny jasper, and the cloak
hanging from his shoulders blazed with Tyrian purple: gifts that wealthy
Dido had made, and interwove the fabric with gold thread.

Conington notes that *atque* in 261 "has . . . the usual continuative force,
implying that Aeneas' Tyrian dress was quite in keeping with the work he had
undertaken as Dido's architect."

Later the Italians will stigmatize Aeneas and his men as Orientals in similar, feminizing terms. Remulus Numanus at 9.598–620 spells out the unwar-
likeness of the Trojans, equating fancy dress, effeminacy, and Orientalness (his
accusation is immediately belied as he himself is killed by Ascanius):

"vobis picta croco et fulgenti murice vestis,
615   desidiae cordi, iuvat indulgere choreis,
et tunicae manicas et habent redimicula mitrae.
o vere Phrygiae, neque enim Phryges, ite per alta
Dindyma, ubi adsuetis biforem dat tibia cantum.
tympana vos buxusque vocat Berecyntia Matris
620   Idaeae; sinite arma viris et cedite ferro."

"Your garments are decorated with saffron and brilliant purple-dye; there
is sloth in your hearts, you like to lose yourself in dances; and your tunics
have sleeves and your *mitrae* laces. O Phrygian women, truly, not
Phrygian men, betake yourselves over the heights of Mount Dindymus,
where the pipe bestows two-toned music on the adepts. The timbrels and
Berecyntian boxwood flute of the Mother of Ida call you; leave warfare to
the men and give up your sword."

These excessive lines (which we shall look at more closely in the next chapter)
strongly recall Catullus 63, and so assimilate the Aeneadae to the emasculated
Attis and his companions (we remember young Atys). Turnus' assertion at 12.12
that the Aeneadae are "cowardly" (*ignavi*) proceeds from the same expectations.
Exhorting his spear at 12.97–100, Turnus reprises the language of Iarbas:

"da sternere corpus
loricamque manu valida lacerare revulsam
semiviri Phrygis et foedare in pulvere crinis
vibratos calido ferro murraque madentis"

"Grant that with my mighty hand I may spread the body of the Phrygian
half-male and tear his corselet away and rend it, and dirty in the dust his
hair, crimped with the curling iron and dripping with myrrh."

Surpassing charges of effeminacy, this is misogyny; he practically intends a rape.[42]

This is how one perspective offered by the poem lets us view the Trojans. We have already noticed Chloreus' carefully Orientalized finery at 11.768–77: his martial apparel is "Phrygian" (769); his weaponry "Lycian" (773); his "foreign" purple-dyed clothing (772 *ipse peregrina ferrugine clarus et ostro*) and the polyptotic repetition of *aurum* at 774–76 recall Dido. He is connected with the worship of Cybele (768), like Attis.[43] His embroidered greaves receive the epithet *barbara* (777): we are looking at him from a Greek-derived ethnic viewpoint (assimilable to Camilla's, despite her own "Oriental" traits elsewhere) and seeing him as the Easterner that he is. The deal that reconciles Juno to the Italians' defeat in Book 12 is supposed to ensure, among other things, that Italian hardiness will expunge the Oriental component contributed by the Trojan victors (note in particular 12.827 "Let Roman posterity take its power from Italian manliness/courage [*virtus*]").[44]

From the beginning, the mutual inclination of Trojan to Carthaginian goes well beyond their common Oriental background, or the eagerness of the Aeneadae to settle down. When Aeneas exclaims at 1.437, "O fortunate ones, whose city walls are already rising!" (*O fortunati, quorum iam moenia surgunt!*), his self-assimilating envy of the Tyrian exiles follows a passage (421–29) in which the rising city is described as if it were Rome, specifically Rome under Augustus:

> miratur molem Aeneas, magalia quondam,
> miratur portas strepitumque et strata viarum.
> instant ardentes Tyrii: pars ducere muros
> molirique arcem et manibus subvolvere saxa,
> 425 pars optare locum tecto et concludere sulco;
> iura magistratusque legunt sanctumque senatum.
> hic portus alii effodiunt; hic alta theatris
> fundamenta locant alii, immanisque columnas
> rupibus excidunt, scaenis decora apta futuris.

Aeneas marvels at the work, once mere huts; he marvels at the gates and the noise and the pavements of the streets. The Tyrians press on, ardent: some are extending the walls, constructing a citadel and rolling up stones with their hands; some are choosing the place for a house and closing it around with a trench; they select laws, magistracies, and a sacred senate. Here some are digging out a harbor, here others are laying deep foundations for a theater and are hewing gigantic columns out of cliff rock, adornments fit for the stage that will be.

---

[42] Cf. 12.14–15.
[43] See p. 75. On Chloreus' affinities to Cybele cf. Arrigoni 1982:51.
[44] Cf. O'Hara 1990:83–84.

The very wording insinuates an ethnic assimilation: the settlement, "once mere huts" (*magalia*, aptly using a word the Romans knew was originally Punic), is now a wonderful *moles* (like the great *moles* that describes the founding of Rome at 1.33?). Carthage now has magistracies and a senate. This vision—Aeneas' (*miratur, miratur*) and ours, unwitting prolepsis and informed hindsight—melds Carthage into Rome. They might both be the same—as might their destinies, not only in ruling the world (as Juno's apprehensions at 1.19–22 assume), but even in the sense of a divine appointment. Ilioneus' rhetoric to Dido gets exactly right the Roman mission later imparted by Anchises in Elysium, but applies it to Carthage: "O queen, whom Jupiter has permitted to found a new city and rein in proud peoples with justice . . ." (1.522–23 *o regina novam cui condere Iuppiter urbem / iustitiaque dedit gentis frenare superbas . . .*).

Why do the two peoples separate? Because of fate, says the poem, insisting on that trick of prolepsis,[45] and not without some relief and disparagement of the Oriental background as finished, over and done with, cleared away in favor of something new and great. One take on all of this would be to show how narrow an escape Aeneas had from remaining Oriental—how narrow an escape Rome had from never being. That attitude the poem makes available, especially as against the subtextual comparison with Mark Antony's dalliance with Cleopatra: will Aeneas go the doomed way of Antony, or triumph like Augustus? Of course he will triumph. Yet the poem also makes available the idea that fate is only what happened, in hindsight, and that Aeneas and his people could have been just as happy in Carthage. The careful assimilation of Aeneas' arrival in Africa to two different passages of the *Odyssey*, Odysseus' arrival at the Phaeacians' island and at the Cyclopes', articulates this ambivalence: "either Carthage is a kind of homecoming and safe harbor for Aeneas in his wanderings, or it is a place of still greater dangers."[46] In the *Aeneid*, the comfortable view of Aeneas' arrival in Carthage is naturally most closely attached to the standpoint of Dido, which the poem often encourages us to adopt (neither intertext nor focalization, of course, pins down a final evaluation).

From the very beginning of her story Dido threatens to forestall Roman identity and meld it with the Other. Her first words in the poem—her long, welcoming response to Ilioneus—introduces the idea of joining Trojan and Carthaginian fortunes and exemplifies this set of possibilities (1.561–78):

> Tum breviter Dido vultum demissa profatur:
> "solvite corde metum, Teucri, secludite curas. . . .
> 565 quis genus Aeneadum, quis Troiae nesciat urbem,
> virtutesque virosque aut tanti incendia belli?

---

[45] On fate as a figure of thought in the *Aeneid*, see Williams 1983:3–16.

[46] Clay 1988:198. See *Od.* 5.451–93, 9.116–48. But the Phaeacians' island also models a place to leave: duty called Odysseus home from a potential marriage among them. A better foil to the Cyclopes' island in this comparison might be Odysseus' arrival back home on Ithaca (13.96–112).

non obtunsa adeo gestamus pectora Poeni,
nec tam aversus equos Tyria Sol iungit ab urbe.
seu vos Hesperiam magnam Saturniaque arva
570 sive Erycis finis regemque optatis Acesten,
auxilio tutos dimittam opibusque iuvabo.
vultis et his mecum pariter considere regnis?
urbem quam statuo vestra est; subducite navis;
Tros Tyriusque mihi nullo discrimine agetur.
575 atque utinam rex ipse Noto compulsus eodem
adforet Aeneas! equidem per litora certos
dimittam et Libyae lustrare extrema iubebo,
si quibus eiectus silvis aut urbibus errat."

Then Dido, with her face bowed, briefly speaks forth: "Release fear from your hearts, Teucrians, dismiss your cares. . . . Who could not know of the lineage of Aeneas' people, of the city of Troy? Their manly qualities, their men, or the conflagration of so great a war? The hearts we Carthaginians bear are not so unfeeling, nor does the Sun yoke his horses so distant from our Tyrian city. Whether your choice is great Hesperia and the fields of Saturn or Eryx's lands and Acestes, their king, I shall send you off in safety and assist you with my resources. Would you, moreover, like to settle with me in these realms on equal terms? The city that I am establishing is yours: draw up your ships. Trojan and Tyrian will be treated with no distinction between them on my part. But would that your king Aeneas were here himself, driven by one and the same South Wind! I shall send out reliable men up and down the shore and order them to search the furthest corners of Libya, in case he is wandering a castaway in some forest or city."

As we hear it, the speech slides from the irony of a Punic welcome to the more enormous instability of Punic Romans. Dido's assurances that everyone has heard of Troy, the Aeneadae, and the exploits they were involved with (565–66) hearken back to the pictures of Trojan War scenes in the temple of Juno, which had given Aeneas that very reassurance (459–60). Watching the scene through his eyes, we are as relieved as he to hear his interpretation of the pictures confirmed as, line by line, she maps her intentions onto his hopes.[47] Her denial of hard-heartedness echoes his inference from the pictures that "here too praiseworthy deeds have their reward; there are tears for things [*sunt lacrimae rerum*] and mortal matters touch the mind" (461–62). And she opens her speech with the same exhortation to put aside fear with which he had ended his there (463 *solve metus*, with the same unusual accusative). She reinforces her

---

[47] On the limits of Aeneas' understanding in this scene, and the double viewpoint the poem gives us on Juno's temple, see Johnson 1976:99–105, Hexter 1992:354–55.

declaration of sympathy by mentioning both cities of origin (565 *Troiae . . .*
urbem, 568 *Tyria . . . urbe*), each closed to its exiles.

The movement from sympathy to identification in her welcoming speech is
underscored by the repetition of *dimittam*: in 571 she will "send away" the
Trojans safely to Hesperia or Sicily; by 577 this intended separation has
changed, under cover of the same verb, into an intention to "send out" scouts
to find and fetch Aeneas so that he can join his people to hers.[48] Line 574 *Tros*
Tyriusque mihi nullo discrimine agetur is the clearest statement of this envisioned melding of the two peoples, underscored by the auspicious alliteration
of the two names:[49] to her there will be no ontological boundary between them.
This denial of difference goes well beyond the *synoikismos* or joint colonization
suggested by the plan she voices (572 *his mecum pariter considere regnis*).[50] There
is a bitter reprisal of the phrase in Jupiter's melding of Trojans and Rutulians
at 10.108 *Tros Rutulusve fuat nullo discrimine habebo*—meaning that he will
maintain impartiality in the general slaughter, but ironically foreshadowing the
divinely approved unification of the two groups. Both passages in a way parody
the combination of ethnicities that will produce Rome; only in Dido's use, we
sense queenly generosity; in Jupiter's, heartlessness.[51]

The futility of this dream of hers is pointed up by a comparison with the
welcome of Latinus, whose people *will* join Aeneas', and who *will* be a Roman
ancestor. He, like Dido, replies (also in a temple) to a speech by Ilioneus in
Aeneas' absence (real this time).[52] Ilioneus uses the language of wooing: "many
peoples, many nations . . . have besought us for themselves and wished to join
us to themselves" (7.236–38 *multi nos populi, multae . . . et petiere sibi et voluere*
adiungere gentes; compare the suitors of Lavinia at 54, *multi illam . . . petiere*)[53]—
appropriately in view of Faunus' oracle, which Latinus will presently recall, and
in sharp contrast to Dido's literal wooing: Ilioneus emphasizes the assent of
fate and the gods (239–42). Once again desire represents and formulates a

---

[48] A cross-language, politically oriented pun may lurk somewhere in this wording: Servius on
11.743 records that *caesar* in Gaulish means *dimitte* (cf. Ahl 1985:81).

[49] Noted by Page ad loc.: "like in name they shall be treated alike." The collocation of the two cities
of origin occurs first at 1.19–20.

[50] On this joint colonization, see Horsfall 1989b:19–20, who notes that the idea "of assimilation
between two groups of colonists or between colonists and indigenes" appealed to the interests of
historians and writers of ktistic literature.

[51] Ovid will use the phrase at *Tristia* 5.10.29 *quippe simul nobis habitat discrimine nullo / barbarus*
("indeed, the barbarian cohabitates with me without difference between us")—this instability leads
naturally to the radical inversion at 35–38, where he says *he* is the barbarian in Tomis, since the
locals do not understand Latin and he cannot understand them.

[52] It is notable that Aeneas' proxy bears a name that makes him a representative of Troy (and also
of the Roman—particularly Julian—future).

[53] The connotations of wooing here are reinforced by comparison with Catullus' marriage hymn,
62.42 (the simile of the flower, compared to the bride) *multi illum pueri, multae optavere puellae*
("many boys, many girls have wished for it").

ktistic program. Latinus, like Dido, starts with assurances that his people well know the Trojans' story and a recommendation of local hospitality (7.196–97, 202–204); but where Dido merely urges the unification of the two peoples, Latinus retails the belief (however old and dim: 205 *obscurior annis*) that Trojan Dardanus originally sprang from Italy. This justification, chiming with that given to Aeneas by the Penates at 3.163–68, trumps Dido's sympathy, let alone the Oriental heritage that the Trojans and Tyrians share. Latinus' promise at 7.262 that Latin soil will restore to the refugees "the opulence of Troy," indeed his whole welcome, partakes of a suggestion that their two peoples are *originally* one. Now Dido's enjambed, climactic application of the epithet "Dardanian" to Aeneas at the very moment of her suicide will have to be reread to include an unwitting (or simply unwilling, since she has heard from him the story the Penates told) acknowledgment of his people's past and future debt to Italy (4.662).

No less radical than 1.574 *nullo discrimine agetur* is 573 *urbem quam statuo, vestra est* ("the city that I am establishing is yours"), and here in hindsight Dido's identification of Carthaginians and Trojans becomes a sinister foreshadowing of the Roman conquest and destruction of the city in 146 B.C.E. With similar irony Ilioneus unknowingly anticipates the plundering of Carthage at 1.527–28: *non nos aut ferro Libycos populare penatis / venimus, aut raptas ad litora vertere praedas* ("We have not come to plunder Libyan homes with the sword or to seize booty and make away to the beaches with it"—not yet, anyway). Dido's words are tortuously Ennian. She offers her guests her city—"*vestra est*"—as Ennius' Hannibal deemed a countryman anyone who fought with him against Rome (*Annales* 234–35 Skutsch):

> "hostem qui feriet †erit (inquit) mi† Carthaginiensis
> quisquis erit, cuiatis siet."

"He who smites the enemy will be Carthaginian to me, whoever he is, wherever he may come from".[54]

He is addressing himself to Italians living under Roman rule, undoing the national identity that the Trojans' alliance with Latinus desiderates and that Augustan ideology declared a reality. The poetic lineage is clarified by *Aeneid* 2.148–49, containing a verbal echo of Ennius and an intermediate idea:

> "quisquis es, amissos hinc iam obliviscere Graios
> (noster eris)."

"Whoever you are, from now on forget the Greeks whom you have lost— you will be one of us".

---

[54] Skutsch ad loc. suspects for syntactical and thematic reasons that *quisquis* conceals *civis* (found in dependent passages in later authors); but the parallel I am about to cite seems to support *quisquis*.

There, Priam welcomes Sinon; both Virgilian offers of citizenship, as Wigodsky notes, bring destruction to the benefactors. Dido's offer is inverted compared to the others, ironically: not "you will be Carthaginian," but "Carthage will be yours," as indeed it was at the end of the three Punic Wars.[55]

Again, comparison with Ilioneus' interview with Latinus is telling: at 7.233 *nec Troiam Ausonios gremio excepisse pigebit* induces ambiguity as to subject: either "the Italians will not regret welcoming Troy into their bosom" (which reflects the force of Ilioneus' speech, and jibes with the gifts that bestow Trojan sacral and kingly offices on Latinus at 243–48) or "Troy will not regret welcoming Italy." The latter, if Troy is read proleptically as "Rome," is the more historically accurate construction. Dido, more subtly, blurs the possessive pronouns in her prayer to Jupiter at 1.732–33: *hunc laetum Tyriisque diem Troiaque profectis / esse velis, nostrosque huius meminisse minores* ("May it be your wish that this day be joyful for both Tyrians and those who have set out from Troy, and that our descendants remember it"). The last clause suggests the real prayer (even before her visit from Cupid), that her *minores* be the same as Aeneas', remembering and celebrating the day that made the two nations one. *Et vos o coetum,* she concludes, *Tyrii, celebrate faventes* (735 "And you, Tyrians, celebrate this union with good will"). *Coetus* has a number of implications: the present gathering to which all have been invited (the same word is used at Catullus 64.33 of the gathering to celebrate the marriage of Peleus and Thetis), the coming-together of the two peoples for which she entertains such high ambitions, and the more personal coming-together of herself and Aeneas that is soon to dominate her life.

Such is her vision of a united people until finally Aeneas turns it inside out at 4.347–50:

> "si te Karthaginis arces
> Phoenissam Libycaeque aspectus detinet urbis,
> quae tandem Ausonia Teucros considere terra
> invidia est? et nos fas extera quaerere regna."

"If the citadel of Carthage and the sight of this Libyan city keep you, a Phoenician, here, why then do you begrudge the Teucrians to settle in the land of Ausonia? We, too, must by divine command seek a realm in foreign lands."

Their likeness now itself prescribes a separation. The ethnic *Phoenissam* (paralleling *Teucros*) simultaneously assimilates the two of them as Eastern refugees and draws a potential ethnic boundary between himself and her. We may already have suspected Aeneas' resistance to a merging. In expressing the

---

[55] Wigodsky 1972:71–72, pursuing the observation of Fraenkel 1954. For the wording and the imperialistic overtone cf. Ovid *Ars Am.* 1.178 *nunc, Oriens ultime, noster eris* ("Now, furthest East, you will be ours").

desire to unite his people with those of Helenus, he uses similar language to Dido's (3.500–505):

500   "si quando Thybrim vicinaque Thybridis arva
      intraro gentique meae data moenia cernam,
      cognatas urbes olim populosque propinquos,
      Epiro Hesperiam (quibus idem Dardanus auctor
      atque idem casus), unam faciemus utramque
505   Troiam animis: maneat nostros ea cura nepotes."

"If I ever enter the Tiber and the fields neighboring the Tiber and see the ramparts that have been bestowed upon my nation, some day out of these kindred cities and neighboring peoples, Hesperia with Epirus (which have the same ancestor, Dardanus, and the same fortune), we shall make a single Troy in spirit. Let that concern await our descendants."

He keeps the nations distinct while promising a spiritual unity for their coming generations (to be fulfilled especially, according to the commentary of Servius Auctus, with the advent of Roman *imperium* in Epirus and Augustus' foundation at Actium). Dido, to whom he is narrating this reminiscence, should take the hint against a literal reading of *unam*.

Dido's welcoming speech ends with an even subtler and more emotional identification. Her last word—*errat*, "wanders"—naturally adheres to Aeneas; in his own words, for example, at 1.333. But *erro* is also *her* word, connected to her by an etymological pun: the third-century Sicilian historian Timaeus had said that the name Dido was applied to her by Libyans because of her wanderings in exile.[56] The connection passes through successive shades of poignancy at 4.211 *femina, quae nostris errans in finibus* ("a woman, who, wandering in our lands . . ."), which refers to her wanderings themselves (the speaker there, Iarbas, in a sense personifies Timaeus' anonymous "Libyans"); at 4.363–64, where she lets her eyes wander up and down Aeneas in disdain (*totumque pererrat / luminibus tacitis*); at 4.684, when Anna seeks a last "wandering" (*errat*) breath on Dido's lips, and 691 as she dies and seeks the light "with wandering eyes" (*oculisque errantibus*); and finally at 6.450–54, in the Underworld: *Phoenissa recens a vulnere Dido / errabat silva in magna* ("Phoenician Dido, fresh from her wound, was wandering in a great forest").[57] The last line of her first speech, in view of this wordplay, makes Aeneas a kind of Dido: perhaps, she fears, *he* wanders a castaway in some wood or city. Her sympathy with the plight of the Trojans can go no further than to cast their

---

[56] Timaeus *FGrH* 566 F 82, *Etymologicum magnum* s.v. Διδώ (which says the etymology is Phoenician). See Huss 1985:41; O'Hara 1996:110–11, 152–53; Brown 2000:336–37.

[57] To the same complex belongs 4.68–69 *uritur infelix Dido totaque vagatur / urbe furens* ("Unhappy Dido burns [with love] and wanders through the whole city in her madness"), with *peragrat* in the simile at 72.

leader as an alter ego; she will do so again in the same terms at 1.755–56 (the last lines of the book) *nam te iam septima portat / omnibus errantem terris et fluctibus aestas* ("for now the seventh summer carries you, a wanderer on land and sea"). When Aeneas becomes visible she pointedly reminds him of their common misfortune, not suppressing a hint that her refuge should likewise be his: *me quoque per multos similis fortuna labores / iactatam hac demum voluit consistere terra* (1.628–29 "A similar fortune intended me, too, buffeted through many toils, finally to settle in this land").[58]

Anna echoes and feeds this hope of unification in Book 4 when, persuading Dido to shed her scruples and marry Aeneas, she moves from the negative advantages that the marriage will bring (the defense of Carthage against Pygmalion and the hostile peoples of Libya: 35–44) to the positive ones (47–49):

> "quam tu urbem, soror, hanc cernes, quae surgere regna
> coniugio tali! Teucrum comitantibus armis
> Punica se quantis attollet gloria rebus!"

"Imagine the city you will see rise here with a marriage like this, sister, imagine the kingdom! With the weaponry of the Teucrians on our side, imagine what great things Punic glory will raise itself to!"

She is speaking now not of defense, but of empire. Her terms are the same as those under which Rome and Carthage were juxtaposed at 1.12–22; instead of a contest between the peoples to be a *regnum gentibus* and *late rex*, Anna envisions—persuasively to Dido—a joint sovereignty (*comitantibus*). She correctly attributes the Trojans' arrival, and the possibility of union, to Juno (45–46 *dis equidem auspicibus reor et Iunone secunda / hunc cursum Iliacas vento tenuisse carinas*). This unification does become part of Juno's plan (102–104), acquiesced in by Venus. The former, complaining of Venus' plots against Carthage (her locution "high Carthage"—97 *Karthaginis altae*—assimilatingly recalls "high Rome" at 1.7),[59] makes the latter a proposal (4.99–104):

> "quin potius pacem aeternam pactosque hymenaeos
> 100   exercemus? habes tota quod mente petisti:
> ardet amans Dido traxitque per ossa furorem.
> communem hunc ergo populum paribusque regamus
> auspiciis; liceat Phrygio servire marito
> dotalisque tuae Tyrios permittere dextrae."

"But why do we not rather cultivate an everlasting truce and a legitimately contracted marriage? You have that for which with all your

---

[58] Cf. Aeneas at 1.3 *multum ille et terris iactatus et alto*. Dido uses *iactatus* of Aeneas again at 4.14.
[59] The phrase is ironically reprised by Mercury at 265–66 *tu nunc Karthaginis altae fundamenta locas . . .* ("Are you now laying the foundations of high Carthage . . . ?").

thoughts you strove: Dido burns with love and has drawn the madness in throughout her very bones. Let us therefore rule over this people in common, with paired auspices. Let her be allowed to serve a Phrygian consort and give up her Tyrians to your hand as a dowry."

Venus, secure in the knowledge that Aeneas will reach Italy one way or the other, avers that no one in her right mind would contend with Juno, but . . . (110–112):

> "sed fatis incerta feror, si Iuppiter unam
> esse velit Tyriis urbem Troiaque profectis,
> miscerive probet populos aut foedera iungi."

"But fate keeps me in uncertainty: whether Jupiter is willing for the Tyrians and those who set out from Troy to have one city, or would approve of their peoples' combining, or of treaties being joined."

Venus casts doubt on Dido's words at 1.732–33 by throwing them slyly back at Juno. Anna and the two goddesses spell out the possibilities more vividly than Dido does—let alone Aeneas, who simply acquiesces in the unification until recalled by Mercury.

Over the course of Book 4 Dido's identification with Aeneas will become more and more antagonistic to reality (just as her sense of "wander" will diverge tragically from his), until at 4.628–29 she will call down war and opposition between her people and his (*litora litoribus contraria* . . .). For a moment in Book 1 it seems quite possible that the ancestors of the Romans will become Carthaginian instead. The viewpoint of the hopeful and unknowing Aeneas, through which we receive these overtures, ominously does not oppose their implications.

III

Virgil's quiet treatment of the Punic Wars abets the illusion that the opposition between Rome and Carthage may be forestalled. The wars do not figure explicitly in any of Virgil's prophetic speeches or scenes, even in connection with the visions of war heroes like the Scipios, Regulus, and Fabius Cunctator (6.842–46); the plainest allusion comes in Anchises' prophecy about the hero of the Second Punic War, M. Claudius Marcellus, who "will destroy the Carthaginians and the rebellious Gaul" (6.858). The great name of Hannibal, remarkably, never sounds in this poem. In the agreement between Jupiter and Juno in Book 12 the Carthaginians never enter Juno's fears or Jupiter's promises; she has apparently[60] abandoned them, their place taken in her care by the

---

[60] Cf. Feeney 1984.

Italians (who will become Romans). The Punic Wars most explicitly enter the *Aeneid* late, in Jupiter's rebuke to the gods quarrelling over the Trojan-Italian war, when he cites the Carthaginian invasion over the Alps (10.11–15). The great struggle between Rome and Carthage that the opening of the poem heralds, and that Dido's curse at 4.622–29 invokes again, is kept firmly in the background—or rather in the subtext. Mere hints keep the opposition between Rome and Carthage before our eyes, even while we are made to blur that line of opposition; possible and real outcomes are constantly juxtaposed.

Either the traumatic, century-long struggle with Carthage is not a formative element in Roman history as Virgil tells it, or Virgil has sublimated its influence, relating it less obviously to his own account of Roman origins and development, making it a subtext for such details as Dido's curse. And in the poem's relations with other poems: the way Virgil constructs his picture of Roman identity in dialogue with earlier Latin poets should be emphasized. The wars between Rome and Carthage constantly shadow the wandering Trojans' travails in Virgil's debt, for a number of crucial scenes relating to Aeneas' mission and the future of Rome, to the earliest generation of Latin poetry, in particular Naevius' historical epic on the First Punic War, the *Bellum Punicum* (later third century B.C.E.).[61] This poem's very fragmentary preservation precludes a close reading of particular Virgilian passages against Naevian ones; its importance for our study lies in the fact that Virgil took from the *Bellum Punicum* large scenes and plot elements that must have helped prepare for Rome's later confrontation with Carthage and thus, transferred to the *Aeneid*, would have aroused consciousness of that purpose. It is at least clear that Naevius included both Roman and Carthaginian foundation legends. "If Naevius did tell the story of Dido and Aeneas as an *aition* of the Punic Wars," Wigodsky speculates, "Vergil's imitations of the earlier poet, in more places than we can tell, may have had ominous overtones for his Roman readers."[62] I suggest that in some places his invocation of Naevius visibly points up the futility of Dido's wishful unification of the two peoples, and reinforces the emergence of a Roman identity distinct from, and opposed to, a Carthaginian one.

Thus Virgil combines Naevius' near abridgement of Roman history in the tempest—located in Book 1 of both epics and in both epics followed by Jupiter's reassurance to Venus of Rome's eventual success—with Naevius' inclusion of Dido, which perhaps had its place in a ktisis of Carthage, paralleling his account of Aeneas' migration and helping to etiologize the enmity.[63] (It is unclear whether Naevius too had brought the two ktiseis together, making the path of the Roman founder intersect that of the Carthaginian; the

---

[61] Wigodsky 1972:22–39.

[62] Wigodsky 1972:34.

[63] Storm: Naevius fr. 13 Morel = Macrobius *Sat.* 6.2.31. For Naevius it would have signified the labors to be overcome before Rome could claim the sea from Carthage. Dido: Naevius fr. 6 Morel = Serv. *Aen.* 4.9 *cuius filiae fuerint Anna et Dido Naevius dicit.* Wigodsky 1972:29–34 reviews the arguments about Dido's role in the *Bellum Punicum*.

meeting—and love affair—between Aeneas and the queen are unattested before Virgil and may be his inventions.[64]) So the ethnic tension that in the *Aeneid* is a complicated separation through identification—a diversion of the proto-Roman path into the proto-Carthaginian, flaunting contingency— intertextually follows the path that leads to the Punic Wars. Narratologically, too, Virgil has followed the *Bellum Punicum*. Naevius fr. 23 Morel (from Book 2), whether or not it refers to Dido, at least shows that *someone* asked to hear Aeneas's most crucial story:

> blande et docte percontat Aenea quo pacto
> Troiam urbem liquerit.

He/she persuasively and shrewdly inquires how Aeneas left the city of Troy.[65]

Thus Naevius, like Virgil starting at the end of *Aeneid* 1, framed Aeneas' subjectivity and viewpoint with another's (a parallel is Virgil's use of Naevius' dialogue between Venus and Jupiter: fr. 13–15 Morel). The *Bellum Punicum*, present just under the surface, reminds us that our viewpoint here, however sympathetic Dido may be and however strongly she may imagine unity between her people and his, is not only that of an ethnic Other, but of the representative of Rome's eventual enemy. If in Dido Virgil is repeating Naevius' interlocutor, the reminiscence is straightforward; if he is substituting another for him or her, he has performed a possibly interesting revision of Naevius' ethnic antinomies. Either way, Virgil uses poetry on the Punic Wars subliminally to complicate the assimilation that he is at pains both to establish and undo.

The arrest and reversal of the ethnic trajectory here is emphasized by another revision of Naevius. In the *Bellum Punicum*, Aeneas and his family, joined by other Trojan refugees, leave their ruined city bringing gold with them (fr. 5 Morel):

> eorum sectam sequuntur multi mortales
> multi alii e Troia strenui viri
> ubi foras cum auro illic exibant.

Many people followed their band out of Troy, many other stalwart men, as they were going away from that place carrying gold.[66]

---

[64] L. Ateius, author of a treatise *An amaverit Didun Aenea* (Charisius p. 162.6–7 Barwick), whatever his conclusions, was Virgil's older contemporary. Varro (d. 27 B.C.E.) may have known and rejected this version, if Servius Auctus' wording is his (*Aen.* 1.482): *Varro ait non Didonem sed Annam Aeneae amore impulsam se super rogum interemisse* (cf. Horsfall 1987:102). Cf. Starks 1999:262–63 nn. 23, 25.

[65] For the various reconstructions of the context see Wigodsky 1972:30–31; cf. Goldberg 1995:54–55.

[66] Naevius fr. 10 Morel, from the first Book of the *Bellum Punicum,* may also belong to this scene: *pulchraque <vasa> ex auro vestemque citrosam* ("and beautiful <urns> of gold, and clothing stored in a citron-wood casket").

In Virgil, Aeneas says he left with only the *penates*, the figures of the ancestral gods (2.717, 747); the gold he might have taken, along with other treasures seized from the city's temples, has fallen prey to the Greeks (763–66). It is rather Dido and her companions, as we have already heard from Venus, who fled their city with a quantity of gold, significant for their story in sharpening the pique of the greedy Pygmalion (1.363). The contrast between Virgil and Naevius reinforces the Romans' origins in piety as against the Carthaginians' in lucre; but this difference fades the longer the former Trojans linger among the former Tyrians. The next chapter will delve more deeply into Trojan treasure and its significance. Observe now that the *Aeneid* carefully restores Trojan gold to its hero through hospitable exchanges by the time he reaches Carthage: at 3.464–69 and 483–85 Helenus packs Aeneas' ships with treasure, much of it gold. Some of this is presumably the "Trojan treasure" that ends up scattered on the waves at 1.119. Among what remains figure Helen's magnificent *palla* and the scepter of Ilione, presented to Dido at 1.647–53, "gifts snatched from the ruins of Troy" (1.647 *munera . . . Iliacis erepta ruinis*—by the resourcefulness of Helenus himself or by the pillaging Greeks?). Thereafter, for the rest of the epic, we find Aeneas lavishing ancestral largess on hosts and allies: he has reclaimed the generosity of a Trojan prince.

The Trojans' recovery of wealth prepares them for their short-lived return to Eastern splendor in Carthage. Significantly, the "purple-dyed covering" that Helenus enjoins him to wear in (an etiological, foundational Roman) sacrifice at 3.405 is answered by "Phrygian covering" (545): the epithets are equivalent. The prizes he promises to victorious contestants at 5.111–12 include silver, gold, and "garments suffused with purple-dye"; the grand prize at 250–51 is a cloak embroidered with gold and dyed with purple, elaborately depicting the abduction by Jupiter's eagle of the Trojan prince Ganymede. At 5.133 his captains wear gold and purple-dyed garments. At 3.354–55 "they sipped cups of wine in the middle of [Helenus'] hall, the feast having been set before them on [dishes of] gold" (*aulai medio libabant pocula Bacchi / impositis auro dapibus*)—prefiguring their experience in Carthage, this banquet is a kind of *mise-en-abyme* in Aeneas' after-dinner narrative in the opulence of Dido's hall (cf. 1.723–30).

A famous simile involves earlier poets (not Naevius this time) to similar allusive effect. At 4.402–405 Dido watches from on high the Trojans loading their ships, preparing to leave Carthage:

> ac velut ingentem formicae farris acervum
> cum populant hiemis memores tectoque reponunt,
> it nigrum campis agmen praedamque per herbas
> convectant calle angusto.

And as when ants, mindful of the winter, plunder an enormous pile of grain and store it under shelter, the black array goes over the fields, and they convey the booty along a narrow file in the grass.

Servius records that the phrase *it nigrum campis agmen* was used by Ennius of elephants (so Virgil neatly reverses the size of the creatures), and of Indians later in the second century by Accius (the adjective in this case brings out the differentiating skin color). Memory of Accius' (not certainly poetic) earlier use of Ennius' hemistich[67] adds something to the Virgilian line, insofar as the Indians were an Eastern people that Augustan literature considered future victims of Roman expansion (as in Anchises' prophecy at 6.794, or implicitly at 8.705, where they, along with other Eastern peoples, flee in terror before Roman arms at Actium); whatever Accius may have said about the "black array of Indians going over the fields," its memory casts forward onto Dido's vision the ethnic inverse of a Roman imperial army. Ennius's intertext may do the same. Skutsch notes that among the enemies who figured in Ennius's *Annales,* "[e]lephants were used by Pyrrhus, Hannibal, and Antiochus" against the Romans, and thinks a Hannibalic context most likely.[68] If this is so, Dido's gaze intertextually assimilates "plundering" Trojans—that is, proto-Romans—to Carthaginians attacking Roman territory, wreaking the queen's vengeance and fulfilling her curse. Here not only are the Romans melded with their conquered enemies, but Rome is cast as Carthage. Consoling from a Roman viewpoint, to see Ennius' frightening vision transformed into its opposite and given a kind of priority; dispiriting to Dido (as the narrator suggests in the following lines), and even more dispiriting than she knows. Yet it is overwhelmingly Dido's viewpoint that we are given here (note the narratological dovetailing: *cernas,* "you [the reader] would see" at 401 and *tibi . . . cernenti,* "you [Dido] seeing" at 408)—not a determining one, but one that colors the intertextual sense, when we read in context. And the destabilization of Roman identity, the confusion with an established Other, comports with Dido's mindset and hopes: what the intertext does is to assimilate the (both metaphorically and proleptically) plundering Aeneadae to Easterners and, by obscuring the ethnic differentiation, force us to think of an Oriental nature that persists in the Roman people long after Aeneas slices the rope that moors him to Carthage.[69] The very trope that reverses Roman defeat and differentiates the Romans from potential Oriental conquerors does so at the price of a Roman identity distinct

---

[67] Accius fr. 26 Morel ("ex annalibus sumptum videtur" according to the editor—Accius' *Annales* seem to have dealt with calendrical rather than historical matter). Presumably Ennius' elephants convert into Accius' Indians on account of their Eastern, not to say exotic quality. This, incidentally, is the only place where Servius cites Accius.

[68] Skutsch 1985:656–57. The fragment is *Ann.* 502 in his numbering.

[69] Even in Dido's savage reproach to Aeneas at 4.366–67 "The Caucasus gave birth to you on its harsh crags, Hyrcanian tigers offered you their teats" (*duris genuit te cautibus horrens / Caucasus Hyrcanaeque admorunt ubera tigres*) there lies within the rejection a claim—potentially hopeful to Dido—of Aeneas' Eastern origins. The speech begins "Neither is your mother divine, perfidious one, nor is Dardanus the author of your race . . ." (365–66), which, read against what she heard of Dardanus' Italian homeland (3.167), contains a denial of Italy's claim on Aeneas (compare her mention of his Dardanian origins at 661–62).

from their opponents. As often, Virgil creates a metaphor that is a dilemma in its own terms.

The most explicit reference to the Punic Wars in the poem, in Jupiter's rebuke to the gods quarelling over the Trojan-Italian War, draws a sharp line between the two peoples who might once have become one (10.11–15):

> "adveniet iustum pugnae (ne arcessite) tempus,
> cum fera Karthago Romanis arcibus olim
> exitium magnum atque Alpis immittet apertas:
> tum certare animis, tum res rapuisse licebit.
> nunc sinite et placitum laeti componite foedus."

"The right time to fight will come—do not hurry it—when savage[70] Carthage will someday[71] unleash upon the citadels of Rome great destruction and a breaching of the Alps. Then, then, it will be licit to vie in hatred, to plunder each other. For now let things be, and cheerfully agree to the pact that pleases me."

Jupiter represents that the Second Punic War in particular will be a legitimate substitute for the unholy war now in progress, when the gods will be permitted to choose sides and fan hatred and rapaciousness against whom they please. One recalls the contrast between Dido's misguided welcome of the Trojans and Latinus' fated welcome. The next chapter will discuss further examples of the narrative perspective that opposes Roman to Carthaginian. Yet despite the ethnic journey the Trojans make and the clarity with which their experience at Carthage ultimately draws the ethnic boundary, the poem never cleanly amputates any past phase from a future cumulative Romanness. Dido's ethnic status has prepared us for the Adonis-figures by pointing up the ambivalence of their ethnic identity. She does not merely reflect this early fluid phase of Roman identity, but carries us forward to the period when Roman identity had been codified (in the great national epics that Virgil hereby revises, and elsewhere), and by recalling the Punic Wars (or Cleopatra and the victory over her and Antony at Actium) makes us think of Romanness as something always definable against an Other, yet always still contestable. The frequent assimilation of Carthage to Rome in appearance, institutions, and potential national destiny not only points up the possibility of a merging of Trojans with Tyrians; it makes Rome fulfill a Carthaginian role. The phrase "happy in the work" at 11.73 (the last mention of Dido in the poem) really has to do with the merged nation—its Easternness there symbolized by the purple-dye and gold embroidery of the robes she wove—that was frustrated by the gods; now Pallas, by the marriage metaphor and by Aeneas' lament at 43–44 and by the rich cloak and by Dido's insinuated viewpoint, represents the failure of another hoped-for merging of nations.

---

[70] Cf. their naturally *ferocia corda*, made kindly toward the Trojans by Mercury, at 1.302–303.

[71] This *olim* echoes the one in Dido's curse (4.627 *nunc, olim, quocumque dabunt se tempore vires*) and helps assimilate the events that Jupiter and she are speaking of.

Chapter Four

ANDROMACHE

I

We have just seen how Virgil uses earlier poetry on the fall of Troy, Roman origins, and the Punic Wars to draw a demarcation between two peoples from the East, Carthaginian and Trojan (Roman-to-be), and to communicate Aeneas' changing sense of national identity. In the present chapter I wish to suggest that in doing so, Virgil extends a Roman tradition—evident, for example, in early Roman tragedy—of freighting intertextuality unavoidably with messages of cultural and national identity, particularly messages that include the radical perspectivity of such an identity.[1] Let us start by reading the *Aeneid* comparatively against the latter two sections of the lament of Ennius' Andromacha over the fall of Troy in his tragedy *Andromacha* (fr. 9 Ribbeck):

> "O pater, o patria, o Priami domus,
> saeptum altisono cardine templum!
> Vidi ego te astante ope barbarica
> tectis caelatis lacunatis,
> auro ebore instructum regifice."

"O father, O fatherland, O house of Priam, precinct enclosed by the high-resounding hinge! I have seen you with barbarian forces standing by, with your carven panelled ceilings, royally appointed with ivory and gold."

The "barbarian forces," of course, are the Trojan army and its allies; like Aeschylus' Persians or Xenophon's Cyrus speaking in Greek of their own "barbarian" soldiers, Ennius' Andromacha takes advantage of the word's basic, neutral sense "non-Greek (in speech and culture)." In Ennius' (unknown) Greek original and the general Greek usage that was his model, *barbarikos* (or *barbaros*: see Jocelyn on his line 89) would have participated in the fifth-century reading of the Trojan War as a prefiguration of the definitive clash between Greece and the East that was the Persian Wars.[2]

---

[1] The passages from Ennius and Naevius that I shall discuss have been assembled and brought into contact with the *Aeneid* by Wigodsky 1972:22–39 and 40–79.
[2] Hall 1989.

At this point Cicero, who preserves the fragment most fully in *Tusculan Disputations* 3.19, interrupts himself and exclaims:

O poetam egregium! quamquam ab his cantoribus Euphorionis contemnitur. Sentit omnia repentina et necopinata esse graviora. Exaggeratis igitur regiis opibus, quae videbantur sempiternae fore, quid adiungit?

Oh, what an extraordinary poet! even though he is despised by these chanters of Euphorion. He feels that all sudden and unexpected events are heavier to bear. So having piled up the riches of the king [*regiis opibus*], which looked as though they would last forever, what does he add?

> "Haec omnia vidi inflammari,
> Priamo vi vitam evitari,
> Iovis aram sanguine turpari."

"I have seen all these things put to the flames, Priam's life taken away by force, the altar of Jupiter befouled with blood."

Every element of this lament emerges in the *Aeneid*,[3] notably in passages attached to Aeneas' persisting identity as a Trojan, thus creating a frame in which we may fruitfully compare the two texts particularly as they carry statements about ethnic identity. Aeneas laments the fall of Troy in a similar outburst at *Aeneid* 2.241–42

> "O patria, o divum domus Ilium et incluta bello
> moenia Dardanidum!"

"O fatherland, O Ilium, home of the gods, and war-renowned ramparts of the children of Dardanus!"

and in his recollection of Priam's death at 499–505 (particularly 501–502):

> "Vidi ipse furentem
> 500   caede Neoptolemum geminosque in limine Atridas,
>   vidi Hecubam centumque nurus Priamumque per aras
>   sanguine foedantem quos ipse sacraverat ignis.
>   Quinquaginta illi thalami, spes tanta nepotum,
>   barbarico postes auro spoliisque superbi
> 505   procubuere; tenent Danai qua deficit ignis."

"I myself have seen Neoptolemus, raging in slaughter, and the two sons of Atreus on the threshold; I have seen Hecuba and her hundred princesses, and Priam over the altar, befouling with blood the fire that he himself had consecrated. Those fifty bridal chambers—great promise of

---

[3] I think of Wills's formulation of the idea of "allusive economy" (1998).

grandchildren—and the doors proud with barbaric gold and war spoils lay low; where fire does not reach, the Greeks hold sway."[4]

The iteration of *vidi* (499, 501), read alongside that in Ennius' play, emphasizes the view that Aeneas and Andromacha share, though in Aeneas' case the pair does not articulate a contrast between the secure past and the recent horrors. Both characters are Trojans recounting the fall of their king's palace to the Greeks, but instead of contrasting glorious past with wretched present sequentially (as Cicero notes Andromacha does), Aeneas works the contrast simultaneously into his view of the disaster, together with an emphasis on the loss of posterity—the loss it is in some way his mission to correct.

Priam's palace has a special significance in Aeneas' story as the scene of Neoptolemus' incursion, which Aeneas is recounting here (469–505). There is a significant shift in focus: Virgil expands Andromacha's hint in "high-resounding hinge," metonymically the door that protected the palace (*saeptum . . . templum*), into an emphasis on the door (*postes superbi*, the "proud doorposts" or metonymically "door"). We are prepared for this focus already at 441–49, where Aeneas looks down to see the Greeks besetting the threshold (*limen*) of the palace; their activity is concentrated "before the very doors" (*postisque sub ipsos*); the defenders "hurl down gilt rafters, the lofty adornments of their ancient forebears" (*aurataoque trabes,*[5] *veterum decora alta parentum*). "Gilt" recalls the wealth Andromacha had emphasized. This focus, and wording, is sustained: Neoptolemus, "grabbing an axe, bursts through the resisting door and rips the brazen doorposts from their hinge" (479–81 *correpta dura bipenni / limina perrumpit postisque a cardine vellit / aeratos*). The terrified matrons within "cling with their arms around the doorposts and press kisses on them" (490 *amplexaeque tenent postis atque oscula figunt*); soon "the door totters with the constant battering of the ram and, disengaged from their pivot, the doorposts topple" (492–93 *labat ariete crebro / ianua et emoti procumbunt cardine postes*). By the time we reach Aeneas' closer echo of Andromacha in 504 (*barbarico postes auro spoliisque superbi*), the palace doors that Andromacha's impressionistic hinge conjured up have been made concrete and endowed with regret and horror.

In the adjective *barbarico* at 504 (for the gold that is the pride of Priam's doorposts), Virgil offers a stance within a long argument over the status of Romans vis-à-vis Greeks.[6] As Andromacha uses it of her own people's armed

---

[4] Clausen 2002:72–73 mentions influence from Ennius; he also sees influence from a hypothetical Hellenistic version of Sinon story used by Triphiodorus in the third century C.E.

[5] This term reminds us of doors, too: it is used for those of Juno's temple at 1.449.

[6] Cf. Bowersock 1965:132, contrasting (in Greek writing of the time of Augustus) *ekbarbarôsthai* at Strabo 6.1.2 "to describe the de-hellenization of Magna Graecia" with e.g. Dionysius' classing of Rome with Greeks against the *barbaroi*. Champion 2000 discusses Polybius' varying uses of *barbaros*, including and excluding Romans.

forces, Aeneas uses it of his own people's wealth blithely, without ascertaina-
ble pejorative overtones. Page ad loc. comments on the phrase, "That Aeneas
a Trojan should speak of Trojan gold as 'barbaric' is curious, but in strict accordance with the literary use of the word as = 'non-Greek,' *e.g.* the Persian messenger in Aeschylus' *Persae* 425 speaks of the Persian host as 'the barbaric
host.'" The boundary that the word draws includes each speaker on the side
of "barbarism," specifically as against Greek. At Rome, of course, and in Latin,
the term has pointed force: a word meaning "non-Greek," whatever its connotations, could mean "Latin" or "Roman" in the right context, as in Plautus'
signature *Plautus vortit barbare*, "Plautus has translated [the Greek play] into
barbarian" (i.e., Latin).[7] It is Plautus who, inserting a topical reference into his
Greek model at *Miles Gloriosus* 211, refers to a Latin poet (possibly Naevius)
as a *poeta barbarus*—almost an oxymoron, in the way the Greek-derived slur
jostles the newly naturalized (possibly by Naevius himself) Greek-derived
noun. In repeating Andromacha's words so straightforwardly, Aeneas is thinking as a Trojan, but also, proleptically, as a Roman of a historically determined
type. His use of the adjective allies Trojan ancestors to Roman descendants on
one side of an ethnic boundary whose other side is occupied by the Greeks.

The intertext between the *Aeneid* and the *Andromacha* thus underwrites the
assimilation of the Trojan refugees to the Tyrian refugees discussed in the last
chapter, and also their subsequent divergence. There we noted that Virgil's
correction of Naevius' *Bellum Punicum*, in which Aeneas flees the wreckage of
Troy bringing its gold with him uses wealth to distinguish, then assimilate, the
two peoples.[8] Emphatically rich in gold, the Tyrians are also "barbarian" in the
same sense that the Trojans were. Aeneas' echoes of Andromacha constantly
pick up her sense of a double loss, of military power and material wealth
(represented in the polysemantic word *opes*), conflating them in an agony of
helpless impoverishment. The very first words of his narration to the
Carthaginians herald the allusive complex (2.3–5):

> "Infandum, regina, iubes renovare dolorem,
> Troianas ut opes et lamentabile regnum
> eruerint Danai."

"An unspeakable sorrow, O queen, you bid me to renew, how the Danaans
overthrew the Trojan forces [or riches] and the lamentable kingdom."

The Trojan *opes* at 2.4 introduces the city's catastrophe as encompassing both
military and material resources, like Andromacha's use of the term (the term is
likewise bivalent at 2.603, Venus' revelation that "the hostility of the gods has
upturned these *opes*," and when at 3.53 Aeneas speaks of the "shattered *opes* of

---

[7] Plautus, *Trin.* 19; cf. *As.* 11, Cicero *Orat.* 160. Cf. *Capt.* 492 *barbarica lege* (of Roman law) and
884 *barbaricas urbis* (of cities in Latium), spoken of course by Greek characters.
[8] P. 98 above.

the Trojans"). In shifting the adjective *barbaricus* at 2.504 from the lost army to the lost gold that adorned the palace (compare Andromacha's "precinct . . . appointed with ivory and gold"), Virgil again implicitly conflates the two senses of *opes*. The double sense of the term recalls 1.14: Carthage is introduced as "rich in *opes* and most keen in zeal for war" (*dives opum studiisque asperrima belli*).[9] The wealth and martial might of the Carthaginians are attributes that the Trojan refugees once had, and wish they still had; Aeneas' references to Trojan wealth and power desiderate and project qualities he might share with his hosts. So echoes of the lament of Ennius' Andromacha in Aeneas' narrative underline the perilous liminality inherent in the Aeneadae's sojourn at Carthage. This is intertextuality as ethnic (re)definition, one part of Virgil's general use of early Latin poetry on the fall of Troy, Roman origins, and the Punic Wars as we discussed it in the last chapter.

By 8.685–88, the prophetic image of the battle of Actium on the Shield, the borderline drawn by *barbaricus* has shifted (in an even closer repetition of Andromacha's phrase):

> hinc ope barbarica variisque Antonius armis,
> victor ab Aurorae populis et litore rubro,
> Aegyptum virisque Orientis et ultima secum
> Bactra vehit.

> On the other side Mark Antony, conqueror from the nations of the Dawn and the ruddy shore, with a barbaric host and motley arms brings with him Egypt and the forces of the Orient and furthest Bactria.[10]

Virgil's reuse of the term implicitly puts Romans, Italians, and Greeks on the same side (observe the Greco-Roman gods at 699–705 who back Augustus, leading the *Itali*)—opposite Easterners led by Egyptians and the renegade Roman general—and implicitly expresses the eventual success of the Aeneadae's merging with the Italians and changing from Trojans to Romans.[11] Aeneas' votive inscription on the site of Actium at 3.288 similarly draws a borderline between Trojans and Greeks that Augustus' victory there (particularly as interpreted on the Shield) will redefine: "Aeneas [took] these [weapons] from the victorious Greeks" (*Aeneas haec de Danais victoribus arma*). If, as the historical syllepsis of the passage invites us to do, we liken Aeneas to Augustus

---

[9] Another such conflation may be signaled by the wording at 2.21–22 *notissima fama / insula, dives opum Priami dum regna manebant* ("[Tenedos was] a most famous island, rich in *opes* while the realm of Priam held . . .").

[10] On the oppositions (including those between East and West, female and male) against which this passage takes meaning, see Quint 1993:23–25.

[11] Wigodsky 1972:78 remarks: "perhaps the only comment required on this implied rejection of Troy as a symbol of the vice and luxury of the East, and the assimilation of Augustus' enemy to the conquered Trojans, is Vergil's own [i.e. Juno's] 'occidit, occideritque sinas cum nomine Troia' (XII 828)."

and Trojans to Romans, we would then liken the "victorious Greeks" to the routed Orientals on the Shield. The tables have turned: the inscription foreshadows a reversal of the Trojan war, and with it a reallignment of nations. Antony on the Shield is made an Eastern conqueror, but in the sense that he is *one of them*: victory itself is troped as defeat. Stigmatized by the Ennian intertext, Antony's rulership over "barbarians" becomes a doomed struggle against history and the fate—the very existence—of the Roman people. By Book 8 and the description of the Shield, the terms of national identity sketched by Andromacha, now attached to Antony at Actium (*ope barbarica*), have fallen on the far side of Roman destiny—though not to Aeneas' knowledge; the prolepsis of his Shield, presupposing a Rome that has subsumed, and assimilated itself to, Hellenism, finds him uncomprehending (8.730 *rerum ignarus*).

Aeneas, indeed, corrects the Plautine construct of Roman "barbarism." Already in his "doors proud with barbaric gold and war spoils" (2.504) lies an ambiguity of identification (again, of course, unapparent to himself). The coupling of "barbaric gold" with "war spoils" makes one think of the former as war spoils, as by hendiadys; yet when we press the adjective, its basic insistence on ethnic boundaries and on a Greek viewpoint raises problems for this interpretation. From what defeated enemy would barbaric gold come? Not from the Greeks, who could not be called *barbari* ("non-Greek"). From nearby Anatolian peoples? But if they are *barbari*, the Trojans are as well. The adjective, in fact, teases us with a proleptic vision, more appropriate to Hellenized imperial Rome, when despoiled Asiatic enemies could in fact be differentiated as "barbarians" from a conquering, Greek-assimilated self. We are left with a sharp sense of the difference between the Romans of Virgil's time and their Trojan forebears. We are already on the way to the vision on the Shield, and to the divisions predicted in an etiology of a Roman practice at 7.601–606, where Juno opens the Latin "twin portals of war" against the Trojans. That account of Rome's inheritance from Latium, which implicitly bonds the Latins and the former Trojans into one nation, names the outsiders against whom the Romans *are* one as Orientals: Getae, Hyrcani, Arabs, Indians, Parthians. Imperial Romans, led by Augustus to a world empire, are opposed both to the Orient and to their own Trojan forebears.

Two remaining details of Andromacha's lament for Priam's palace appear soon after Aeneas' arrival in Carthage. There are seven hinges in the *Aeneid*,[12] and the first appears on Dido's temple to Juno in Carthage, as seen by Aeneas at 1.448–49

> aerea cui gradibus surgebant limina nexaeque
> aere trabes, foribus cardo stridebat aënis.

---

[12] *Aen.* 1.449; 2.480, 493; 3.448; 6.573; 7.621; 9.724. Figurative at 1.672.

Its threshold of bronze rose upon a flight of stairs, and its beams were
bound with bronze, and its hinge screeched on brazen doors.

He perhaps omits to notice that the appointments there are not of gold, but
rather—curiously for the gold-rich Tyrian exiles—brazen.[13] In this they are
like the brazen doors of Priam's palace at 2.480–81. Now the similarity is
comforting; a terrifying inversion of the image comes if we hear Ennius' compound adjective *altisono*, "high-resounding [hinge]," behind the "hair-raising-
sounding" hinge of the Tartarus of Juno's Furies (6.573 *horrisono*). By now it
should come as no surprise that when we encounter a royally appointed paneled ceiling in the *Aeneid*, it is the one beneath which Aeneas tells his tale: that
of Dido's banquet hall (1.726 *laquearibus aureis*, "golden ceiling panels"), hint-
ing to the aware at both the sympathy of the surroundings—will this be the
Trojan guests' new homeland?—and, in retrospect, the impossibility of such
sympathy, once the line of "barbarism" has been redrawn. Here again we
reprise a topic of the last chapter, the sojourn in Carthage as a pivot—a
hinge?—of the Aeneadae's movement away from Trojan identity. In the doors
and the paneled ceiling, we remember Troy, and in the assimilation of Dido's
temple and palace to Priam's ruined temple-palace (*templum*), there is a
reminder both of Dido's death and funeral pyre and of the more remote devastation of Carthage. Aeneas will leave the attributes of Troy for Carthage to
assume, to her detriment. Orientalness means obsolescence and destruction.

There are further tokens of evolving nationhood in Dido's argument at
4.311–13:

> "quid, si non arva aliena domosque
> ignotas peteres, et Troia antiqua maneret,
> Troia per undosum peteretur classibus aequor?"

"What if you were not heading for foreign people's farmlands and
unknown homes, and ancient Troy still remained: would you head for
Troy in ships over this billowing [i.e. stormy] sea?"

But now she clearly has it all wrong: he is no longer looking for Troy. Troy is
not comparable to his present object, Italy (as it is in his encouragement of his
people at 1.206 *illic fas regna resurgere Troiae*, "There [in Latium] it is divinely
decreed for the kingdom of Troy to rise again"). Her effort to assimilate and
reflect Aeneas' viewpoint in the epithet *antiqua*, which he had used of Troy at
2.363, brings this message home to the reader: the sentimental and venerable
associations of the word (as at 4.633, in Dido's orbit of focalization: *namque
suam patria antiqua cinis ater habebat*, "for black ashes held her own [nurse] in
their ancient homeland [Tyre]") are easily ousted by the connotation "has-
been, no longer relevant," as the next chapter will explore.

---

[13] The "substitution" of bronze for gold here emerges especially from a comparison of the polyptotic and polymorphic repetition of "bronze" with that of "gold" at 4.138–39.

His answer (especially 340–50) suggests that he is beginning to understand
this. The assimilation to Dido's people now contains its own arguments for his
departure:

> 340   "me si fata meis paterentur ducere vitam
> auspiciis et sponte mea componere curas,
> urbem Troianam primum dulcisque meorum
> reliquias colerem, Priami tecta alta manerent,
> et recidiva manu posuissem Pergama victis.
> 345   sed nunc Italiam magnam Gryneus Apollo,
> Italiam Lyciae iussere capessere sortes;
> hic amor, haec patria est. si te Karthaginis arces
> Phoenissam Libycaeque aspectus detinet urbis,
> quae tandem Ausonia Teucros considere terra
> 350   invidia est? et nos fas extera quaerere regna."

"If fate allowed me to lead my life under my own auspices and find my
own resolution for my woes, first I would be living in the city of Troy and
caring for the sweet remnants of my people; the high halls of Priam
would stand, and I would have planted a revived Pergamum for the
defeated. But now Grynean Apollo and the oracles of Lycia have bidden
me to make for great Italy—Italy. That is my love, that is my fatherland.
If the citadel of Carthage and the sight of this Libyan city keep you, a
Phoenician, here, why then do you begrudge the Teucrians to settle in the
land of Ausonia? We, too, by divine decree must seek for a realm in foreign lands."

In the summarizing last sentence he answers her welcome at 1.628–29, "A
similar fortune intended me, too, buffeted through many toils, finally to settle
in this land" (*me quoque per multos similis fortuna labores / iactatam hac demum
voluit consistere terra*). The resort to an architectural figure at 4.343 "Priam's
high halls would remain" underlines his steady revision of the Andromachan
persona. Notice also the epithet: the fallen "high" halls of Troy foreshadow the
ramparts of "high" Rome that will replace them (1.7). The ethnic differentiations are sharp but agonized. "Italy, Italy," urge the god of the Grynean grove
and his Lycian oracles: as at 3.85 (*da propriam, Thymbraee, domum*), Aeneas
persists in calling his charter god by the epithets of his old Anatolian home,
here in pathetic contrast to the as yet unknown new home. He has just called
Dido "Elissa" (335): "Here, for the first time, he uses her old Phoenician name,
creating an impression of distance and estrangement."[14] The name expresses
the Orientalness that persists in her and that he is leaving behind.

It is fate (340), according to this view, that separates him from his Oriental
past: he does not make for Italy (he concludes the speech by declaring) of his

---

[14] Clausen 1987:48.

own volition (361 *Italiam non sponte sequor*); and we have heard of the various oracles and prophecies that confirm this circumstance. But fate here becomes a figure for a reconstructed self, replacing his love for Dido with a love of an unknown country where he will cease to be Trojan. A telling wordplay is perhaps detectable in Mercury's final order to Aeneas at line 569: *rumpe moras*, literally, "break delay." The word for "delay," *mora*, is an anagram of *amor*: subliminally, Aeneas is to break off his love affair with Dido. But it is also an anagram for *Roma*: Aeneas is to replace his lingering in the comfort of the familiar and the happy with the quest that he cannot hope to see achieved, but which must become his new love.[15] In Carthage we see Aeneas sloughing the Andromachan persona. Folding his personal into his national aims, the phrase *hic amor, haec patria est* signals a rethinking of the sentiment in Andromacha's *O pater, o patria*: Italy replaces Troy.

II

In redistributing and revising the meaning of Andromacha's speech in the way we have seen, Virgil is taking up an old practice in Latin translations from Greek (I use the word "translation" in the broadest sense, to include both close translations for sense, with minimal additions and omissions, and looser adaptations that claim some identity to an original). Early translations often carry—unavoidably, automatically—a message about Roman ethnic identity as against Greek, as in Andromacha's use of *ope barbarica* for her own husband's troops. When Ennius transforms the Homeric imprecation ὦ πάτερ ἡμέτερε, Κρονίδη, ὕπατε κρειόντων (*Iliad* 8.31) into a newly minted Latin hexameter, the first part retains its sense "Our father, son of Saturn" (*Annales* 444 Skutsch *o genitor noster Saturnie*), but the second changes from "highest of the ruling [gods]" to "greatest of the gods" (*maxime divom*), insinuating the Roman, specifically Capitoline, deity: "Zeus is now Jupiter Optimus Maximus," observes Feeney, "and the world he rules is now a Roman world."[16] Moreover, there is a sly insinuation that Homer—Ennius' authority according to the prologue to the *Annales*, indeed Ennius' own self in a past life—knew that Zeus always *was* Jupiter Optimus Maximus and the sphere of the Trojan war the domain of a Roman god, and that it took only the genius of Homer's

---

[15] This particular (and potentially reversible) construction of synonymy and antonymy, of course, depends on Mercury's control of the wordplay, and his equation of Aeneas' stay in Carthage with *mora*. On the anagram *amor-Roma* see p. 43 above; on *amor-mora-Roma*, see Pucci 1978:53–54 (exploring its meaning in Propertius 1.8). The locution *rumpe moras* reappears at the moment when Aeneas turns to single combat with Turnus: *praecipitatque moras omnis, opera omnia rumpit* ("12.699 and he hurled aside all delays, broke off all his operations").

[16] Feeney 1991:128, reading the line against the background of Naevius' similar use of Homer. Ennius is almost certainly the author, although the line is unattributed (Priscian 3.205).

own later incarnation to make the identity plain. The very first verse of the very first Latin epic, Livius Andronicus' intricately learned translation of the *Odyssey*, inscribes its poem with self-consciousness about translation: *virum mihi, Camena, insece versutum*. The final word, from *vertere*, not only renders the Greek epithet *polytropos*, "of many turns" (and thus unavoidably brings into Latin the revisionary poetics of the *Odyssey*), but also picks up the sense "translate" (as in *vortit* in the Plautus lines cited above).[17] "Tell me, Muse, of the *translated* man": the tropics of the *Odyssey* are bonded to those of the Roman appropriation of Greek culture, and the problems of the resulting double perspective.

Early Roman drama almost automatically works out Roman identity through translation (as in the large number of tragedies concerned with the Trojan War and thus, potentially, Roman national origins). Observe, for example, what happens when a drama on Antigone goes into Latin (Accius, *Antigona* fr. 1 Ribbeck):

> Quid agis? perturbas rem omnem ac resupinas, soror.

> What are you doing? You are upturning the state, sister, and laying it flat on its back.

Ismene's sentiment alone would have a home in any Greek tragedian we may imagine as Accius' original. Yet the simple, obvious transition from *polis* to *res* promotes a commentary on late second-century Roman culture, and implicitly on its relation to Greek (the elision in *rem omnem*, producing the syllable *rom-*, helps direct this commentary). Similarly Ennius' *o pater, o patria* (which because of context first recalls Euripides, *Andromache* 394 ὦ τάλαιν' ἐμὴ πατρίς, "O my poor fatherland!") helps effect a Roman revision of the closer model, which has *polis*, not "fatherland": Euripides, *Medea* 166 ὦ πάτερ ὦ πόλις ("O father, O city!").[18] The comparison with the spectacularly un-Greek Medea, of course, opens up a rich, compound intertext on "barbarity" versus Hellenism, further complicated by the new Roman context and modulated by the themes of exile and alienation that Medea and Andromache share. Jocelyn notices the way Roman protocols shape the Ennian Andromacha's whole lament: "Ennius makes his Andromache speak of herself as a stateless person in terms of Roman law and social practice"; and he discerns "Roman sacral language" in the lines on the destruction of the palace.[19] The obvious etymological relationship between *pater* and *patria* conjures up a sense that *polis* never could of Roman senatorial authority—and patriarchy in general:

---

[17] Livius Andronicus fr. 1 Morel; see Hinds 1998:61–62 (and on his technique Goldberg 1995:64–73). On the poetics of *polytropos* see Pucci 1987.

[18] Later poets use the phrase in Roman and Trojan contexts: Ovid *Tr.* 2.574 (on Augustus) *o pater o patriae cura salusque tuae*, Petronius *Sat.* 89 (*Troiae Halosis* 11) *o patria*.

[19] Jocelyn ad loc.

Rome as the domain of the *paterfamilias*—and projects it into the Trojan, proto-Roman past, creating a sense of ethical prolepsis. Compare a simple line of Naevius' Hector (line 15 Ribbeck):

> Laetus sum laudari me abs te, pater, a laudato viro.

I am happy, father, to be praised by you, a much-praised man.

Whatever the original Greek context had made of this, the Roman connotations of *pater* and *laudare* wrench the scene out of the realm of the Trojan Other and reinstate it in that of the Trojan forebear formulating and predicting a future ethos, the *mos* of his *minores*. This anticipates a Virgilian motif: compare Aeneas' words to Ascanius at *Aeneid* 12.438–40, "You be sure to remember, when in the near future your young age grows to maturity; look back in your spirit to the models among your people, and let both your father Aeneas and your uncle Hector inspire you" (*tu facito, mox cum matura adoleverit aetas, / sis memor et te animo repetentem exempla tuorum / et pater Aeneas et avunculus excitet Hector*). One could make similar claims about the new meaning that accrues to ideas rendered by strongly ethical, and ideologically charged, Latin words like *maiestas* and *virtus* (Andronicus 13 and 16 Ribbeck).

In this inherent commentary, moreover, is a deeper one on the instability of ethnic boundaries, and their dependence on language. We find it in Naevius, in a septenarius probably from his *Lucurgus* (Naevius, *Incertarum fabularum* fr. 4 Ribbeck):

> diabathra in pedibus habebat, erat amictus epicroco.

He wore *diabathra* on his feet, he was wrapped in an *epicrocon*.

One does not need to know what exactly *diabathra* and *epicrocon* mean; the imported words function almost purely as signs for "egregiously foreign apparel." This line recalls scenes of contempt from Euripides' *Bacchae*, and probably refers to Liber (the Italian wine god by whom Naevius translates Dionysus). Notice how the language tropes the traditional "effeminacy"—which in the original ideology and presumably the original drama was "barbarian," Oriental, anti-Greek—as Greek, with the connotations of the attire underscored by Greek loan words (framing the line), and those of the Greek loan words underscored metrically by Greek-sounding resolved longs. Metonymy thickens immediately to metaphor. Greek Orientalism translates into Latin, almost inevitably, as a contrast between Roman and Greek, with Greek and Easterner together cast as the Other now that Roman is the self. This contrast is simply inscribed in the Romans' way of talking about themselves among nations. There are similar moments in the *Aeneid*: Varro felt the word *mitra*, meaning the Oriental head-dress with which Iarbas taxes Aeneas' masculinity (4.216), as Greek.[20]

---

[20] See p. 85 above. This article of clothing had special Bacchic associations: Tatham 1990.

The female devotees of Liber are similarly stigmatized in a fragment known
to come from the *Lucurgus* (lines 31–32 Ribbeck):

pergite

thyrsigerae Bacchae <. . .> Bacchico cum schemate.

Onward, Bacchants, bearing *thyrsoi*, in Bacchic dress!

(as a model for the sense one thinks of Euripides' ἴτε Βάκχαι, ἴτε Βάκχαι).
Punctiliously pronounced, the un-Latin aspirates, like the resolved longs in the
other fragment, would underscore the trope. And when Naevius comes to
name the melody whereby the unruly throng seduce new converts, he does not
bother to Latinize, but calls it a *suavisonum melos* (20 Ribbeck), no more than
transliterating the Greek noun. There is a parallel in Naevius' contemporary
Livius Andronicus, from an unknown play (30 Ribbeck):

florem anculabant Liberi ex carchesiis.

From chalices they were serving the bloom of Bacchus.[21]

There, not only does the Greek loan word advertise the opulence of the cups,
but the metonymy for wine—*florem*, "bloom"—is a calque on Greek *anthos*, the
"bouquet" of wine (as we say). That verse, however, lacks the sexual distur-
bance that enriches Naevius' line on the *diabathra*.

We find a similar technique of ethnic and gender differentiation at the end
of the longest such statement in the *Aeneid*, Remulus Numanus' harangue
against the Trojans (9.614–20):

"vobis picta croco et fulgenti murice vestis,
615   desidiae cordi, iuvat indulgere choreis,
et tunicae manicas et habent redimicula mitrae.
o vere Phrygiae, neque enim Phryges, ite per alta
Dindyma, ubi adsuetis biforem dat tibia cantum.
tympana vos buxusque vocat Berecyntia Matris
620   Idaeae; sinite arma viris et cedite ferro."

"Your garments are decorated with saffron and brilliant purple-dye;
there is sloth in your hearts; you like to lose yourself in dances, and your
tunics have sleeves and your *mitrae* laces. O Phrygian women, truly, not
Phrygian men, betake yourselves over the heights of Mount Dindymus,
where the pipe bestows two-toned music on the adepts. The timbrels and
Berecyntian boxwood flute of the Mother of Ida call you; leave warfare to
the men and give up your sword."

---

[21] In Virgil's two instances of *carchesium* a similar metonymy points back to Andronicus: *Georg.*
4.380 *cape Maeonii carchesia Bacchi* and *Aen.* 5.77 *hic duo rite mero libans carchesia Baccho.* Cf.
Wigodsky 1972:18.

This diatribe (intended to illustrate the difference between the Trojans and the tough, austere Italians: 603–613)[22] is a rich compendium of Orientalist motifs. We have, first of all, the clothes, with their expensive dyes and such damning elaborations as sleeves and laces. Again we meet with stigmatizing *mitrae*.[23] Gender is inverted. The orgiastic side of the cult of Cybele (compare the Bacchism in Naevius) is taken full advantage of, her devotees identified with her self-castrating priests—and their mythological prototype Attis: lines 617–19 uncannily recall the treatment of the myth in Catullus 63. We are far from the stately, kindly Mother Goddess, *alma Cybebe* (10.220), as Anchises describes her at 6.784–87 or as she appears when she rescues Aeneas' ships at 9.80–117. In Remulus' slur, dances and musical instruments take the place of arms and warfare. But in the proliferation of Greek-derived names for Anatolian geography in 617–19, we hear a proliferation of breathy aspirates and mincing upsilons, audibly marking the Oriental as Greek (also in *tympana*; and the learned reader could calque Greek *pyxos* on its Latin derivative *buxus*).[24] The linguistically and culturally Greek *choreis* in 615, denoting the dances in which these decadents lose themselves, already heralds this program, which is consonant with the way Remulus at 602, in a kind of argument a fortiori, casts Greek and Trojan together as antitypes of the virile Italians: "Here there are no sons of Atreus, no Ulysses, fashioner of speech" (*non hic Atridae nec fandi fictor Ulixes*).

The boundary is immediately redrawn, not only by Ascanius' prompt slaying of Remulus, but by the response of Apollo, watching from a cloud, to the boy's sharpshooting (9.641–44):

> "macte nova virtute, puer, sic itur ad astra,
> dis genite et geniture deos. iure omnia bella
> gente sub Assaraci fato ventura resident,
> nec te Troia capit."

"Blessings on your newfound valor, boy—this is the way to the stars, O descendant and ancestor of gods! Rightly all future wars will subside under the rule of Assaracus' lineage. And Troy cannot contain you."

On the one hand, Apollo—the young god of male coming-of-age, as signaled by his epithet *crinitus*, "with flowing, unshorn hair," at line 638—reverses

---

[22] At 603 he calls his people a *durum genus*, a hard, tough, enduring race (as does Anchises' prophecy at 5.730 and Aeneas at 11.48)—a characterization mirrored by the Trojans at 3.94 *Dardanidae duri* (see p. 85 above) and 9.468 *Aeneadae duri*, recalling the sufferings endured by Aeneas' people and belying Remulus' sharp opposition.

[23] This taunt is difficult: Remulus speaks as if the laces (*redimicula*), not the *mitrae* themselves, were the target. Perhaps a compressed argument a fortiori: not only do you wear *mitrae*, but they have laces. *Redimicula* would then carry a connotation of ladylike ribbons; cf. Juvenal 2.84.

[24] Likewise in his violent harangue against Aeneas at 12.99, with its rape-like imagery, Turnus takes care to call him *semiviri Phrygis* ("half-male Phrygian"), using a toponym that has not only marked "Oriental" connotations, but a distinctly Greek-sounding aspirate and upsilon.

Remulus' assessment by congratulating the boy Ascanius on his newly earned *virtus*, "valor," literally "manliness" (courage in battle being the preeminent virtue for men in archaic society). His last remark seems to do the same in the ethnic sphere, by recalling that this very Trojan race will master the warring world—that is, they will impose peace by shooting down the "proud" (Ascanius calls Remulus' words "proud" at 634), agreeably to Anchises' dictum at 6.853. On the other hand, Apollo immediately qualifies this prophecy by making Troy too small for Ascanius' manliness (so too Anchises addressed himself to "you, Roman"). This in effect endorses Remulus' characterization.[25] Indeed, Apollo's rhetoric accepts Remulus' terms, as in *nova virtute*, which could even imply "new" manliness of the Trojans in general; he just redraws the line to exclude Ascanius, and by extension his posterity, from the side that the Trojans had inhabited (the identification between growing toward Romanness and growing into manliness is negatively and tragically expressed in the fallen warriors we reviewed in chapter 1). This Greco-Roman god (compare his opposition to motley Egyptian deities on the Shield) implicitly corrects Remulus' schema by replacing the Italians with Greco-Romans as foils to a rejected Orient, and thereby helps introduce into the *Aeneid* an antithetical tradition within the dialogue that Naevius had promoted.

The verse from Naevius' *Lucurgus* parallels the controversy over the Roman cult of Bacchus in Rome, which culminated in the proscription of 186 B.C.E. Both the verse and the legislation lump Greek and barbarian together as alien to Rome—trope Greek as Oriental, in fact. The fact that this "Greek" opponent of Bacchus is the Thracian Lycurgus complicates matters; it is unclear what dynamics of national identity underlay Aeschylus' drama about him (and even in the *Bacchae* of Euripides, Pentheus' Thebes, founded by Phoenician Cadmus and famously a foil for Athens,[26] is at best a heuristic antitype to "barbarism"). A King Lycurgus is mentioned at *Aeneid* 3.14 as a one-time ruler of Thrace, in connection with the refugees' first stop (and first attempted settlement) after escaping from the Troad. Priam's gold is at issue here too: the present king murdered Priam's son Polydorus for the gold left with him (3.49–57). He and his country are part of the world that Aeneas must learn somehow to detach, with much agony, from his own identity.

Naevius' play dramatizes tragedy itself—indeed, drama as a whole—and its problematic position in Rome in a different way from Euripides' dramatization of the problematics of tragedy at Athens. Yet it is not only in tragedy that one finds this kind of translation. There is a close parallel to the Naevius passage a few generations later in a speech by Scipio Africanus the Younger (fr. 17 Malcovati = Gellius 6.12):

---

[25] I owe this last point to Brian Calabrese.
[26] Vidal-Naquet 1989:175–211, Zeitlin 1990 and 1993.

Nam qui cotidie unguentatus adversus speculum ornetur, cuius supercilia radantur, qui barba vulsa feminibusque subvulsis ambulet, qui in conviviis adulescentulus cum amatore cum chirodyta tunica interior accubuerit, qui non modo vinosus sed virosus quoque sit, eumne quisquam dubitet quin idem fecerit quod cinaedi facere solent?

For if a man, anointed with scented oils, primps himself in front of a mirror every day, and his eyebrows are trimmed, and his beard is plucked and he goes about with plucked thighs and, in his youth, reclines with his back up against his lover at dinner, wearing a long-sleeved tunic, and is not only mad for wine but mad for men, can anyone doubt that he does the same thing that pathics customarily do?

Scipio is deploying against P. Sulpicius Gallus a charge common also to Greek rhetoric[27] (the *femini-* in *feminibus*, "thighs," is a nice coincidence); in Latin the effeminacy is troped as distinctly Greek. The use of *chirodyta*, "long-sleeved" (for which Gellius quotes this passage, emphasizing the *indecorum* of a man wearing such a tunic "at Rome and anywhere in Latium") recalls the Greek clothing words in Naevius; Courtney 1999:119 notes: "This last item is contemptuously cited by a Greek term rather than the Latin manicata, man-uleata" (as in the speech by Virgil's Remulus quoted above), and he cites a scathing satirical catalogue of such terms by Scipio's friend Lucilius (fr. 71 Marx). Gellius concludes his discussion by observing that Virgil too uses long-sleeved tunics as evidence of effeminacy (*Aeneid* 9.616, discussed above), and that Ennius spoke of the "tunic-clad youth" of Carthage, "evidently not with-out reproach" (*non videtur sine probro dixisse*).[28]

Another example from oratory is instructive (Cicero, *Pro Caelio* 8):

Quo loco possum dicere id quod vir clarissimus, M. Crassus, cum de adventu regis Ptolemaei quereretur, paulo ante dixit: "Utinam ne in nemore Pelio. . . ." Ac longius mihi quidem contexere hoc carmen liceret: "Nam numquam era errans" hanc molestiam nobis exhiberet, "Medea animo aegro, amore saevo saucia."

At this point I can say what Marcus Crassus, that illustrious man, said a little while ago when he was complaining about the arrival of King Ptolemy: "Oh, would that in the Pelian forest never . . ." And if I were permitted to pursue the poetic context further: "For then my wandering mistress never" would have given us this trouble, "Medea, sick at heart, wounded by savage love."

---

[27] E.g. at Aeschines 1.131, aimed at Demosthenes.

[28] *Annales* 303 Skutsch (who suggests a speech, perhaps by Scipio Africanus the Elder, as the context).

His quotations come from the nurse's opening speech in Ennius' *Medea Exul*
(fr. 1 Ribbeck), modeled after the opening of Euripides' *Medea*:

> Utinam ne in nemore Pelio securibus
> caesae accidissent abiegnae ad terram trabes,
> neve inde navis inchoandi exordium
> cepisset, quae nunc nominatur nomine
> 5 Argo, quia Argivi in ea delecti viri
> vecti petebant pellem inauratam arietis
> Colchis, imperio regis Peliae, per dolum:
> nam numquam era errans mea domo efferret pedem
> Medea, animo aegra, amore saevo saucia.

Oh, would that in the Pelian forest the firwood beams had never fallen
to earth, struck by axes, and the ship had never taken from there its origin of departure—the ship that is now called by the name of Argo,
because in it, chosen men of Argos came seeking by trickery from the
Colchians the golden fleece of the ram, by order of King Pelias. For then
my wandering mistress would never have set foot from home, Medea,
sick at heart, wounded by savage love.

Cicero is talking about Clodia, the "Medea of the Palatine," a Roman lady he
assimilates to a notable "barbarian" from the East. He is taking advantage of a
mythological game that had already been introduced into the trial: Fortunatianus
tells us that in his speech, Cicero's opponent Atratinus had called Caelius a
"pretty-boy Jason," *pulchellus Iason*; the ingenuity of Caelius, quick to capitalize
on the mythological allusion, came back with "curly-haired Pelias," *Pelia cincin-
natus.*[29] These allusive epithets cast their targets as effeminate (as Austin notes
in his commentary), but they do not work any play with ethnicity: it is not the
Greekness of Jason or Pelias that generates opprobrium, but their characters,
respectively that of a thief who filched the golden fleece (as Caelius was alleged
to have fleeced Clodia of her gold) and that of a murderer who attempted to
destroy his nephew. It is left to Cicero to draw the irresistible parallel between
Clodia and Medea, and in doing so he ties these earlier jibes to Ennius through
Crassus' quotation from the *Medea Exul*, which identified the embassy from
Egypt with the Greeks arriving on barbarian shores.[30] The Romans take the
place of the barbarians, the anti-Greeks, as Clodia takes the place of Medea. The
strong viewpoint of Ennius' Medea, expressed through her nurse, coincides with
the Roman perspective; the Ennian quotation carries us back to the world of
Plautus vortit barbare. The implicit casting of a (Greco-Egyptian) Ptolemy as
Greek Jason in an encounter with *barbaroi* also opens up an intertext with

---

[29] Fortunatianus 3.7 (p. 124 Halm).
[30] So Austin 1960:68, citing other possibilities.

Apollonius' *Argonautica* and the cultural reconciliations of Ptolemaic poetry in general.[31]

In Ennius' concluding phrase *amore saevo saucia* we see one stage on the route by which the distressed heroines of Euripidean tragedy came down through Apollonius to Virgil, who makes us read Ennius' Medea as a prefiguration of his own Dido. *Aeneid* 4 opens with the same metaphor using the same word: "But the queen, now wounded by a grievous care . . ." (*at regina gravi iamdudum saucia cura*). There *regina* replaces *era*; Dido too is an *era errans*, a wandering mistress (as we observed in the last chapter, *erro* is her special verb, connected to her name by a venerable etymology—which subtextually replicates Ennius' sound-based wordplay). It is specifically Ennius, not his Greek original, that the Virgilian text fruitfully engages with here. With *errans* and *amore saucia* Ennius divides Euripides' phrase "stricken with love" (*Medea* 8 ἔρωτι . . . ἐκπλαγεῖσα) between its ostensible meaning and a perfectly possible secondary one, "driven into exile because of love." The opening wish of *Medea Exul* echoes in the *Aeneid* when Dido, about to die, wishes the Trojans had never arrived (4.657–58):

> "felix, heu nimium felix, si litora tantum
> numquam Dardaniae tetigissent nostra carinae."

"[I would have been] happy, alas, all too happy, if only the Dardanian ships had never touched our shores."[32]

In this intertext the Trojans are like the Greeks, and Dido is like the barbarian Medea (of course). Especially after the break with Aeneas becomes final, this reinforces from that perspective the gradual division between Trojans and Carthaginians that we have been tracing. The assimilation to Jason (in these little allusions as in the grand imitation of Apollonius that Servius on 4.1 claims for the whole of Book 4), in putting Aeneas over on the Greek side, also predicts the future Greco-Roman identity that will be clearest in the depiction of the Battle of Actium on Aeneas' Shield.

The ethnic dichotomy, accepted from Greece, between Hellenes and barbarians involves a tough choice for a Roman poet recounting his history: either a denial of Trojan origins, or a vindication of them from a Greek stereotype, and the task of constructing a new ethnic paradigm. The efforts of Dionysius of Halicarnassus in the first book of his Roman history to prove the Trojans—and thus the Romans at their very origins—to be *Greek* show that in Virgil's time the debate over where the Romans stand versus the Greeks was still alive. From the perspective of Greek historians and diplomats, Rome is the problem

---

[31] Stephens 2003.

[32] The echo here is partly filtered through Catullus 64.171–72 (Wigodsky 1972:76). See also Wigodsky 1972:93 on the influence of Ennius' *Medea Exul* on Virgil, and Thomas 1999:12–32 (first published in 1982) on the long tradition of literary borrowing that these texts belong to.

in this question.[33] In the *Aeneid*, as we progress from the simple Trojans-versus-Greeks schema of the late war, Greek emerges as the problem: either part of Rome as against the East, or part of the Eastern world that the Romans reject (and that Aeneas left behind). One message of the *Aeneid* is that Apollo and Octavian settled that question at the Battle of Actium. From other angles, however, the poem interrogates the Greek-derived categories themselves and offers a meditation on what an astonishing and contested self-reflexiveness Greek culture had introduced into Rome. For centuries the very dynamic of Latin poetry was translation from (and confrontation with) Greek poetry, entailing both impersonation and a consciousness of alterity; thus national-ity becomes a function or aspect of the ancient dynamics of literary mimesis, which involved imitation (*mimêsis, imitatio*) with studied divergence (*zêlôsis, aemulatio*).[34] The examples from Andronicus, Naevius, Ennius, Accius, Scipio, and Cicero illustrate the power of linguistic translation to effect a cultural translation from Greek to Roman terms, whether by simply giving an idea special Roman implications (e.g. *res* versus *polis*) or more subtly, as in the case of *barbaricus*, by using a word that in the new context maps out a new ethnic perspective. In building on and renovating this tradition, Virgil insinu-ates into the *Aeneid* not only commentaries both on earlier literature and on Roman identity, but one on the changing definition of Roman identity through words.

There is room here for a complicated ethnicized literary history: Andronicus, Naevius, Ennius, and Accius began as non-Romans, with a spe-cial sense of the shifting lines that mark out nationhood; and it is in their acquired Latin that we have been tracing those lines as they pertain to Roman identity. Feeney speaks of non-native Latin speakers creating a Roman version of Greek literature "in the interstices" of Central and South Italian culture[35] (in this regard the alien origins and essential emptiness of Romanness in the *Aeneid* mimic the nature of Latin poetry). Virgil does not just engage with the contemporary debate on whether Romans were to be classified as Greeks (as Dionysius of Halicarnassus and others would have it) or barbarians; he builds on an even more powerful poetic tradition. In the way his Aeneas negotiates Roman identity in the palace of Dido and later, the *Aeneid* tests the terms of Ennius' *Andromacha* and revises them, balancing Rome between a Greek and a "barbarian" identity; embedded in its literary borrowings is a commentary on the way poets have created Roman identity out of Greek. And the tradition continues: Silius, for example, will interrogate Virgil's ethnic boundaries, test-ing them in the Punic Wars that they are to result in.

---

[33] On Dionysius see Gruen 1992:7–8. See also the discussions in Bowersock 1965, Momigliano 1975.

[34] See Russell 1979 on the ideas and the sources.

[35] Feeney 1998:52–53 and elsewhere, e.g. 68.

Look again at the fragment from the *Andromacha*. Cicero's appreciative read-ing of Ennius places him at odds with the "chanters of Euphorion": Roman lovers of Hellenistic poetry, presumably the likes of Cinna and other members of his generation, the Latin poets who rejoiced in distressed mythological hero-ines, extremes of gender-bending, and the combination of love and death, the voluptuous and the macabre, that descends especially from Euphorion through Parthenius and has left its traces in the passages we reviewed in chapter 1.[36] In appropriating Ennius' voice (and Andromacha's) does not Virgil, the disciple of Cinna and Parthenius, collapse Cicero's polarity? In the pathos of Troy, in its destruction and its gradual recession into the past and the realm of what is alien, Virgil instills both a new way to read Roman identity and a new way to read his Latin precursors. *O poetam egregium!*

III

In thinking about the perils of false settlements, whether in Carthage or else-where, one recalls as the signal metaphor for that peril the little settlement of Virgil's own Andromache in Book 3, which represented a literal recovery of the Trojan past as a pathetic dead end. Together with her new husband, Helenus (a brother of Hector and thus Aeneas' and her own former brother-in-law), she has tried to rebuild Troy—in line with her feeling, in Ennius, for the architectural losses. The result is a reduced-scale simulacrum of the origi-nal, an amusement-park or miniature-golf version. Aeneas, who refers to this as "a little Troy," takes note of "false" and "dry" rivers with the old names Simois and Xanthus, and a citadel that "simulates great Pergamum" (3.302, 349–50). Virgil's own Andromache—whose lacrimosity has only increased, if anything, since the scene Ennius scripted—thinks too exclusively of a restora-tion of Troy itself, of staying Trojan; without an Astyanax, her expectations have become limited to her memories. Her speeches inevitably come around to Ascanius, as at 339–43:

> "quid puer Ascanius? superatne et vescitur aura?
> quem tibi iam Troia—
> ecqua tamen puero est amissae cura parentis?
> ecquid in antiquam virtutem animosque virilis
> et pater Aeneas et avunculus excitat Hector?"

"What about your boy Ascanius? Does he survive and batten upon the living air? Whom you, now that Troy . . . Does he care at all about the loss of his mother? Does his father Aeneas stir him to antique valor and manly spirit—does his uncle Hector?"

---

[36] Cf. Clua 1988, and on the *cantores Euphorionis* Courtney 1993:213.

Touching is her inversion of her own situation: she has lost a son; of first importance to her is that a son should mourn his lost mother. Her next concern is that the "ancient" Trojan qualities pass down to the next generation (of men: the terms *virtutem* and *virilis* etymologically suggest a molding of gender roles on the "antique" model); Aeneas will reprise this concern on his own terms at 12.438–40. Through the implicit contrast with Ascanius, the paradigm of successful male initiation, Astyanax joins our roster of Roman ancestors *manqués*.

Similar is 3.482–91, where, making her assimilation of Ascanius to Astyanax explicit (489 *o mihi sola mei super Astyanactis imago*, "O sole surviving image of my Astyanax"—the ethic dative *mihi* is as usual untranslatable), she loads the boy with ancestral articles of clothing: robes embroidered with gold and a Phrygian *chlamys* (the Greek term here recalls Naevius' conflation of Greek and Oriental through clothing terms).[37] Some of the other *chlamydes* in the poem are given Oriental connections: Sidonian herself, Dido wears a "Sidonian" one as she goes to the hunt attired in purple-dye and gold at 4.137; Aeneas awards a purple-dyed one at 5.250; Evander recalls at 8.167 that he was given a gold-embroidered one (along with "Lycian arrows") by Anchises; and a saffron-dyed one figures at 11.775 amid the finery, coveted by Camilla, that bedecks Chloreus. Andromache is emphasizing generational succession as national survival. So too does Aeneas, but his yearning for Troy is becoming more complicated than hers. He is not to rebuild Troy literally; his new "Troy" must be different. Already the ghost of Hector, giving Aeneas the first hints of his mission, had suggested the end of old Troy (2.291–92):

> "sat patriae Priamoque datum: si Pergama dextra
> defendi possent, etiam hac defensa fuissent."

"Our homeland, and Priam, have been given enough. If Troy's stronghold could be saved by a warrior's arm, this arm of mine would have saved it."

This answers the words Ennius had given his widow (*o patria, o Priami domus*). At 3.86–87, praying to Thymbraean Apollo for a new home and "a city that will last" (*mansuram urbem*), Aeneas refers to his band of refugees as "a second stronghold for Troy" (*altera Troiae / Pergama*): although he may not fully recognize the implications, his people is the only "Troy" he needs for now. The contrast with Andromache's Troy, when it arises later in the book, is sharp. By contrast with the real Andromache, Aeneas loses the Andromachan persona he had displayed in his narration of (and sometimes speeches in) Book 2.

---

[37] Wiltshire 1989:54 surmises that this garment was "surely originally woven by Andromache for her son Astyanax."

At 5.632–34 an echo of Ennius' *Andromacha* introduces another new little Troy:

> "o patria et rapti nequiquam ex hoste penates,
> nullane iam Troiae dicentur moenia? nusquam
> Hectoreos amnis, Xanthum et Simoenta, videbo?"

"O fatherland, and household gods saved from the enemy to no avail! Will they say the ramparts of Troy are annihilated? Will I nowhere see the rivers of Hector, Xanthus and Simois?"

The speaker is the false Beroe (really Iris in disguise), who partially succeeds in persuading the matrons among the Aeneadae in Sicily to burn their ships, working upon their anxiety and despair; most of the women of the company end up staying in a Buthrotum-style ersatz Troy in Sicily instead of proceeding to Italy with Aeneas and thus participating in Roman destiny. Iris plays Beroe as a combination of Ennius' Andromacha and Virgil's Andromache. Her appeal cannily suggests an exact repetition of Troy in its dead, "Hectorean" glory. "Who says we must not lay walls," she asks just before, "and give our fellow citizens a city?" (631 *quis prohibet muros iacere et dare civibus urbem?*). The settlement that Aeneas is thus forced to establish is laid out and named like Andromache's imitation city: "He gives word that this is to be Ilium, that this place is to be Troy" (756–57 *hoc Ilium et haec loca Troiam / esse iubet*).

Beroe is emphatically "Rhoetean" (646), which is to say, Trojan. She (and presumably her Tmarian husband: 620) joined the Aeneadae at Helenus' settlement, doubtless after enslavement and other tribulations. But her name occurs in Nonnus as the name of Beirut, a Phoenician city, and of its personifying nymph (a daughter, interestingly, of Aphrodite and Adonis in his version); and Nonnus, as often, is most likely to have taken this name from Hellenistic ktisis poems knowable also by Virgil.[38] The city name makes Iris' impersonation of Beroe an ethnological correction of an early Greek story that the instigator of the ship-burning was a Trojan prisoner of the Greeks named Rhome, and that it led to the founding of Rome on the site[39] (one recalls Virgil's subsitution of Ardea for Rome as a foundation of Danae, discussed above on p. 64). The real Beroe presumably stays behind in Acesta; for us, Iris has made a significant onomastic choice in the vehicle of her scheme.

---

[38] Chuvin 1991:196–221. The name "Beroe" echoes a Macedonian place name and suggests a punning homotoponymy typical of the poetics of Diadochan colonialism. Compare Stephens 2003:91–95 and 207 on homonymy of cities and other geographical features as a trope of colonialist etiologies in Ptolemaic poetry. Ovid *Met.* 3.278 uses "Beroe" as the name of Semele's nurse (whose identity is taken by Juno for destructive purposes), a Phoenician colonist who has migrated west (to Thebes).

[39] Hellanicus *FGrH* 4 F 84 in Dionysius of Halicarnassus *A.R.* 1.72.2, Heraclides Lembus in Festus p. 329 Lindsay = fr. 1 Müller. On these and other versions of the story, see Bickerman 1952:66–67; Gruen 1992:10–11, 17–18; Malkin 1998:194–98.

Beroe's name functions analogously to the dying-god names discussed in the last chapter—in contrast, for example, with that of young Atys, whose progeny are to become the Atii of Augustus' maternal side. Add Mnestheus, Sergestus, and Cloanthus, whose names (as we are told at 5.116–23) will evolve into the gentilics of Memmius, Sergius, and "Roman Cluentius." These semantics were in fact set at the very opening of the poem, in the most vivid way possible. From Aeneas' original company of sea captains, whose names will emblematize the change from Trojan to Roman nationality, the one who is lost bears a river name that represents a whole nation: Orontes (1.113–17). Juvenal will use the Orontes River as the source of unassimilable Asiatics, poisoning Rome by their influx (3.62). The name of Trojan Orontes points up the special fate of the Trojans who will make it to Italy, and contrastively defends against an anxiety about Rome's Asiatic origins. The extrusion of Orontes, and synecdochically Orientalness, from among the forebears of Rome resonates within the mythological substructure of the *Aeneid*: Strabo records that the original name of the river was Typhon (because the monster Typhon created it with his dragging claws as he fled from Jupiter's lightning). The poet has chosen a river name allligned against the Olympian gods (and against Rome) in the Gigantomachic scheme that Hardie traces in the poem.[40] Orontes is like Beroe, an emphatically Trojan character bearing the name of an Oriental place—and one who is left behind. The symbolism is not without ambivalence: O'Hara, for example, notes that the *Arae* (literally "altars") near which Orontes' ship founders make him and his men "the first of many sacrifices in the *Aeneid*," like Marcellus (cf. 6.870–71) and the doomed warriors we studied in chapter 1.[41] Sidonian Dido too, and the Turnus whom similes compare to Oriental rivers and beasts, may be added to the list: all die that Rome may rise one day. We get a sympathetic, though passing, glimpse of Orontes' shade in the Underworld (6.334).

This allusion to the Typhon myth has a complicated pendant at 12.458 (a verse mentioned several times already): the last battle of the Italian war begins with the slaying of the Italian Osiris (homonymous with the Egyptian god and thus also the Egyptian river[42]) by Trojan Thymbraeus (with a name recalling Trojan and Roman rivers)—but the god Osiris was the victim of Typhon, the Greek interpretation of his Egyptian rival Seth.[43] Again we are made to look back from a post-Actium, de-Orientalized Rome. The suggestion

---

[40] Strabo 16.2.7; Hardie 1986. O'Hara 1994a:219–20 alerts us to the long-standing poetic associations between Gigantomachy and the repulse of foreigners.

[41] O'Hara 1990:19–22. Otis 1963:303–304 develops the idea of Euryalus and the others as sacrifices. Indeed, Hardie 1986 finds a measure of ambivalence in the support the poem's Gigantomachic mythological underpinning gives to the Roman mission.

[42] For Roman awareness of the identification of Osiris with the Nile, see Koenen 1976:138–57 on Tibullus 1.7.27.

[43] As e.g. at Plutarch *De Is.* 13.356c.

of Orientalness in an Italian is by no means isolated, as we noted in chapter 2. What particularly complicates this allegory is Virgil's melding of the Trojan Thymbris with the Roman Thybris (Tiber)[44]; this wordplay leaves some of Troy coursing through Rome, inalienable. One is tempted to collate the metonymy river-as-ethnicity with the metaphor river-as-poetic-style, especially as Callimachus uses the Euphrates at the end of his hymn to Apollo, a passage Virgil carefully alludes to thrice.[45] The intersection of the two figures should be in the third of these allusions, at *Aeneid* 8.726: the defeated Euphrates, among other rivers emblematic of pacified nations, is paraded in Octavian's triple triumph of August 29 B.C.E.[46] The message here recalls the dialogue between Latin poets in a contest for defining Roman identity, discussed above—here in connection with the way Hellenizing revolutions in Latin poetry "operate through a revision of previous Hellenizing revolutions"[47] (like, for example, Virgil's response to the Callimachean poetics of the generation of Catullus).

All of these negotiations operate according to a triangle of Roman, Greek, and Oriental ethnicity (with the last term, whatever its relation to the first two, encompassing Trojan, Phoenician, Punic, Egyptian, and so on); and the version of these negotiations that involves Ennius' tragedy augments and confirms the abandonment of Trojan—as Oriental—identity that the last chapter traced in the whole Carthage episode. Yet one would not wish to underestimate Virgil's capacity for nuance and ambiguity in drawing ethnic boundaries as he defines a Roman identity out of the broad Mediterranean world. The ethnopoetic triumph he hints at, like the ethnic viewpoint he constructs, is never left unproblematic or definitive. We have been tracing only one message in the poet's use of Ennius' *Andromacha*. Doorposts—like rivers, another ready symbol of transition—may carry another message. On the Shield, at the climactic moment of his triple triumph over Egypt and the peoples of the Orient, Augustus "acknowledges the gifts of the nations and affixes them to the proud doorposts" of his temple to Apollo on the Palatine (8.721–2 *dona recognoscit populorum aptatque superbis / postibus*). Commentators usually compare the doors of the temple to Apollo at Actium on which Aeneas hangs a captured Greek shield at 3.287; yet at the same time, Augustus' spoil-laden doorposts are the closest equivalent, in imperial Rome, to those of King Priam in Troy as Aeneas himself remembers them at 2.504, "the doorjambs proud with barbaric gold and war spoils." *Dona populorum*, "the gifts of the nations," are tribute from conquered peoples, just as at 2.504: the *Aeneid* ultimately

---

[44] See pp. 5–6 above.

[45] Scodel/Thomas 1985. Cf. Catullus 95 (with Clausen 1987:6–7), Ovid *Fasti* 1.24.

[46] Cf. the swollen Nile at *Georg.* 3.29, in a passage that is programmatic for Virgil's engagment with both Augustan ideology and Ptolemaic poetry.

[47] Hinds 1998:55. He continues: ". . . a revision which can be simultaneously an appropriation and a denial."

divides the image of Andromacha's *saeptum altisono cardine templum* between Priam's palace and Apollo's temple. There is a suggestion on the Shield that Troy really has been restored—though in the requisite combination with Latin tradition, as we see if we compare the spoil-laden "sacred" doorposts of King Latinus at 7.183 (his palace is itself a *templum* at 174).

The *populi* who send their gifts to Rome recall those that Anchises urges the "Roman" to rule imperially, as his proper art, at 6.851. Both Augustus' and Priam's, notably, are "proud" doorposts, *superbi*; the epithet is more usually attached to the enemies of Aeneas and of Rome, most famously in Anchises' defining injunction to spare defeated enemies, but to "war down the proud" (6.853 *debellare superbos*).[48] At 9.634 Remulus Numanus becomes the first *superbus* (Ascanius' term there) to be "warred down." The word characterizes actual tyrants at 8.481 (Mezentius) and 11.539 (Metabus); Circe's house at 7.12; Italian opponents of the Aeneadae at 7.630 (Tivoli) and 8.613 (the Laurentians). But there are more piquant instances; the evaluative force of the epithet ultimately depends on viewpoint—an instability that complicates Anchises' doctrine. In Dido's mouth the word characterizes Aeneas as arrogant, unresponsive, unsympathetic at 4.424; his ships at 540. At 12.877–78 Juturna calls the divine decree of Turnus' death "the proud command of high-hearted Jupiter" (*iussa superba magnamimi Iovis*). The ambivalence of the term is most glaring in Evander's story of the battle between Hercules and Cacus on the future site of Rome. Both the hero and the monster are "proud with spoils," Hercules with the cattle stolen from Geryon (8.202 *tergemini nece Geryonae spoliisque superbus*) and Cacus' doors, no less, with the putrefying heads of his victims (196–97 *foribusque adfixa superbis / ora virum*). If Priam's and Latinus' treasure-laden palaces are models for Augustus' Palatine temple, Cacus' lair on the neighboring Aventine furnishes an antitype, and Hercules, as often, provides a divine precedent.[49] But the line can be drawn fine between these varieties of *superbia*.

The characterization (that of Juno's informants, as the indirect discourse suggests, and thus involved in a dialectic of focalizations)[50] of the future Roman nation as "a people widely sovereign [literally "king"] and proud in war" (1.21 *populum late regem belloque superbum*) not only likens Rome to the image of Carthage expressed just before, but conceives of Rome in terms of its detested last king, Tarquinius Superbus—Tarquin the Proud. The double-edged pride of Priam's doorposts will become Rome's. Again we see military might conflated with wealth in a vision of empire—lost and regained. Significantly, this characterization makes Rome a superior replacement of

---

[48] Lloyd 1972:126–29 reviews Virgil's use of *superbus*.

[49] It is noteworthy that Virgil has moved Cacus' lair to the Aventine from the Palatine, where it was traditionally said to have been (Propertius 4.9.3; cf. Dionysius of Halicarnassus *A.R.* 1.39; cf. Livy 1.7.4–5).

[50] Cf. Fowler 2000b:48.

Carthage, with the same traits as Carthage (13–18 *dives opum studiisque asperrima belli . . . hoc regnum dea gentibus esse, si qua fata sinant, iam tum tenditque fovetque*). Juno's prophetic imagination is perhaps too limited to envision a Rome that goes beyond the hopes of empire she has established for her Carthage (unlike Jupiter's vision, which at least begins to unite worldly sway with moral authority: 1.278–96). But the broader point here is that under Augustus (really since conquerors like Pompey, but especially, here, under Augustus) Rome has become literally an Eastern power, and a powerful, gold-rich imperial city on the Oriental model: compare Virgil's flash-forward to the Roman Capitol, "now golden" (8.348 *aurea nunc*). This trajectory was in a sense predicted, in terms of *superbia*, at 3.1–5, Aeneas' summary of the fall of Troy:

> "Postquam res Asiae Priamique evertere gentem
> immeritam visum superis, ceciditque superbum
> Ilium et omnis humo fumat Neptunia Troia,
> diversa exsilia et desertas quaerere terras
> auguriis agimur divum."

"After it had pleased the gods above to destroy the empire of Asia and the undeserving nation of Priam, and proud Ilium fell and all of Neptunian Troy lay smoking on the ground, we were driven by the oracles of the gods to seek scattered places of exile and lonely lands."

Troy's *superbia* (implicitly linked to King Laomedon's one-time deception of Neptune) seems to be blamed for its fall and loss of empire. Yet its people are "undeserving" of such a misfortune: so whose *superbia* was this?[51] Or was the "pride" of Troy not at fault at all, but only the will of the gods? Compare line 2 with line 5: the same gods destroyed Troy and guide the refugee Trojans, including the Aeneadae. Here in embryo is Aeneas' sense of a split, in theodical terms, between his own fate and that of his old city. Implicit in his formulation of Troy's fall is the possibility not only that divine favor will have followed him toward whatever new settlement he establishes in Troy's place, but that that favor may restore to the new nation the imperial pride of Troy, whose last king was "once the ruler of Asia, proud over so many nations and lands" (2.556–57 *tot quondam populis terrisque superbum / regnatorem Asiae*). And the Eastern spoils affixed to Augustus' temple doors accommodate the dubious alterity of Priam's "barbaric gold." The future nation's ruler will in fact ascend to heaven, according to Jupiter, "loaded with the spoils of the Orient" (1.289 *spoliis Orientis onustum*); he will join the gods still burdened with the ethnic ambivalence of Priam.

---

[51] The argument that in line 2 Aeneas uses two different focalizations, his own in *immeritam* and (ironically) that of the gods in *superbum* (Fowler 2000b:50), reveals by the abruptness it introduces into Aeneas' affect the problem with letting focalization decide an interpretive question (a problem that Fowler's paper recognizes).

At last Rome ends up like Troy and like Carthage, *dives opum studiisque asperrima belli*, possessing abundant *opes* in the material and military senses (and justifying Aeneas' initial envy of Carthage).[52] The blurring of ethnic lines complements the ambiguity we noticed in the "barbaric gold" of Priam's door—and on top of predicting the separation of Roman from Oriental, the earlier, Trojan passage in a sense predicts Roman *imperium* and the final difficulty of deciding where to draw the line between self and Other. Rome does not leave Eastern identity behind; aside from the persistence signaled by proper names, traditional ceremonies, and the like, she ends up regaining and subsuming it from the outside, especially (this is the drift of the description of Augustus' triumph on the Shield) after conquering Egypt. Self-definition against an antitype collapses ultimately into assimilation, and acceptance of the terms of the Other. The architectural imagery in our texts comes to represent an imperial city, and the imagery of doors in particular suggests in this context themes of liminality, admission, accession to (or exclusion from) one's rightful place.

The boundary between Trojan-Oriental and Roman, drawn as it is by the assumption of a Greek perspective, is unstable, and has been so in literature ever since the Romans first presented themselves to the Greeks as the descendants of Trojans. Cato the Censor warned his son about Greek physicians, who "have sworn an oath amongst themselves to kill all barbarians with their drugs. . . . they call *us* barbarians too!" (Cato, *De Medicina* fr. 1.6–9, in Pliny *Historia naturalis* 29.14: *iurarunt inter se barbaros necare omnis medicina. . . . nos quoque dictitant barbaros*). Implicit in his indignation is Cato's refusal to be classed with the barbarians; that is, he classes himself with the Greeks (although, impatient of Greek constructs of identity as well as of Greeks themselves, he might not have phrased it that way). Polybius 39.1 has Cato rebuke the Hellenophile Aulus Postumius' fears that he βαρβαρίζη (might commit, as a foreign speaker, a solecism in Greek); here, if Polybius' Greek reflects the original Latin (and the whole passage breathes the searing sarcasm we know from Cato's extant rhetoric), it is a pointed acknowledgment by Cato of the perilous status of being a Roman who has accepted Greek cultural terms.[53] Plautus' use of *barbare*, too, can attract the suspicion of ironic self-deprecation.

Cato was himself a canny ironist of ethnicity. In his speech *Pro Rodiensibus*—delivered in 168 after the defeat of Perseus of Macedon, so at a cardinal moment in the history of the cultural Hellenization of Rome, when Aemilius Paullus imported in triumph the Macedonian royal library—we hear the conqueror assuming the perspective of the conquered, provisionally and strategically.[54] The people of Rhodes, seeking to mediate between the Romans

---

[52] The opening of the poem (1.12–22) assimilates Carthage to Rome in warlikeness and imperial sway; the first characteristic of Carthage, *dives opum*, pointedly finds no Roman analogue. It is left to us to supply this detail from the prophetic passages of the poem.

[53] Cf. Gellius 11.8.

[54] Cato fr. 95 Peter = 163–69 Malcovati.

and Macedonians, had been caught unawares by the Roman victory and found themselves the objects of Roman rancor and of a possible declaration of war. Portraying himself as deeply skeptical of Roman success and its consequences, going through the logical steps of his argument as though he thought his audience of noblemen were children, Cato imaginatively assimilates the mindset of the Rhodians and other nations in their position of subordination to Rome in order to vindicate them. Latent here is a broad, unsparing vision of the Republic at the moment of its greatest success so far—of Rome's ascension over a wider world. His mock-legalistic analogy between what the Rhodians wanted and what the average Roman noble wants (at section 167 Malcovati) connects the putatively punishable attitude of the Rhodians with the attitudes of the Roman noble class in a century of increasing disputes over property regulation; here class distinctions complicate the ethnic boundaries (one recalls Cato's notorious sumptuary preoccupations). He makes the Rhodians a foil to the Romans, or more particularly to the increasingly rich, powerful, and Hellenized Roman upper class who become the target of this speech. The beginning and end of our fragment should be key texts on the term *superbia*, the "pride" of the conquerer. He knows, Cato begins by saying, that men's *superbia* and cruelty increase with prosperous times; he ends: "They call the Rhodians *superbi*, imputing to them what I would least wish to be imputed to me and my offspring. Let them be *superbi*: how does that affect us? Are you angry if someone is more *superbus* than we?"[55] Implicitly he connects the good fortune of the Roman nation with the decadent haughtiness of an Eastern, Hellenic people and warns that with power and prosperity, the Romans will fall into the same ethical category. The self-assertion "to me and my offspring" (*mihi et liberis meis*) inserts a message of generational succession and the need to preserve a certain "Romanness." For a moment Romans and Greeks switch roles: seldom have the ethnic borders been crossed so deftly or tellingly.

Before we move on in the next chapter to the nature of this Rome, assimilated to its imperial predecessors, and to the question whether Rome thus achieves a permanent, quasi-Platonic ideal of an imperial city or is just the latest in a series, let us for a brief moment reintroduce the theme of *amor*, which this chapter has almost neglected. A previous instance of "proud doorposts" in Latin poetry, in a poem often in the background of the *Aeneid*, is Lucretius 4.1178 *postisque superbos*, the metonymically "proud" doorframe of the beloved, inhabited by the hopeful but "weeping, excluded lover." The doors of empire as the domain of the inaccessible beloved: the intertextually produced metaphor coincides with Aeneas' effort, in the second half of the poem, to gain power in Italy by marrying Lavinia,[56] and generally with the erotic metaphor that so often underlies his mission. Lucretius' skeptical presentation

of this scene jibes with the destructive consequences of passionate love in the
Aeneid, and viewed from the Lucretian subtext, various analogies, more fruitful than frivolous, suggest themselves. Augustus is a kind of suitor leaving gifts
at the door of Apollo (the sculptures on display in the portico as one
approached the door of this temple, depicting the doomed marriage of the
sons of Aegyptus to the daughters of Danaus, juxtapose in the Roman reader's
mind a counter-message of originary East-West conflict and failed generational succession). The Greeks, from Aeneas' vagrant and capacious point of
view at 2.504, violently claim an erotic prize. And we are invited to ask
whether Virgil's patient paraclausithyron at the portals of earlier Latin poetry
has been a success.

Chapter Five

ANCIENT CITIES

I

Carthage is a new city, still under construction, when it appears on our horizon, but Virgil calls it old (1.12–14):

> Urbs antiqua fuit (Tyrii tenuere coloni)
> Karthago, Italiam contra Tiberinaque longe
> ostia, dives opum studiisque asperrima belli.

"There was an ancient city (colonists from Tyre possessed it): Carthage, far opposite to Italy and the mouths of the Tiber, rich in wealth and most fierce in zeal for war."

At 1.366 Venus gives Carthage a more appropriate epithet: "and the rising citadel of new Carthage [*novae Karthaginis*]"; it is described as *nova* also at 1.298 and 522. At 4.670, where a simile has the population react to Dido's suicide as if their city were falling to an enemy, the contrast between their new city and their old home ("Carthage or ancient Tyre") is eloquent. These qualifiers involve wordplay: according to information current among the Romans since at least the time of Cato the Elder, the name *Karthago* meant "new city" in Punic. Perhaps the slyest appeal to this etymology occurs at 4.260, when Mercury arrives in Carthage to find Aeneas "establishing new buildings" (*tecta novantem*). At 1.12 it makes *urbs antiqua* an etymological game of the antiphrastic type, pointing up the original sense of the name by contradicting it.[1] A similar pun occurs at 6.448–49, where Caeneus (cf. Greek *kainos*, "new"), born a woman, then changed to a man, has reverted in death to her "old" form (*veterem figuram*).[2]

"There was an ancient city" paradoxically reaffirms the newness of Carthage, and at the same time makes the discrepancy all the more jarring. If we try to explain *antiqua* in 1.12, an appeal to the rhetorical device of prolepsis is obviously available—for example, "Virgil is narrating from his own temporal standpoint, when Carthage *is* ancient, obliterated, replaced by a Roman colony"—and is often prescribed by commentators, like Austin, who suggests

---

[1] Cato *Orig.* fr. 37.4; Maltby 1991:111 s.v. *Carthago*; Brown 1995:119 (with remarks on "old cities" in the Phoenician sphere), 334; O'Hara 1996:115 (see 66 on etymologies κατ' ἀντίφρασιν). The Phoenician name of Carthage, *qrt ḥdšt* (*KAI* 68.2), "new city," supports the etymology.
[2] Norden ad loc., O'Hara 1996:172–73. Feldherr 1999:99–100 gives a subtle analysis of the pun.

an affective twist: "*Antiqua* implies not only age, but the honour due to age: cf. 6.648 . . . *G.* 2.174 . . . ; so of Troy, 375, 2.363 . . . 4.312; of trees, 2.626, 714, 6.179, *G.* 2.209, *G.* 3.32. In this way Virgil suggests to his contemporaries the respect due to an old and honourable foe." Servius, whose commentary on line 12 anticipates this approach, finds a similar solution for 23 *veterisque memor . . . belli* ("[Juno] remembering the old war"), referring the epithet to Virgil, for whom the Trojan War was indeed old.[3] In the case of 1.12, Austin's "to his contemporaries" reflects a proleptic interpretation: the "antiquity" of Carthage suggests age, and the honor due to age; but also, from an ineluctable perspective, the "over-and-done-with" quality of the city and the fact of Roman conquest. "There was a city long ago . . ." is one sense that emerges at 1.12.

The prolepsis, however, only raises more questions: first, why the anomalous focalization here? For that is what a prolepsis is; the figure gives the reader a particular subject position involved with the metaphorical dynamics we have traced in the poem's narratology, intertextuality, and engagement with Roman ideology. Secondly, how does the trope square with the grand proleptic frame of the whole poem,[4] whose episodes will only acquire their full meaning in the reign of Augustus? Ahl discusses the "peculiar time-perspective" in terms not only of the later enmity of Rome and Carthage, but of the poem's different levels of narrative awareness thereof.[5] *Tiberinaque longe ostia* is likewise a kind of prolepsis—though using space, or rather troping space as time—since the perspective from Rome's entrance to the Mediterranean Sea gives us a Roman standpoint, which is the telos of the epic. The sixth line of the poem summarizes a similar paradox: *inferretque deos Latio, genus unde Latinum . . .* ("and introduce his gods to Latium: and from this came the Latin race . . ."). The place is already called Latium before Aeneas gets there (see, for example, 1.205 and 265), and the adjective "Latin" is used often in the poem of its people and institutions (not to mention King Latinus), yet the "Latin race" will only arise from Aeneas' sacred foundation. The paradox foreshadows that of the Latin nation itself, bearing the name of the indigens but accommodating the contributions of the Trojan newcomers and their gods.[6] These questions are inseparable from a network of prolepses that the phrase *urbs antiqua* raises in the *Aeneid*. The phrase recurs in connection with three more modest polities.

[3] Fowler 1997:75–76.

[4] And with the poem's other individual prolepses? A famous example occurs in Aeneas' resort to the port of Caieta (6.900 *tum se ad Caietae recto fert limite portum*), whose name is immediately explained as deriving from Aeneas' nurse (7.1–2 *tu quoque litoribus nostris, Aeneia nutrix, / aeternam moriens famam, Caieta, dedisti . . .*); that anachronism served as a productive irritant for later poets (see Hinds 1998:107–13 on Ovid's response).

[5] Ahl 1976:186–88.

[6] A perhaps milder anachronism—or prolepsis—occurs already in line 2: the Italian destination of the refugees can be called "Lavinian shores" only in hindsight, since the city they are to establish there, Lavinium, will only be named after Aeneas' wife Lavinia (12.193–94). The name of the city occurs in prophecies at 1.258, 270; 6.84.

Behind them lies a sixth "ancient city": Troy. The epithet, always picking up meaning from its contexts, intertwines all their various stories. Moreover we are invited to think of another city—also ancient in Virgil's time, though not even founded at the dramatic date of his poem—that nevertheless figures prominently in it. Although the phrase under discussion is never applied to it, the text provides enough parallels and links to create a mirror effect, full of meaning on all levels, between these ancient cities and the future ancient city of Rome.

Ardea is another city ruled, like Carthage, by someone who stands in the way of Aeneas' mission. We are concerned here with the conclusion of the episode in Book 10 that yielded so much for our discussion of Turnus in chapter 2. Juno diverts him from battle with a phantom Aeneas and traps him on a ship. At the conclusion of a soliloquy that on pp. 65–66 we compared to those of distressed heroines in mythological poetry, he wonders whether to kill himself in disgrace or try to swim back to shore and rejoin the battle (10.685–88):

> ter conatus utramque viam, ter maxima Iuno
> continuit iuvenemque animi miserata repressit.
> labitur alta secans fluctuque aestuque secundo
> et patris antiquam Dauni defertur ad urbem.

Thrice he tried either route; thrice great Juno checked the young man and held him back, pitying him in her heart. He glides away, cutting the deep with the surge and swell speeding him on, and is carried down to the ancient city of his father Daunus.

Antiqua reinforces an image of Turnus as a child, rescued from danger and helplessly returned to the parental nest—the ancestral nest. Something *antiquum* can be "old" in the sense of "existing for a long time and continuing to exist" (as Juno's *antiquus dolor* at 5.608 is her long-lived and still abiding anger) or, as we have already started to see, "no longer existing, no longer what it was" (as at 4.670 with Tyre, the Carthaginians' former homeland, or Dido's former marriage to Sychaeus: 4.431 *coniugium antiquum*, 458 *coniugis antiqui*).[7] These senses tend to drift into evaluations, "revered" (Austin's "old and honourable")[8] or "no longer relevant." A single usage can suggest both, as in Andromache's phrase *antiquam virtutem* at 3.342 (of Trojan heroes, Aeneas

---

[7] See E. Evrard in *EV* I.195–96 (s.v. *antiquus*) on the usages of the term. On Dido's "ancient" marriage see Williams 1968:383; cf. 264 (note the ambivalence of this term when used of Sychaeus, especially in view of Dido's reunion with her *coniunx pristinus* at 6.473). At 7.365 Amata appeals to Latinus' kingly sense of responsibility as "your ancient concern for your people" (*cura antiqua tuorum*)—that is, customary to him, but (she charges) forgotten. There Horsfall glosses, "which was and is no more," comparing 2.137; 4.431, 458, 633.

[8] Ancient commentators (like Servius on 2.363, quoted in n. 16 below) routinely gloss *antiquus* as "renowned" (*nobilis*), both where the adjective is applied to cities and elsewhere.

and Hector, to be emulated by Ascanius): is this old-time courage, worthy of being handed down (as she thinks), or outmoded courage (as the parallel with her ersatz Troy might suggest)? Both senses can generate complicated emotional associations when used of cities.

In "ancient" Ardea, the sense "revered" coexists with a sense "obsolete": this latter reinforces the pathos connoted by his father. Compare 1.12 *urbs antiqua fuit* with the verdict on Ardea at 7.413: once a great city, "but its fortune *has been*" (*sed fortuna fuit*); that is, has come and gone. Compare Dido's valedictory perfect tense: *vixi*, "I have lived" (4.653). And Camilla's: *potui*, "I have prevailed" (11.823). In the case of Carthage, the variation in tense from the narrative (often ecphrastic) commonplace[9] "there *is* a city . . ." or imperfective ". . . was . . ." makes *fuit*—which in these passages contrastively jerks the reader into the time of, or since, Virgil's narration—striking. Taken together, the antiquity of Carthage and Ardea describes the temporal scope of the poem: the Carthaginian proleptic *antiqua* looks ahead to the Punic Wars and Rome's mastery of the Mediterranean; the Ardeatine *antiqua* delves back into Italian history, the world that the Trojans are disrupting. But a trope of hindsight informs Ardea too: this city is more conspicuously "ancient" from Virgil's own standpoint than from that of Aeneas or Turnus. Ardea has, after all, only a modest claim to antiquity, having been founded by Danae three or four generations earlier (7.409–13). As with Carthage, the epithet *antiqua* reflects Ardea's desuetude from the standpoint of Virgil's own time, when it was barely inhabited. One effect of this focalization is to remind us of the early Roman dominance of Latium and the consequent decline of other Latin towns.

It transpires that Camilla's home city too is "ancient" (11.539–43):

> "pulsus ob invidiam regno virisque superbas
> Priverno antiqua Metabus cum excederet urbe,
> infantem fugiens media inter proelia belli
> sustulit exsilio comitem, matrisque vocavit
> nomine Casmillae mutata parte Camillam."

"When Metabus was leaving the ancient city of Privernum, expelled from his kingdom on account of hatred for his violent pride, in flight through the midst of battle he brought away his infant child as a companion in exile, and he called her Camilla, changing part of her mother Casmilla's name."

The city itself may well be considered literally ancient in Metabus' time (no founding legends are attested), but awareness of its conquest by the Romans around 329 B.C.E. and removal of its rebellious senate to the other side of the

---

[9] The commonplace, found in a number of ancient literatures, occurs first in Greek at *Il.* 6.152, 11.711 (West 1997:259, 365).

Tiber[10] superimposes on the epithet at 11.540 some of the same proleptic connotations and feelings that attach to *antiqua* as used with Carthage or Ardea. "Antiquity" here represents heritage, origins—particularly in time of trouble, a homeland cut off and denied. As in the passage on Turnus we get an emphasis on fatherhood (not to mention Camilla's absent, perhaps dead, mother), and like that passage this one too offers us the viewpoint of a protective goddess—here Diana, who is narrating Camilla's history to her nymphs. Metabus, Diana will go on to say, tied his infant daughter to a spear and launched her across a river to safety: she too, like Turnus, is saved by a passage over water. But unlike the ancient city of Daunus, her home city is depicted in a state of tumult, its ruler driven into exile. In the midst is a child in danger of her life and cut off forever from the paradise that was Privernum. Baby Camilla, unlike Turnus, is leaving, not going home.

A couple of less conspicuous lands that the poem describes as *antiqua* are telling. We have already glanced at "ancient Tyre"; here is the passage in full (4.669–71):

> non aliter quam si immissis ruat hostibus omnis
> Karthago aut antiqua Tyros, flammaeque furentes
> culmina perque hominum volvantur perque deorum.

. . . just as if all Carthage or ancient Tyre were to fall at the incursion of an enemy, and raging flames roll over the rooftops of men and gods alike.

Tyre is indeed an ancient city in the poem's time frame, as we can see from the successive generations of Dido's "ancient" Tyrian ancestry and their deeds, which are chased in gold on her dinner service (1.642 *antiqua ab origine gentis*; at 9.266 Ascanius promises Nisus, among other rewards, an "ancient wine bowl" that was a gift from Dido). There is a sense here of the immemoriality of the Orient (from a certain Greco-Roman standpoint); compare the Phoenician city Byblos, reputed to be the oldest city in the world (Strabo 16.2.18). And yet the use of a future-less-vivid condition, rather than one contrary-to-fact, brings before our eyes the possibility of the destruction of both Tyre and Carthage, which did come about in each case: that of Carthage at the hands of Scipio in 146 B.C.E., that of Tyre at Alexander the Great's in 332. Within ten lines of the introduction of "ancient Carthage" we learn, with Juno, that Tyre's successor Carthage is doomed to that very fate (1.22 *excidio Libyae*). Tyre is also *antiqua* at 4.633: Dido's nurse is long dead and "black ashes held her in their ancient homeland" (*patria antiqua cinis ater habebat*). Here, as with Privernum, the antiquity of the lost homeland is associated with the security and comforts of childhood.

---

[10] Livy 8.20.9.

The fifth ancient city is Calydon (7.304–307):

> "Mars perdere gentem
> immanem Lapithum valuit, concessit in iras
> ipse deum antiquam genitor Calydona Dianae,
> quod scelus aut Lapithas tantum aut Calydona merentem?"

"Mars was able to destroy the mighty race of the Lapiths; the father of the gods gave up ancient Calydon to the rage of Diana. What great sin did either the Lapiths or Calydon commit?"

Here Juno renews her complaint from 1.39–45 that other gods, but not she, are permitted to wreak vengeance against offending mortals (*ast ego* at the opening of both 1.46 and 7.308 marks the parallel). She is talking about the gigantic boar that Diana sent against Calydon (where Oeneus had neglected to honor the goddess: *Iliad* 9.533–37); the curious thing here is that she involves Jupiter as approving the punishment. It calls to mind both the indulgence of Zeus toward Artemis in Callimachus' *Hymn* 3 and Jupiter's treatment of Turnus (with Juno's acquiescence) in *Aeneid* 12. The origins of this Aetolian city are indeed mythological in the accounts known to us;[11] but a vantage point from Virgil's own time, when Augustus had removed the inhabitants to Nicopolis, gives "ancient" the overtones of the other *urbes antiquae*, which are targets of destruction, or lands of origin now forbidden, or both. They negatively embody the comforts of somebody's heritage. Only in the case of Ardea is the ancient city a place of (temporary) safety.

Carthage should surprise us at 1.12. One expects to hear Troy, especially as the cause of Juno's anger (Virgil has just prayed, "Muse, tell me the cause . . ."). After the main caesura the reader learns what city this is (". . . colonists from Tyre possessed it") and understands that Virgil is going to follow Naevius in juxtaposing the origin of Rome with that of Carthage (indeed, Virgil's prolepsis is something of a transformation of a grand Naevian narrative trope, if—as is probable—Naevius related these origins in a flashback). This substitution heralds the assimilation between Troy and Carthage that we traced in the last two chapters. From the literary-historical perspective, Troy is privileged as an "ancient city": it is the only one of Virgil's *urbes antiquae* to receive such an epithet before the *Aeneid* (otherwise this is a striking habit on the part of Virgil). Aeschylus at *Agamemnon* 710 refers to "the old city of Priam" (Πριάμου πόλις γεραιά), a phrase embellished by Horace at *Carmina* 1.15.8 as "the old kingdom of Priam" (*regnum Priami vetus*).[12] Virgil attaches *antiqua* to Troy often, each time more deeply etching the image of Aeneas' fallen homeland with the associations we have observed in the other cities. At 1.375–77, in the first

---

[11] See [Apollodorus] *Bibl.* 1.7.7 and Stephanus of Byzantium s.v. Καλυδών on its eponym, Calydon, a son of Aetolus (the eponym of Aetolia) and grandson of Endymion.
[12] Cf. Sophocles *El.* 4 παλαιὸν ᾿Άργος.

account of his wanderings, Aeneas tells Venus that "from ancient Troy . . . a storm has driven us by its mischance to the shores of Libya." At 4.312 Dido wonders what Aeneas would be doing "if ancient Troy were still standing." At 2.626 a simile likens the falling city to an "ancient ash tree" in the mountains beset by axe-wielding farmers.[13] At 2.634–35 Aeneas' destination amid the ruin of Troy is the "threshold of [his] paternal seat and the ancient house [*antiquasque domos*]," where he finds his aged father ready to give up hope. Camilla, a "precious burden" (*caroque oneri*) to her fugitive father at 11.550, is like Anchises, carried out of fallen Troy in Book 2 (he is *carus* to Aeneas at 707; he is an *onus* at 723 and 729): the parallel points up the status of each city as a homeland cut off (and, simultaneously, the different fates of their survivors). Trojan antiquity has a cunning mirror image in the sympathy-arousing speech of Troy's destroyer, Sinon, at *Aeneid* 2.137: "nor do I have any hope left of seeing my ancient homeland" (*nec mihi iam patriam antiquam spes ulla videndi*).[14]

The destruction of Troy also attracts declarations of the kind we noticed attached to Carthage and Ardea, using qualifiers like "once" and "formerly" or the perfect tense of "to be." At 2.556–57 Priam is described as "once the ruler of Asia, proud over so many nations and lands" (*tot quondam populis terrisque superbum / regnatorem Asiae*). As we noted at the end of the last chapter, this complex of themes, whose wording recalls the language of Trojan imperial "pride" that invests Virgil's appropriations of the lament of Ennius' Andromacha, also recalls the opening of the poem (1.12–22): Troy was the wealthy, warlike empire Carthage and Rome will be. Each use of *urbs antiqua* is a miniature example of the genre "lament for a fallen city."[15] Compare Panthus' anguished insistence at 2.325–26, "We *were* Trojans; Troy, and the immense glory of the Teucrians, *was*" (*fuimus Troes, fuit Ilium et ingens / gloria Teucrorum*). At 3.16 we hear of an "ancient" guest-friendship that had existed between the Trojan and Thracian ruling houses "while [Troy's] fortune *was*" (*dum fortuna fuit*). Aeneas echoes this line when at 6.62–65 he asks Apollo for an end to Trojan fortune—that is, the Trojans' ill fortune:

> "hac Troiana tenus fuerit fortuna secuta;
> vos quoque Pergameae iam fas est parcere genti,
> dique deaeque omnes, quibus obstitit Ilium et ingens
> gloria Dardaniae."

[13] Cf. the "very old [*veterrima*] laurel" at 2.513 and the refugees' meeting place at 714, an "ancient cypress" by the "old" (*vetustum*) temple of Ceres, "preserved for many years by the reverence of my forefathers." This Ceres herself is called *antiqua* at 742.

[14] Sinon comes from somewhere in Greece (78 *neque me Argolica de gente negabo*); Virgil leaves the place unspecified and other sources do not offer decisive clues. His kinsman Palamedes is a descendant of Belus (2.82).

[15] The examples given by West 1997:554–56 constitute a brief history of this type from Near Eastern through Classical Greek poetry. The lament of Ennius' Andromacha, discussed in the last chapter, is a conspicuous Roman example.

"Let Trojan fortune have dogged us only up to now. And now it is right for you to spare the people of Pergamum, O gods and goddesses all, to whom Ilium and the immense glory of Dardania were offensive."

But for us the most critical summing-up of Troy's antiquity in the "has-been" sense comes at 2.363:

> urbs antiqua ruit multos dominata per annos.

An ancient city is falling, having held sway for many years.

The line opening takes us back to 1.12, *urbs antiqua fuit* . . . (again with an emphasis on the imperial power that characterizes Carthage—and Rome—in the opening to Book 1). For a moment *ruit* glosses *fuit*, brings out the finality of the perfect tense, reminds us how exactly the opulence and vigor of Carthage will come to an end. Read from 2.363, there is a retroactive pun in 1.12 that does not bode well for the city in which Aeneas is recounting his ordeals, especially if we glance again at 4.669–71, where Carthage does fall (*ruat*) in the simile upon Dido's death. In this backward reading, perhaps, lies part of the meaning of the anomalous antiquity of the new city in 1.12: Carthage is described as *antiqua* there in order to be likened to Troy in its ruin.

Troy at its fall is not really much older than Carthage, and certainly no older than Ardea: there were only two generations of kings before Priam, whose grandfather Ilus founded it and whose father Laomedon gave it new walls. When Aeneas refers at 2.484 to "Priam and the kings of old" who dwelt in the palace (*Priami et veterum . . . regum*), he is referring to only three kings. His "for many years" at 363 is entirely relative.[16] It is always Aeneas who calls Troy "ancient" (the exception is 4.312, where we can imagine Dido opportunistically adopting the viewpoint she has heard Aeneas express).[17] We could invoke prolepsis again to explain his hyperbole at 2.363; but it is also complemented, from the characters' own temporal perspective, by the poem's treatment of Italy, which experiences a proliferation of instances of *antiquus*, as if to suggest the genuine "antiquity" of Dardanus' homeland as against the relative newness of Troy, which Aeneas mistakenly considered his *patria*. At *Georgics* 2.157 and 174, in the encomium of Italy, we already hear of "ancient walls" and "ancient praise": a vision of the country is developing. In the *Aeneid* Italy as a whole, and all within it, is repeatedly characterized as *antiquus* from almost the beginning of the Trojans' journey. At 3.96 Apollo directs the refugees, "Seek out

---

[16] Servius' alternative suggestion that Troy is so described "because it is affirmed to have ruled for two thousand eight hundred years" (*vel nobilis, vel quia duobus milibus octingentis annis regnasse firmatur*) does not fit the data given by the *Aeneid*.

[17] Servius Auctus on 2.363 invokes Aeneas' focalization in the form of an argument *ex persona loquentis*: "This is [the sentiment] of a mourner, not a narrator" (*sane hoc dolentis est, non narrantis*).

your ancient mother."[18] On Italian ground we hear of an "ancient field" (11.316 *est antiquus ager*), an "ancient king" (11.850–51 *regis . . . antiqui*), the "ancient names" of the royal Latin lineage of Murranus (12.529), and "the ancient Ausonians" (11.253 *antiqui Ausonii*, used by Diomedes to address the Rutulian ambassadors). Shortly after reaching Latium, Aeneas' men chop wood for Misenus' funeral pyre in "an ancient forest" (6.179 *antiquam silvam*). In Latinus' palace, which shelters a laurel tree "maintained with holy dread for many years" (7.60 *multosque metu servata per annos*), the long row of carved ancestral portraits contrast with the few kings who ruled over Troy (7.177–81).

Finally cornered by Aeneas, Turnus looks in desperation for an opportunity (12.896–98):

> nec plura effatus saxum circumspicit ingens,
> saxum antiquum ingens, campo quod forte iacebat,
> limes agro positus litem ut discerneret arvis.

Saying no more, he spies a great stone, a great ancient stone that happened to be lying on the plain, placed in the field as a boundary to decide disputes over farmland.

In the *Aeneid* the stone's epithet adds new ideas, lacking in the Iliadic models, to the traditional epic stone-throwing motif.[19] The futility of Turnus' gesture is a thematic link with the "great stone" (*saxum ingens*) that "some"—we are to think of Sisyphus—roll (*volvunt*, which also describes Turnus' action at 906) as a punishment in Tartarus at 6.616. This boundary stone has a touch both of the Trojan boundary stone, set by "men of a former time" (ἄνδρες πρότεροι), that Athena hurls at Ares at *Iliad* 21.403–404 and of the washing places of 22.153–56 (the scene corresponding to the showdown between Aeneas and Turnus), a sign of former normality overwhelmed by war. The epithet makes the rock part of some primordial heritage. Wills, observing the epanalepsis of *saxum ingens*, compares "the brutal stone-thowing society of Lucretius" 5.948–52:

> denique nota vagi silvestria templa tenebant
> nympharum, quibus e scibant umoris fluenta
> lubrica proluvie larga lavere umida saxa,
> umida saxa, super viridi stillantia musco,
> et partim plano scatere atque erumpere campo.

Finally in their wandering they learned of, and settled in, the sylvan precincts of the nymphs, from whom they came to know that streams of

---

[18] Anchises' mistaken understanding that this means Crete is abetted for the reader at 3.131, where the voyagers approach the "ancient shores of the Curetes." An analogue to the phrase, with the connotation "revered," is Aratus 99 (on Astraeus) ἄστρων ἀρχαῖον πατέρ', "the ancient father of the stars."

[19] Cf. *Il.* 5.302–10, 12.445–62, 21.403–406.

water, dripping over green moss, wash over wet stones, wet stones, slippery with voluminous overflow, while in other parts they spread and burst out over the level plain.

"If rightly connected," Wills says, "the allusion to the Lucretian passage recalls an older, simpler Italian life which the Trojans have undermined."[20] But Virgil's ancient boundary stone is a marker too of a normality to come, the agrarian future of the *Georgics* and the peace that is supposed to emerge with the death of Turnus and the establishment of the Trojans in Italy, and reemerge under Augustus.

If we put Troy at the center of our group of "ancient cities," the little tales of Privernum, Tyre, and even Calydon become contrastive doublets of the great story of the epic. Our ancient cities are metaphors for each other, participating in a meaningful interplay of repetition and difference, and the anxiety and despair that attend all of their names in the poem diffract the feelings of Aeneas and his followers at the fall of their own city. Carthage is of course such a doublet, with Dido's founding a counterpart to Aeneas' task. And now we come to Rome. *Urbs antiqua fuit* jolts us out of the age of origins into Virgil's present precisely to remind us that as the city's antiquity will make sense only hundreds of years later, this whole network of associations that surround Carthage—and the Trojans' relations with it—will only make sense once Rome wins the Punic Wars. One can say much the same about the temporal perspective invited by the same epithet with the other cities: they are *antiquae* in the sense of "finished," but Rome continues. And it should be noted that the perspective is not only temporal, but implicitly political: Carthage, Tyre, Ardea, Privernum, Calydon, and the Troad now are all subject to Rome, their populations uprooted at the command of Roman generals, their land occupied by Roman colonists. The contrast established by prolepsis makes Rome the distant goal in this poem, an ancient city to be added to the others we have looked at, but superior. Rome takes on meaning through a play of comparison and contrast with other cities. At 10.42–43 Venus reproaches Jupiter in rhetorical despair: "I am no longer motivated by [hope of Roman] empire. That was my hope while fortune existed" (*nil super imperio moveor. speravimus ista, dum fortuna fuit*). "That," *ista*, means specifically "*your* promise" of Roman *imperium* at 1.278–79. Her last phrase—*dum fortuna fuit*—momentarily likens Rome to Ardea, Troy, and Carthage. But unlike them, in Rome there will be no interruption to the steady handing down of traditions from father to son. There will be no flight, no destruction, no enemies barring a return. There will only be empire without end. Rome will be the true ancient city; all the others are imperfect foreshadowings of Rome, like the pathetic mini-Troy of Helenus

---

[20] Wills 1996:156–58. He sees Virgil's *antiquum* as an "external marker" "that a rock from an older text is involved"; cf. the intertextual reading (with the *Iliad*) of Quint 1993:74.

and Andromache in Book 3. One recalls Anchises' list of future cities of Latium at 6.773–75: Nomentum, Gabii, Fidena, Collatia, Pometii, Castrum Inui, Bola, Cora—all has-beens from the standpoint of Virgil's time.[21] Not Rome. As cities go, the passages we are looking at set up a sort of contest for antiquity, ultimately to be won by Rome alone.

One further ancient city is that of Corythus in Etruria, which we discussed in the Introduction as complicating the question of Roman origins in this poem.[22] The Trojan Penates at 3.170 make it the destination of the Aeneadae, explaining that Apollo's oracle meant this place when it said to "seek out your ancient mother" (96); Latinus at 7.209 calls it the original home of Dardanus. At 10.719 we hear briefly about a "Greek man," Acron, who had come "from the ancient territory of Corythus" (*antiquis Corythi de finibus*). Read against the other ancient cities, particularly Aeneas' more immediate homeland Troy, the epithet "ancient" at 10.719 makes the city of Corythus both the venerable origin of Aeneas' people and a homeland irrevocably in the past, to be replaced—like Troy—with something more valid, more permanent. This characterization underscores (but does not resolve) the troubling disparity between the Dardanids' origin and their destination that the Introduction discussed.

But there is more to the "antiquity" of Aeneas' once and future homeland. Transmitting Apollo's charter at 3.163–66 (in words repeated by Ilioneus to Dido at 1.530–33), the Trojan Penates characterize Aeneas' destination as "ancient":

> "est locus, Hesperiam Grai cognomine dicunt,
> terra antiqua, potens armis atque ubere glaebae.
> Oenotri coluere viri; nunc fama minores
> Italiam dixisse ducis de nomine gentem."

"There is a place—the Greeks call it by the name of Hesperia—an ancient land, prevailing in arms and in wealth of soil. Oenotrian men cultivated it; now the report goes that their descendants have called their nation Italy, after the name of their leader."

The description supplements a *Georgics*-compatible emphasis on farming (*terra, ubere glaebae, coluere*) with the *arma* endemic to this epic poem. But how can a *land* be "ancient," as opposed to a settlement founded at a determined point in time? Servius glosses: "'renowned'; a land cannot be new, even if the Athenians call their land the first land" (*nobilis; nec enim nova esse potest, licet primam terram suam esse dicant Athenienses*). Comparable is "ancient Latium" in Virgil's appeal to the muse Erato at 7.37. This usage suggests a metonymy, identifying a land with its people, as do the Penates and Ilioneus, who seem to

---

[21] Ahl 1976:216–18, Feeney 1986:7–8.
[22] See Introduction pp. 10–12.

be referring to the *terra* as a "nation" (*gens*).[23] "Antiquity" here is validating, authenticating: a land cannot be over and done with as a city can be (or a homeland or a marriage). By closely identifying a people with their land, the poem here not only channels and mitigates the connotations of *antiquus*, but emphasizes that this land is ancestral to Aeneas' people. The usage here establishes the Trojan's claim to Italy, concealing the seams between Trojan (and Roman) and Italian.

II

Five lines above the pun on "ancient Carthage," the first sentence of the *Aeneid* closes with the phrase "the walls of high Rome," *altae moenia Romae*: the sentence has led to the name of the city as the wanderings and travails that it enumerates will lead to the founding of Rome. The epithet here may pun on *this* city's name. Bernal has proposed that *Roma* comes from a West Semitic word meaning "high place, ἄκρον, citadel"; for obvious reasons this was a popular city name, attested a number of times in the Hebrew scriptures in the form Ramah, most notably as the birthplace of the prophet Samuel (1 Samuel 1:19, etc.). In the Phoenician form the first syllable would have been pronounced *Rōm-*. Brown has brought these facts into connection with *Aeneid* 1.7.[24] Whether or not this is the real origin of the name of Rome, it would have been a folk etymology easily assumed by any Phoenician or Punic speaker, such as those who frequented the city as merchants for much of its early history;[25] the Capitoline cliffs beetling over the Tiber, along with the other six hills (to which Virgil's *altae* refers), would have given the etymology a foothold and suggested that Rome was one of many cities bearing a name that meant "high place." One would like to know for sure whether this assumption had entered Roman lore (as the etymology of Carthage had), and whether Virgil has knowingly worked into the opening lines of his Roman epic, here at the very source of Roman origins, already a hint of an alien point of view, a hint pointed up by the complementary Semitic pun on Carthage a few lines below.

The *Aeneid* has other Semitic puns that parallel Latin or Greek puns and relate to the defining contest with Carthage. In the next chapter we shall look at one at 6.842–43 *duo fulmina belli, Scipiadas*, which etymologizes the name

---

[23] The implicit identification of Italy with its inhabitants has a parallel, far opposed to the mouths of Tiber, in Venus' apposition at 1.339: "the land of Libya, a people unbeatable in war" (*fines Libyci, genus intractabile bello*; cf. Anna at 4.40 *genus insuperabile bello*). Both cases concern newcomers faced with indigenous inhabitants.

[24] Bernal in Brown/Levin 1986:95, Brown 1995:24 n. 72.

[25] For example, Phoenicians in the eighth century established a cult of Melqart down in the *Forum Boarium*—the site of the Ara Maxima cult of Hercules that is celebrated in *Aen.* 8 (van Berchem 1959–60, Huss 1985:23, Hexter 1992:347).

"Scipio" from Greek *skêptos*, "lightning bolt, *fulmen*" but also, by a wordplay with Semitic *brq*, makes the Scipios the onomastic counterparts to the house of Barca (originally a cognomen of Hannibal's father Hamilcar). The name Dido apparently meant "beloved";[26] again one wonders if this etymology, which gives the poem two suicidal queens—each hostile to Aeneas—named *amata*, was known to Virgil. It resonates in ways that complement, without contradicting, Timaeus' interpretation, "wanderer" (which we have seen Virgil take full advantage of).[27] These puns are syllepses: giving us simultaneous standpoints in two languages, they sharpen the line of demarcation between two cultures (Phoenician and Latin), while at the same time uniting them.[28] We are dealing with a potential self-definition against an ethnic Other that also reinforces the mirror effect that obtains between Rome and Carthage. This all takes us a step beyond the view of translation that Virgil's use of Ennius' *Andromacha* brought us to in the last chapter, where the perspective given by translation shifted between Roman and Greek. In these Semitic-Latin puns, too, a general Greek perspective is conceivable, even when it is not obvious (as in the one on *Scipiadas*), since Virgil had Greek models in this practice; the first line of Sophocles' *Oedipus*, referring to "the new brood of old Cadmus" (Κάδμου τοῦ πάλαι νέα τροφή), plays on a Semitic etymology, "old," of Cadmus' name (with a pointed antiphrasis in "new brood").[29]

It is not strange to find an alien viewpoint worked in like this. Roman origins in the *Aeneid* are an unstable combination of different elements, represented on the narrative level by the contested viewpoints and ambiguity that so often contribute to "Virgilian melancholy." There is certainly enough melancholy in the passages on "ancient cities," but we would do well to remember that the tender feelings of loss that readers often detect in Virgil's account of the cost of Aeneas' mission can be as much an aesthetic channeling of true indignation as they are an acknowledgement of ambivalence about the triumph of Rome.[30] Here the more one pities the fall of Troy, the impending fall of Carthage, or the exile of Camilla from Privernum, the more one hears with relief Jupiter's recurrent prophecies that Rome will have a more secure

---

[26] Bauer 1917:411 (following Gesenius 1837:406). See Frazer 1914:1.19 n. 2 for a remote and speculative connection between Adonis and Dido's name (through "David").

[27] See p. 93 above.

[28] A similar example is the "striped" cloaks of the Gauls on the Shield, interpretable in their own language as "purple-dyed": both linguistic standpoints yield a picture of exotic luxury; see p. 56 above. It is worth remembering that the language in question was the one traditionally spoken in Virgil's homeland, Cisalpine Gaul.

[29] Brown 1995:37; on the sense of "old" in "Cadmus" see West 1997:448–50.

[30] Cf. Empson 1935:1: "Pope said that even the *Aeneid* was 'political puff'; its dreamy, impersonal, universal melancholy was a calculated support for Augustus"; Habinek 1998:164: "Through its central movement of lamentation [the *Aeneid*] distances the author and reader from their responsibility in the losses generated by imperialism while foreclosing the possibility of resistance on the part of the defeated."

future. And in this poem, where "to be Roman" is a dialectic, Rome does not just oppose the alien cities; it absorbs them. Rome is more of an heir to Oriental empires than their strict opponent. When we hear about those other cities we "become" Carthaginian or Ardeatine or whatever—think how often we hear their tales related from a sympathetic viewpoint, often divine—and our feelings then supplement those we have about Troy and Aeneas' people, and persist as the poem transfigures us into Romans. Gathering up many viewpoints and geographical perspectives, Virgil implicitly subsumes them within a larger, Roman viewpoint—a Roman identity—and gives it to us. There is an analogy with the replacement of the original Carthaginians or Ardeatines or whomever with Roman colonists. This is a narratology of empire: all these "ancient" cities will be reborn as Roman cities. The value of our network of ancient cities is not just to tell us that unlike them, Rome will survive; we knew that already. It is rather to ensure that Rome emerges from the *Aeneid* as the sum of the history, geography, and complicated human loyalties of its world.

There are of course two aspects to this subsumption. On the one hand, Rome obliterates these cities and makes them Roman; their subjectivities are lost within a bigger one. On the other hand, the metaphorical exchange that makes Rome the ultimate ancient city requires that Rome accept the terms of those cities, including her origin, Troy, and her enemy, Carthage. Anchises, as we shall observe in the next chapter, represents Augustus' *imperium* as such an accommodation. This tension is typical of the *Aeneid*. In the case of Italian cities like Ardea and Privernum, the places of origin of many Romans of Virgil's time, the tension is subdued, and the obliteration of their several histories and outlooks may easily present itself as Rome's generosity in bestowing her own national identity as a generally "Italian" one; in the cases of more unarguably foreign cities, the tension is more urgent. When Carthage is described as possessing a Roman-style senate, theaters, and so on, does the assimilation make Dido's city over into the pre-fab Roman colony it will be in Virgil's day, or does it disturb Roman assumptions by making the reader see the alien in the looking glass? This kind of choice arises immediately in the quasi-paradox at 1.12, in the parenthesis that identifies the poem's first "ancient city": *Tyrii tenuere coloni*. The Roman term *coloni*, "colonists, settlers, land-grantees," makes Dido's Tyrians prefigure the veterans of Caesar's wars who one day will settle the deserted site of Dido's city;[31] but the specification "Tyrian" inserts the possibility that Phoenicians could be stalwart, battle-hardened, glebe-loving Roman-style *coloni*.[32]

---

[31] This scenario is that of Dido's nightmare at 4.465–68 (where her focalization is an open possibility); there the sense of a reversal of ktisis is underscored by dense echoes of Ennius *Ann.* 34–50 Skutsch, Ilia's dream of the conception of Romulus and Remus (see below, p. 191). Cf. the reversals implicit in the ant simile at 4.402–405 (discussed on pp. 98–100 above).

[32] Cf. the references to Dido's *penates* (1.525, 4.21), distinctly Roman tutelary gods—like the Trojan ones at the center of Aeneas' colonial mission (2.293). Cf. Fletcher 2005:142–51 on Ovid's ethnopoetics of *penates* in non-Roman contexts.

The answer to these questions obviously depends on one's perspective. The feelings of Aeneas and his followers do not constitute the only viewpoint that the text makes available on the various cities. The inconsistency among these viewpoints persists, if we let it, and complicates the Roman identity that the poem insinuates. Even the "ancient homeland" in Greece of the mendacious Sinon is to be taken over by Rome someday. The poem guarantees that Rome embodies a living, never-ending dialectic among the nationalities of which it emerges as the sum.

With this potential for slippage in mind we might revisit the Romans' trajectory, traced in the last two chapters, from an "Oriental" identity in Troy to one allied with Greeks and opposed to the Orient, as when we read of the battle of Actium on Aeneas' Shield, "on the other side Antony, conqueror from the nations of the Dawn and the ruddy shore, with a barbaric host and motley arms" (8.685–86 *hinc ope barbarica variisque Antonius armis / victor ab Aurorae populis et litore rubro*), opposed to Augustus, the Italians, and Greco-Roman gods—where once Aeneas had used that language for his own people. Yet if Antony, as ruler of the Orient, can thereby be conceived as "Oriental," conquerable, un-Roman—so, on the same logic of the poem, can a Caesar who, Jupiter prophesies, will ascend to heaven loaded with the spoils of the Orient (1.289 *caelo spoliis Orientis onustum*). As we saw in the last chapter, to be loaded with the spoils of the East can mean to have conquered the East; or it could mean to be an Eastern sovereign, like Priam of Troy, whose doorposts were "proud with barbarian gold and spoils." The difference between them turns out not to be ethnic, whatever criteria one used for ethnic identity, but based on something else, something more like power (whose visual symbols are always Oriental, like gold and purple-dye, and the general opulence and architectural grandeur) or mere perspective—and the two prove to be closely related. The line drawn and redrawn between the ethnic self and the Other in this poem can always be redrawn again. Another potential paradox: in chapter 2 we noted how the Italian enemies of Aeneas are sometimes made to seem Oriental; above we noted that the *Aeneid* compulsively applies the term *antiquus* to Italy and to things and people within it. From different angles, either characterization could signal an opposition between the Trojan newcomers and their foes, or collapse the distinction between them—since both peoples that will together become Rome are already in some sense both native and Eastern. What makes the difference is which truth one accepts among the several offered by the poem.

We have now begun refining the sense, arrived at by the end of the last chapter, of Rome as an heir to the imperial power of its predecessors and rivals, a sense connected with that of Rome as still in some way Oriental, having retained some such quality from Troy and confirmed it through a self-defining antithesis with Carthage. According to Ilioneus' boast to Latinus at 7.217–18, Troy once had the greatest realm in the world; so too, considers Latinus at 258 on the basis of Faunus' oracle, may the nation destined to emerge from this refugee band.[33] Along with "antiquity" Rome inherits a dream of empire. At 3.156–57 the Penates say they follow Aeneas and his *arma* over the tumid sea—this predicts god-favored Roman military conquest, as they make clear in the next lines: "we will also exalt your future descendants to the stars and give imperial power to their city" (*idem venturos tollemus in astra nepotes / imperiumque urbi dabimus*).

The next chapter will come around to a comparison between the vicissitudes of empire and the passage of ideas from one poet to another (as part of that dialogue on Roman identity that the last chapter emphasized): the image of a greater Rome that coalesces from its constituent nations has a counterpart in the image that Virgil synthesizes from his precursors' images and words. What is left of Troy, Ardea, and the rest lives only in Rome—and in the *Aeneid*—and one day, perhaps, what is left of Rome will live on, transfigured, in some other poet, and some other nation. For now it is worth a brief digression to see how two later poets continue the dialogue, by picking up Virgil's "ancient city" motif. First, look at how Ovid reworks Virgil's opening description of Carthage, in *Ex Ponto* 1.8.11–16, on the Danubian city of Aegisos (which, like the "ancient cities" of the *Aeneid*, has also fallen under Roman control):

> Stat vetus urbs ripae vicina binominis Histri,
>   moenibus et positu vix adeunda loci.
> Caspius Aegisos, de se si credimus ipsis,
>   condidit et proprio nomine dixit opus.
> hanc ferus Odrysiis inopino Marte peremptis
>   cepit et in regem sustulit arma Getes.

There stands an old city beside the bank of the double-named Hister, unapproachable on account of its ramparts and geographical position. Caspian Aegisos, if we are to believe the stories they tell about themselves, founded it and called his work by his own name. This city the savage Gete took in sudden war, killing the Odrysians, and raised arms against its king.

Even in distant exile the resourceful Roman finds fodder for a Hellenistic mini-ktisis. The parallels with Virgil's Carthage pile up: not just the opening phrase, but the position on a shore, the foundation by an Eastern wanderer, the situation amid threatening savages, and the (almost gratuitously mentioned) dubious *fides* of the inhabitants.[34] Who is Ovid here? He calls himself *profugus*

---

[33] The expression the oracle uses, "everything . . . where in its returning course the sun beholds either ocean" (7.100–101 *omnia . . . qua sol utrumque recurrens aspicit Oceanum*), is a common figure for world empire; Ilioneus also uses it (217–18). See Brown 2001:75, 333 (tracing the topos back to Persian usage); Horsfall ad locc.

[34] On the way the *Aeneid* uses the proverbial (among the Romans) bad *fides* of the Carthaginians, see Starks 1999.

in 50, an irresistible reference to Aeneas in *Aeneid* 1.2; thus the banished poet arrives in an ancient city from Rome as Aeneas once arrived in such a city from Troy, and Ovid's yearnings for Rome (of which this epistle is as keen an advertisement as the others) appear as a new version of Aeneas' yearnings for Troy—or (though Aeneas does not realize it until after Anchises' instruction, if then) for Rome, the new Troy.[35]

Yet Ovid seems to identify with the city of Aegisos, comparing its brave isolation amid savagery to his own (the poem unfortunately goes corrupt at line 20, just where we would expect the analogy of Aegisos with Ovid to become explicit): he is thus like Aeneas in Carthage, melting into the local population. Ovid has accepted the Virgilian model with all its ambiguities for a Roman. The city's "double-named" river (Hister and Danube) recalls not only Virgil's Tiber (Thybris), but Troy's river Xanthus, also known as the Scamander, according to *Iliad* 20.74: the characterization furthers the Virgilian analogy between the three great cities of the *Aeneid*. This performance is one little variation on Ovid's typical pose, in the letters *Ex Ponto*, of the Roman carrying on the struggle for Romanity and empire at the very edge of the ordered world. As always, he is patrolling—ostentatiously, for the emperor and other Romans to see—the Roman-barbarian border within himself.[36] Here the shifting boundaries of identity make that message a dialectic, and part of a larger dialectic between successive visions of national identity. We might observe that the prolepsis in Virgil's *antiqua* becomes reality here: Ovid is living long after the foundation of Aegisos, and is looking back on its origins as he knows Virgil looks back on those of Carthage.

We may compare the way such a tough, insatiable reader of the *Aeneid* as Silius adapts the pathos of Virgil's *urbs antiqua ruit* (*Punica* 2.654–56):

> urbs, habitata diu Fidei caeloque parentem
> murorum repetens, ruit inter perfida gentis
> Sidoniae tela.

A city that was long inhabited by Loyalty, and that looked back to heaven for the founder of its walls, is falling amid the perfidious weaponry of the people of Sidon.

The city is Saguntum, besieged by Hannibal's army on its way to Rome; this comes amid a pervasive and complex assimilation, in Books 1 and 2, of Saguntum to Virgil's Rutulians (based on the alleged Rutulian origin of the Saguntians). Hannibal's pursuit and slaying of Theron, with its identifications Theron-Hector-Turnus and Hannibal-Achilles-Aeneas, reminds us that Silius' complications of Virgil's ethnic oppositions build on Virgil's own complications of the *Iliad*'s. If Lucan (as his recent critics have reminded us)

[35] On Ovid's assumption of the Virgilian thematics of exile, see Putnam 2001.
[36] Cf. *Pont.* 1.2.20–21, 59, 65–66, 93, 104.

presses Virgil's ambiguities to make them explicit, Silius presses them to exacerbate their ambiguity. When Murrus threatens Hannibal, he uses the sarcasm of a Rutulian warrior taunting one of the encroaching Aeneadae: "Take the reward owed you for your deceit, and seek for Italy far below the earth" (1.484–85 *fer debita fraudum / praemia et Italiam tellure inquire sub ima*).[37] Yet as his sarcasm mounts, he traces his Roman allies, and by implication assimilates his own city, to Troy: "The gift of my right hand is your long journey into Dardanian territory and the snowy Pyrenees and the Alps" (1.486–87 *longum in Dardanios fines iter atque nivalem / Pyrenen Alpesque tibi mea dextera donat*). Of most interest to our present question is Silius' replacement at 2.654–55 of the *antiqua* of *Aeneid* 2.363. "A city that was long inhabited by Loyalty, and that looked back to heaven for the founder of its walls": the first characterization contrasts the city with the proverbially faithless Carthaginians (whose weapons are as perfidious at 655 as the trick of Sinon and the Greeks at Troy); the second mythologically assimilates Saguntum to Troy.

From the perspective that sees Virgil's "ancient cities" as imperfect prefigurations of Rome, their *fuit* quality contrasts with the durability or eternity of Rome. The loss and reacquisition of empire is the main thing about this contrast.[38] Troy is the object of several laments for lost empire, as in the line we discussed above, 2.363 *urbs antiqua ruit multos dominata per annos* ("an ancient city is falling, having held sway for many years"). In the last chapter we noticed a significant example at the very beginning of Book 3: *postquam res Asiae Priamique evertere gentem immeritam visum superis . . .* (1–2 "After it had pleased the gods above to destroy the empire of Asia and the undeserving nation of Priam . . ."). This is the way Aeneas sums up the fall of Troy; the notion is paralleled in such places as 2.556–57 *tot quondam populis terrisque superbum / regnatorem Asiae* ("once the ruler of Asia, proud over so many peoples and lands"). This theme often uses the word *res* (singular or plural) in the sense "state, power, empire," as in Jupiter's promise to Juno at 1.278 *his ego nec metas rerum nec tempora pono* ("for them [the Romans] I set no spatial or temporal limits of power [*res*]"), and even in Aeneas' famous verdict on the Trojan War images in Juno's temple at Carthage: *sunt hic etiam sua praemia laudi, / sunt lacrimae rerum et mentem mortalia tangunt* (1.461–62 "here too praiseworthy action receives its due reward; there are tears for things [*res*], and mortal matters touch the mind"). *Res* there could be as broad as English "things," but in context—in a commentary on the fall of Troy—the term points especially to the sense in which Aeneas will use it at 3.1: there are tears in Carthage, he means, for the lost empire of Troy, whose restoration is his goal.

---

[37] Cf. Turnus to Eumedes at *Aen.* 12.359–61 *en agros et, quam bello, Troiane, petisti, / Hesperiam metire iacens: haec praemia, qui me / ferro ausi temptare, ferunt, sic moenia condunt* ("Here is your land, Trojan; measure out with your dead body the Hesperia that you sought to gain by war. This is the reward earned by those who dare to test me in sword fighting; this is how they establish city walls").

[38] With the Aeneadae's steady reacquisition of treasure compare their equally emblematic reacquisition of horses, i.e. war horses (Quint 1993:65–66).

Yet it takes only a slight shift in perspective to reverse this effect and turn this contrast into an assimilation. In the *Georgics* Virgil had anticipated the end of Rome, as of all nations: "Roman power [*res* again] and the realm fated to perish" (2.498 *res Romanae perituraque regna*).[39] If we read *Aeneid* 1.462 (*sunt lacrimae rerum et mentem mortalia tangunt*) against that line, the Rome that is to redeem the Trojan loss becomes all too like Troy. "Mortal matters" glosses, as it must, the fallen power of Troy, but by analogy it touches any future empire as well. In the *Aeneid,* too, there is no guarantee that Rome is destined to be eternal. Reassuring Venus at 1.278–79, Jupiter does not say "the Romans will have no spatial or temporal limits of power; they will have empire without end"; instead he says "*I* set them no spatial or temporal limits of power; I have given them empire without end" (*his ego nec metas rerum nec tempora pono, / imperium sine fine dedi*), with emphatic *ego*. They might set limits for themselves, or receive them from elsewhere. Jupiter's gift partakes of the same dubiety or selectivity that colors other parts of his prophecy (as at 292–93, where he falsely predicts that Romulus and Remus will together "give laws" when Caesar is taken up to heaven), and leaves open the possibility that all nations are mortal, including Rome.[40] At 8.355–58 Evander points out two abandoned, ruined towns, Janiculum and Saturnia, still visible near his settlement of Pallanteum—where Rome will be. They are a token of the fate of all cities: "the remnants and reminders of men of old" (356 *reliquias veterumque . . . monimenta virorum*).[41] The poem offers a vision that assimilates Rome to, as well as one that contrasts her with, the ruined hilltop habitations remembered by Evander. Rome inherits the ambivalence of Virgilian "antiquity."

---

[39] Cf. Thomas 1988 ad loc., reading the phrase as a kind of hendiadys, which at the very least coexists with and threatens to reverse the oppositional meaning "Roman power [on the one hand] and realms fated to perish [on the other]."

[40] An Ovidian reflex of this suggestion, too, exists: at *Met.* 15.426–30 Pythagoras, expounding the inevitable rise and fall of cities and the changefulness of things in general, prefaces an account of Rome with the fates of Troy, Mycenae, Athens, and Sparta (here too within a striking prolepsis: Athens and Sparta should not be considered fallen in Pythagoras' time). On the trustworthiness of Jupiter's predictions (and predictions in the *Aeneid* generally), see O'Hara 1990.

[41] Compare Sulpicius Rufus' consolatory comparison of ruined cities with human mortality (in Cicero *Ad fam.* 4.5), with Shackleton Bailey 2001:405.

Chapter Six

MARCELLUS

I

This chapter is the third that proceeds from chapter 3 in exploring the idea of Carthage as a foil for Rome in the *Aeneid*; it also brings us back to the themes of youth, death, and desire with which we started in chapters 1, 2, and 3. Now we approach them from the other end, through their connection with national identity, benefiting from the discussion of prolepsis in chapter 5. Anchises' prophecy in Book 6, tailored to meet Aeneas' persisting Trojan identification and understanding of his mission, couches Roman history in terms of a recovery of Trojan empire. That is what Aeneas' desire should be.

Even more complicated a prolepsis than "ancient Carthage" is Anchises' lament for Marcellus in the Underworld, which concludes the Pageant of Heroes, his review of future Romans. According to Anchises, the souls of the dead in Elysium must drink from the water of the River Lethe in order to forget their past selves and to "begin to wish to revert to physical bodies" (6.748–51). The youth stands before them on the bank of Lethe as he will appear in life, while Anchises laments his future death extravagantly. This is Augustus' nephew, son-in-law, and heir, who died at nineteen in the autumn of 23 B.C.E.[1] It is Aeneas who points him out (860–66):

> 860 atque hic Aeneas (una namque ire videbat
> egregium forma iuvenem et fulgentibus armis,
> sed frons laeta parum et deiecto lumina vultu):
> "quis, pater, ille, virum qui sic comitatur euntem?
> filius, anne aliquis magna de stirpe nepotum?
> 865 qui strepitus circa comitum! quantum instar in ipso!
> sed nox atra caput tristi circumvolat umbra."

Here Aeneas said (for he was observing a youth going along together [with the elder Marcellus], extraordinary for his beauty and flashing armor—but far from happy were his brow and the eyes in his downcast face), "Father, who is that who accompanies the hero as he goes? Is it his son, or one of the grand stock of his descendants? What a clamor his companions make! What quality there is in him! But black night swirls around his head with a mournful shadow."

[1] Dio 53.27–28, 30–32.

Before Pallas, Lausus, and Camilla have made their appearance, and when Nisus and Euryalus are still no more to us than zealously devoted prizewinners in *Aeneid* 5, we already have a lush description of a (proleptically) dead youth. Armed in glittering gear and accompanying a bellicose ancestor, he is ready to go to war, but in contrast with the dynamic Euryalus, Pallas, Lausus, and Camilla before their deaths, we see only his voiceless passivity and lugubrious beauty. He is potentially the first object of the appreciative gaze that will fall suddenly on them—only in his case the desire it represents is commandeered for the push toward Roman identity. In Anchises' subsequent eulogy Marcellus, not yet born, is treated as a valued and exemplary Roman corpse. Aeneas' aversion to him, in fact, together with Anchises' tearful response—the fullest commentary in the *Aeneid* on the tragedy of young death—is a confluence of the very themes that our Adonis-figures gather as well, notably the pathos of young death for the prospects of a family stock and, on a larger scale, the fate of a nation.[2]

In Book 6, desire in general is more or less explicitly directed toward lineage, nation, succession. Anchises' instruction about the Roman future begins with Aeneas' question about the souls waiting to ascend to the upper world from Elysium: *quae lucis miseris tam dira cupido?* (721 "What so terrible desire do these piteous beings have for the light?"). "Terrible desire" (*dira cupido*) already has significance in this Underworld. At 133 the Sibyl incredulously referred to Aeneas' wish to visit his father as *tantus amor, tanta cupido* ("such love, such desire") to visit the shades; at 373, not long after we see the unburied dead stretching out their hands *ripae ulterioris amore* (314 "with love for the further bank"), she questions Palinurus' *tam dira cupido* ("so terrible desire") to get across Acheron. These phrases piquantly trope as love a sort of death-drive, the urge that impels into the Underworld, naturally deemed shocking or *dira* by the living; at 721 Aeneas inverts this metaphor. Why would anyone "love" life; that is (in context), desire to leave Elysium and rejoin the world of the living, with its pain and trouble and obscure, seemingly endless national mission? His father never fully answers his question, and does not directly address the terms in which Aeneas couches it. The closest he gets is the last lines of his exposition of reincarnation, "and [the souls] begin to wish to revert to physical bodies" (751 *et incipiant in corpora velle reverti*). "Wish" (*velle*) answers—better, channels and reformulates—his son's question about the souls' *cupido*, a much stronger word. Anchises reduces his son's metaphor, strips the question of its accretion of meaning.

It should be clear by now that the *Aeneid* as a whole frequently tropes desire as part of the dynamics of nation building and gives love a peculiarly ktistic import. On the theological level, the love goddess herself is promoter of the

[2] He is often discussed with them: cf. Heinze 1915:159; Otis 1963:303; Hardie 1994:14–19, 23–34; Petrini 1997 *passim* (esp. 8–9, 108–10).

Roman future; one may even speculate on a ktistic sublimation in the loves of
Dido and Turnus, lethally thwarted so that Rome might be. In the *Aeneid* love
between persons tends to oppose the Roman mission.[3] Already at 4.347
Aeneas equates his journey to Italy with *amor*, a substitute for the love affair
with Dido (*hic amor, haec patria est*, "That is my love, that is my fatherland").[4]
The poet's invocation of Erato, the muse of love poetry, at the opening of the
second half of the poem in connection with the Italian war (7.37) may have as
much to do with this trope as with the contest for Lavinia that will secure the
future for Aeneas. But the text also weaves a less conspicuous web of desire and
nationhood through striking expressions that infuse desire into the motivations of crucial actions in the narrative, particularly expressions of the type
magnus amor, tantus amor, tanta cupido, dira cupido, and the like, with a genitive
of object.[5] At 1.171 the Trojans step onto the Libyan shore "with great love of
the land" (*magno telluris amore*)—this will prove a misdirected love, analogous
to Aeneas' for Dido. Latinus perceptively uses one such phrase of Aeneas' wish
to settle in his territory (7.263 *nostri si tanta cupido est*, "If you have such great
love for us"); contrary to this purpose, at 7.57 Amata is said to favor Turnus'
suit *miro amore*, "with wondrous love" (where the literal meaning also threatens to come alive). At 7.496 Ascanius aims at Silvia's stag *eximiae laudis suc-
census amore* ("kindled by a desire for extraordinary praise") and so starts the
war with the Latins; at 9.197 the same phrase (*magno laudum . . . amore*)
describes Euryalus' yearning to join Nisus' adventure (a yearning that is easily
made to answer the *amor pius* that unites Nisus to him: 5.296). Anchises similarly characterizes the dire patriotism of Brutus (823): "Love of his country
and immense desire for praise—*laudumque immensa cupido*—will prevail [over
paternal affection for his sons, whom he will put to death]."

Cumulatively these desires, apparently shooting in various directions in
human blindness, elaborate an almost Empedoclean or Platonic love, psychol-
ogy as cosmology, and particularly trope love as the force behind the progress of
Aeneas' journey and the founding of his new nation, or as the force that
opposes it. It becomes theology in Nisus' question to Euryalus at 9.184–85, the
one that launches their adventure: "Do the gods put this burning desire [*ardor*]
in our minds, Euryalus, or does each man's terrible desire [*dira cupido*] become
his god?"[6] The different kinds of love (literal and metaphorical, or in different

---

[3] Wiltshire 1989:115–19.

[4] A striking Greek precedent for the metaphor is Thucydides 2.43.1 (Pericles' *epitaphios logos*): one
should be *erastês* of one's city. I thank Brian Calabrese and Richard Apóstol for raising these points.

[5] These metaphors are complemented by similar phrases that speak of the literal loves of Dido:
Venus refers to her "immense love" for Sychaeus (1.344 *magno . . . amore*) and plots her "immense
love" for Aeneas (1.675 *magno . . . amore*); at 5.5 the same phrase puts an end to Dido's story.

[6] Aletes' response at 247–50 convinces Nisus that the former alternative is correct (cf. Lennox
1977:340). Makowski 1989:8 notes how, against the background of Platonic *erôs* (and especially
Phaedrus' speech on heroic partnerships in the *Symposium*), the desire to do great deeds of valor

metaphorical senses) are not necessarily matched or commensurate. Anchises, in subduing and redirecting the *dira cupido* questioned by his son into the wish to return to the upper world to become mighty Romans, focuses on the building of a nation; by the end of his exposition, when Aeneas himself reascends from the Underworld to the light, "kindled" by "love of the fame that was to come" (889 *incenditque animum famae venientis amore*), national foundations have been troped back again as a new, politically acceptable kind of love.

The treatment of Marcellus exemplifies a similar substitution. At their joint introduction in battle both Lausus and Pallas are "extraordinary for beauty" as well as doomed (10.433–36):

> hinc Pallas instat et urget,
> hinc contra Lausus, nec multum discrepat aetas,
> egregii forma, sed quis Fortuna negarat
> in patriam reditus.

"On this side Pallas attacks and pushes on, on the opposite side Lausus, and there is not much difference in age between them; both extraordinary for beauty; but to both Fortune had denied homecomings."

The neutral beauty denoted by *egregii forma*, here tinged with martial connotations, will at their deaths become real voluptuousness when our gaze, through Aeneas', lights on Lausus' *ora, ora,* and Pallas' "snowy" body and "smooth" chest. Marcellus shares this phrase, with its erotic implications firmly latent: "a youth extraordinary for his beauty and flashing armor" (6.861 *egregium forma iuvenem et fulgentibus armis*). Brenk compares the line with the same one from the epitaph of L. Cornelius Scipio Barbatus, "whose beauty was equal to his courage" (*quoius forma virtutei parisuma fuit*), that Thomas brings into contact with Turnus.[7] Of the traits noticed by Aeneas at 861, Anchises' epicedium does not pick up Marcellus' beauty, but only the military prowess it accompanies and emblematizes. Anchises' lament also ignores the suggestive detail in line 862 "but far from happy were his brow and the eyes in his downcast face" (*sed frons laeta parum et deiecto lumina vultu*):[8] part of the boy's sadness, which seems to contradict ("but . . . ") his martial splendor, is the demure downward gaze that we will observe in Turnus, along with his "downy cheeks" and "youthful body," as he approaches the altar (12.220 *demisso lumine*), the subdued, negated gaze that he shares with Lavinia at 11.479. Coupled with *egregium forma*, this feature might easily pass into the self-enclosed, tantalizing beauty of the *erômenos*.

---

melds with the more concrete love between Nisus and Euryalus. See Fowler 2000a:96–97 on the sexual background of such phrases in Lucretius (e.g. 3.1077 *quae mala nos subigit vitai tanta cupido?*) and on the variations Virgil rings on it.

[7] Brenk 1986:224. See p. 48 above.

[8] Some commentators take *deiecto vultu* as an ablative of description, parallel to *laeta* and predicate with *lumina*: "but far from happy was his brow, and his eyes had a downcast expression."

But the text does nothing with this possibility. Anchises focuses on the mourning of the whole people (6.868–74), transvaluing his son's preoccupations from a personal to a national sorrow buttressing national interests; he touches on the boy's body only to lament his "right hand unvanquished in war" (878–79). Anchises takes off from the flashing arms, the beauty of the warrior, and redirects Aeneas' sadness to the service of that Romanness he has just been expounding (875–81):

> 875 "nec puer Iliaca quisquam de gente Latinos
> in tantum spe tollet avos, nec Romula quondam
> ullo se tantum tellus iactabit alumno.
> heu pietas, heu prisca fides invictaque bello
> dextera! non illi se quisquam impune tulisset
> 880 obvius armato, seu cum pedes iret in hostem
> seu spumantis equi foderet calcaribus armos."

"No boy of the Trojan race will exalt his Latin ancestors so high by his promise, nor will the land of Romulus ever glory so in any of her nurslings. Alas for the piety! Alas for the old-time trustiness and the right hand unvanquished in war! When he was in armor no one would ever have come against him without paying a price, either when he went against the enemy on foot or when he spurred his foaming horse's forequarters."

"Boy" is pathetic, especially as juxtaposed with the values—the *spes*, his promise, his anticipated but unfulfilled qualities—that Marcellus would have grown to embody: *pietas*, of course, and *fides* (*prisca*, but not *antiqua* in the sense "outdated"), and above all prowess in war. He is an Astyanax-figure, and his traditional manly qualities recall the way Andromache projected her grief for her son into hope for Ascanius' *antiqua virtus*, "antique valor," literally "manliness" (3.342). His potential battle-worthiness not only exemplifies the warlike nature of Rome (851–53), but anticipates Anchises' instructions concerning the war in Italy (890). The tragedy that Anchises emphasizes is in the loss of a potential Roman hero and savior; in this pageant of *exempla* or national paradigms Marcellus is an *exemplum manqué*, a point made syntactical by the unfulfilled wish in Anchises' concluding pitch of emotion: *heu, miserande puer, si qua fata aspera rumpas! / tu Marcellus eris* (882–83 "Alas, pitiable boy, if only you could somehow break through harsh fate . . . ! You will be Marcellus").[9]

The death of Marcellus, Augustus' chosen heir, assimilated nation to family as bereft of hope and future, at risk of a return to civil war.[10] "With the lament for Marcellus," O'Hara notes, "the possibility is raised that . . . [Augustus] may instead come to resemble an Alexander—to whom the description of

---

[9] See Goold 1992:101 on the syntax.

[10] Dufallo 2007, chapter 5, discusses the ideology of this assimilation.

Augustus in the underworld implicitly compares him—whose death without a clear heir led to the kind of struggle for power that might well have attended an early death of Augustus."[11] Anchises' epicedium blurs the distinction between the Julian line and the other Roman families by juxtaposing the boy to his paternal ancestor, also named Marcus Claudius Marcellus, and thus making Marcellus a sort of universal Roman heir (and Augustus a sort of universal *paterfamilias*).[12] His beauty picks up notes of connubiality rather than eroticism; one recalls the introduction one hundred lines later of Turnus as "most beautiful" of all Lavinia's suitors (7.55). In Marcellus' case marriage—to Augustus' young daughter Julia—means legitimate succession, and peace and order for Rome; his death means the opposite.[13] The deaths of our Adonis-figures, who also represent the lost chances of their families and nations, will reprise, then unpack Marcellus' beauty. Beginning his speeches over the corpses of Lausus and Pallas (10.825 *"quid tibi nunc, miserande puer..."* 11.42 *"tene" inquit "miserande puer..."*), Aeneas echoes his father's *"heu, miserande puer..."* over Marcellus (6.882): the themes of familial and national survival that Marcellus problematizes and that resonate in Aeneas' views on the boys[14] displace, in Marcellus' case, the amorous grief of Bion's Aphrodite (her view, remember, is the model for that of Aeneas in each of those passages).[15]

Although Marcellus does not receive an Adonis-moment—he is not even dead, exactly, when gazed upon—it may be possible to trace a debt to Bion's lush imagery at the end of Anchises' epicedium (6.883–86):[16]

> "manibus date lilia plenis,
> purpureos spargam flores animamque nepotis
> his saltem accumulem donis, et fungar inani
> munere."

[11] Cf. O'Hara 1990:169. On the assimilation of Augustus to Alexander see e.g. Norden on 6.791–805; cf. pp. 158–9 below.

[12] Virgil was preceded in this juxtaposition by Augustus' own funeral speech for Marcellus: Augustus fr. 14 Malcovati = Plutarch *Comp. Pelop. Marc.* 1.7; cf. Horsfall 1989a:266.

[13] Anchises translates Roman anxiety into a melancholy hope that Marcellus' death was a necessary sacrifice; so too Euryalus, Pallas, Lausus, and Camilla have been discussed together as sacrifices to the Roman future, as well as for their more general thematization of premature death: see especially Otis 1963:303 (particularly on 6.870–71).

[14] Especially Pallas: see p. 38 above on 11.43–44. On other echoes of Anchises in the Pallas speech, see chapter 7, pp. 182–4.

[15] The intertext with Bion prompts a comparison between phrases like *dira cupido* and the explicitly erotic αἰνὸς ἔρως ("terrible love") of Aphrodite for Adonis at *Ad.* 39. Notice in that connection the potential interlingual pun on Aeneas' own name (cf. *Il.* 13.481 and *Homeric Hymn* 5.198–99, with O'Hara 1996:8, 242).

[16] A debt to Bion may also exist in Horace, *Carmina* 1.12.45–48 (on the dead Marcellus) *micat inter omnis / Iulium sidus velut inter ignis / luna minores* ("the Julian star twinkles among them all like the moon among lesser lights"), which recalls the double comparison in Bion fr. 11.3 (from a poem echoed by Virgil at 9.403 and for Pallas at 8.590–91: Reed 2004:34–38).

"Give lilies in armloads; let me strew crimson [*purpureos*] flowers[17] and ~~heap over the soul of my descendant these gifts at least, and fulfill the~~ empty duty."

Brenk has explored the similarities between Anchises' behest in these lines and Bion's appeal at *Adonis* 75–76 to heap flowers on the corpse of Adonis (which is also described as reclining "among purple-dyed sheets": 79 ἐν εἵμασι πορφυρέοισιν):

βάλλε δέ νιν[18] στεφάνοισι καὶ ἄνθεσι· πάντα σὺν αὐτῷ,
ὡς τῆνος τέθνακε, καὶ ἄνθεα πάντ᾽ ἐμαράνθη.

And strew him with garlands and flowers: all flowers too have wilted, all, since he is dead.

An assimilation of Marcellus to Adonis, Brenk observes, both idealizes the youthful beauty of the Roman and places "the tragic loss of Venus' descendant in the context of her earlier sorrow for the Adonis of myth."[19] Except for the verbs for "strew" (which are not close equivalents) there is no verbal resemblance between the two passages. The situation is not the same, since Adonis is actually dead, whereas Marcellus, who is standing below and in front of them, fully armed, looking as he will in life, will not die for another thousand years or more. Bion's narrator urges the strewing as part of a pathetic fallacy, a personification of flowers begun in line 35, where "flowers turn red from grief" for Adonis. But the motif of heaping up a dead body with flowers is rare, and not only Virgil's other echoes of Bion at moments of pathos, but more particularly Anchises' "crimson flowers" invite a connection with Bion's poem, where red flowers are prominent.[20] There is a reciprocal link with the *purpureus flos* to which Euryalus is likened at 9.435 and Pallas' hyacinth (describable as *purpureus*) at 11.68–69; at least by association, even the *purpureus color* that leaves Camilla's dying *ora* at 11.819 shares in this significance. And like Pallas, Marcellus ends up cloaked in Dido's color; one could see the crimson color here not only as associated with death,[21] but as a transfusion from the rich crimson hangings, furniture, and attire habitual among the Tyrians in Book 4, products of Phoenician *purpura*, emblematic of Dido's Phoenician wealth and, emotionally, her passion.

---

[17] The reading that takes *spargam* as a subjunctive dependent on *date* ("Grant that I may strew lilies, crimson flowers, with full arms . . ."), with no stop after 883, produces a jejune apposition; and Anchises should not be asking anyone's permission, but rather inviting his guests to join in.

[18] See Reed 1997 ad loc. for discussion of the text.

[19] Brenk 1990:222–23.

[20] Lines 35, 66.

[21] Brenk 1990:223. Cf. Servius on 884, explaining the epithet: "On account of the similarity to blood, because it is either the soul or the seat of the soul" (*propter sanguinis similitudinem, quia aut anima est, aut animae sedes*).

The resonance of these ethnic overtones will emerge in the discussion to follow. As far as the rest of his Adoniac persona goes, Marcellus hovers on the verge of desirability, but ultimately suggests desire only as the ktistic metaphor that is so potent in this Book especially. The sensuality of the initial observation at 860–66 gets displaced, diffused into the sensuous armfuls of flowers. More fundamentally, as with the fallen warriors we looked at in chapter 1, the comparison of Marcellus to Adonis casts him as a quintessential beloved, perpetually desirable because perpetually inaccessible—a quality his death ensures. This image parallels his virtues, which are nothing more than *spes*, promise, expectation, hope; it is as if the perfect Roman, the ultimate Roman, were necessarily the Roman who will never be. It is striking that in inspiring his son at last with ardor for the great nation he must found, Anchises directs Aeneas toward unfulfillable desire.

II

Anchises makes Marcellus embody the ethnic history, crucial to his lesson, of the Roman people (6.875–77):

> "nec puer Iliaca quisquam de gente Latinos
> in tantum spe tollet avos, nec Romula quondam
> ullo se tantum tellus iactabit alumno."

"No boy of the Trojan race will exalt his Latin ancestors so high by his promise, nor will the land of Romulus ever glory so in any of her nurslings."

Iliaca, Latinos, and *Romula* unite the dual past and unified future of Aeneas' people. The whole Pageant of Heroes whose exposition ends (for the reader anyway) in the vision of Marcellus has presented the projected Roman nation as a composite; and this long attempt to define the Roman ultimately involves a series of oppositions. Anchises makes the nation fundamentally mixed, with Trojan and Italian as the basic ingredients, as in its first representative (761–63):

> "primus ad auras
> aetherias Italo commixtus sanguine surget
> Silvius, Albanum nomen, tua postuma proles."

"Silvius (an Alban name) will ascend first to the air of heaven, your posthumous offspring, commixed with Italian blood."

The Trojan element in this mixture is at the fore, as when Procas, the second king of Alba, is "the glory of the Trojan race" (767 *Troianae gloria gentis*), or when the introduction of Romulus relates the Roman future to a Trojan ancestor: "Romulus, of the blood of Assaracus" (778 *Romulus, Assaraci . . . sanguinis*). The lines drawn are between Trojan and Greek, with Trojan now comprehending

Italian—in line with the claim that Italy was the original home of Dardanus, the founder of Aeneas' line. Greeks appear as enemies; Anchises emphasizes the conquest of Greece (836–40) over that of Carthage (which figures in a few details but is plain only to the reader). The character of the future nation is defined for Aeneas as un-Greek—as it is also, implicitly, in the remarks on the superior creative arts (sculpture, oratory, astronomy) of "other nations" with which Anchises concludes his lesson (847–53).

As at the opening of the epic, the exposition operates through successive cities; Alba is the immediately introduced example, almost the test case, of this mixed nation, the city where, starting from the Trojan-Italian son of Aeneas, "our race" will rule (766). It is from here, significantly, that Augustus' own Julian clan allegedly arose: as in the lament for Marcellus, the emperor's family implicitly figures for the whole nation. The clan implicitly enters the *Aeneid* at 1.6, *Albanique patres* ("the elders of Alba"): they are thus already part of that matrix of nationhood outlined in the opening words of the poem. Jupiter (whose prophecy to Venus also offers a Trojan viewpoint) onomastically traces the change from Trojan to Roman in the founder of their family (1.267–71):

> "at puer Ascanius, cui nunc cognomen Iulo
> additur (Ilus erat, dum res stetit Ilia regno),
> triginta magnos volvendis mensibus orbis
> imperio explebit, regnumque ab sede Lavini
> transferet, et Longam multa vi muniet Albam."

> "But the boy Ascanius, who now receives the extra name of Iulus (he was Ilus while the state of Ilium stood in sovereignty), will complete thirty great cycles in power, with the months revolving, and will transfer the kingdom from the seat of Lavinium and fortify Alba Longa with great strength."

He *was* Ilus (compare other statements of finality, like *fuit Ilium* at 2.325 and at 12.828 Juno's *occidit, occideritque sinas cum nomine Troia*). "Ascanius" is left behind (appropriately: How and Wells on Herodotus 7.73 derive the name from a Phrygian ethnic). Iulus is the name that will become Roman Julius; compare the Trojans whose names become Roman gentilics in Book 5, including Ascanius' friend Atys (5.116–23, 568). Troy, in Apollo's view, would no longer be capacious enough for Ascanius' qualities (9.644 *nec te Troia capit*).[22] But the fact that the name Iulus is equally Trojan, differing by only one letter from Ilus (also the name of the founder of Troy), secures the continuity of Trojanness in the name of his descendants, including Julius Caesar and Augustus. His name moves away from the Oriental and immediately comes back to it. In Ascanius—the heir, the "promise" or "hope" of the new nation (12.168 *spes*)—Oriental qualities pass down to Rome. We have seen him riding in the etiological "Troy" spectacle beside his friends Atys and young Priam.

[22] See p. 114 above.

O'Hara notes "the Eastern preciousness of the simile applied to him at 10.132–38," where he is compared to an elaborate and costly jewel.[23] We trace in the poem's portrayal of Augustus' clan the same trajectory of nationhood we have been tracing elsewhere in the poem's account of Roman power.

Reaching for an image wherewith to register the all-embracing empire of Rome, Anchises compares the city to the Anatolian goddess Cybele (6.781–87):

> "en huius, nate, auspiciis illa incluta Roma
> imperium terris, animos aequabit Olympo,
> septemque una sibi muro circumdabit arces,
> felix prole virum: qualis Berecyntia mater
> 785 invehitur curru Phrygias turrita per urbes
> laeta deum partu, centum complexa nepotes,
> omnis caelicolas, omnis supera alta tenentis."

"Look, son: by his [Romulus'] auspices that famous city of which you have heard, Rome, will make its empire equal to the whole earth, its spirit to heaven, and within its wall will encircle seven citadels as one city, blessed with manly offspring: like the Berecyntian Mother as she is conveyed in a chariot through the cities of Phrygia, crowned with towers, blessed with divine offspring, embracing one hundred grandchildren, all of them heaven-dwellers, all of them possessing the realms above."

The strong image continues the emphasis on the Asiatic character of Rome; the Asiatic component, in fact, becomes a model, guarantee, and justification for Roman imperialism (first over seven adjoining hills, then over the whole world). The analogy might reassure Aeneas of continuity with his old life, or speak to him of future need in terms he can understand.[24] This is Cybele as embracing mother goddess, as she appears when she rescues her pines in Book 9: *alma Cybebe* (10.220), or *alma parens*, as Aeneas invokes her (10.252), or the "Phrygian mother" of his prayer at 7.139 (where "Jupiter of Mount Ida" also reflects a Trojan viewpoint). Her identity as the fierce lover of Attis is far in the background, and of the language of ecstatic goddess-cult such as Remulus Numanus will use against the Trojans (9.617–20) there is no trace. It is important to remember the Punic subtext here: the glorious procession that Anchises describes reenacts the conveyance of the image of Magna Mater to Rome from Mount Ida in 204 to help decide the war against Carthage.[25] That event, on

---

[23] Cf. O'Hara 1990:145 n. 43. There is a vague sensuality in the "throat or head" on which the jewel rests. Compare the sensual description of the Gauls on the Shield (p. 56), who merge with the costly materials in which they are depicted.

[24] The goddess's lions and Mount Ida, "most gratifying to the Teucrian refugees" (*profugis gratissima Teucris*), form the figurehead of Aeneas' ship at 10.156–58.

[25] See Gruen 1992:47 on the connections between the importation of Magna Mater and the Aenean origins of Rome.

the Aeneas myth of Roman origins, gathered some Easternness back into Rome in the effort to defeat an originally Eastern people; here, the maternal benevolence shown by the Great Goddess toward her divine grandchildren and the cities of Phrygia alike prefigures a conciliatory, embracing—not vanquishing—model of Roman imperialism toward the peoples of the Orient (for which *nepotes* and the *urbes Phrygiae* are divided analogues, respectively metaphor and metonymy).

Anchises' exegesis of Augustus and his Eastern conquests at 6.794–800 seems to draw the boundary differently, putting the future Romans implicitly on the side of the Greeks against Oriental barbarians, and potentially to leave Troy behind on the far side of national identity:

> "... super et Garamantas et Indos
> proferet imperium. ...
> huius in adventum iam nunc et Caspia regna
> responsis horrent divum et Maeotia tellus,
> et septemgemini turbant trepida ostia Nili."

"... and he will extend imperial power over the Garamantians and Indians. ... Both the realms of Caspia and the land of Maeotis already tremble at the oracles of the gods in anticipation of his coming, and the sevenfold mouths of the Nile are in a turmoil of fear."

One is reminded of the description of Antony's unassimilably Eastern army on the Shield. India is a desiderated, Egypt an actual conquest of Augustan Rome. The Scythian realms of Maeotis (the Sea of Azov) and the Caspian Sea fall into the same ethnic category, as do the Garamantians of North Africa, whom Herodotus describes as a timid, unwarlike people (4.174).

Yet Anchises' next lines give this conquest a different character (801–805):

> nec vero Alcides tantum telluris obivit,
> fixerit aeripedem cervam licet, aut Erymanthi
> pacarit nemora et Lernam tremefecerit arcu;
> nec qui pampineis victor iuga flectit habenis
> Liber, agens celso Nysae de vertice tigris.

"Truly, neither Alcides covered so much country, for all that he shot the bronze-footed deer, or pacified the woods of Erymanthus and made Lerna tremble at his bow; nor Liber, who steers his chariot with vine-leaf-covered reins, driving tigers down from the high peak of Nysa."

This contrast conceals a fundamental assimilation: Anchises accepts the terms of the Other. Augustus as Eastern conqueror is compared to two gods, Hercules and Bacchus, of whom the second was especially well known in this role and became an emblem and model for Alexander the Great. They have Oriental overtones; the detail "Nysa" especially recalls the syncretism of

Bacchus with Osiris, who, in a detail that may have entered Osiris lore from Dionysus lore, was supposed to have been born on a Mount Nysa.[26] The very name "Liber" (Virgil follows the syncretism that Naevius had pioneered) sets up a metaphorical chain: Italian-Greek-Egyptian. Moreover, these two gods were Antony's divine models; along with them Anchises has bestowed on Augustus Antony's role (in Octavian's propaganda) as an arch-Oriental. Antony had actually claimed descent (along with his whole *gens*) from a son of Hercules, Anton, thus giving himself a pedigree equal to that of Alexander and other Macedonian aristocrats who claimed descent from Heracles—including Cleopatra and the rest of the Ptolemies.[27] This makes Augustus' conquests immediately not conquests but absorptions, self-assimilations, a presentation that contrasts with that on the Shield (as discussed in chapter 4): the image of Antony and Cleopatra, hopelessly Oriental, routed by a Greco-Roman *imperator* and his gods. The underlying subsumptive model of Roman imperialism comports with Anchises' Cybele simile shortly before.

Hercules is a famous traverser of the West; the two gods thus complement each other geographically and suggest the sweep of Augustus' empire. Yet in the context of ktisis literature and imperial foundations, Hercules may be considered as much an Eastern conqueror and founder god as Bacchus, if, as is most likely, the stories about him retailed in the early third-century C.E. *Cynegetica* ascribed to Oppian go back to Hellenistic poetry.[28] There he fights the river Orontes and deposits the cattle of Geryon at Syrian Apamea (2.109–58); Nonnus too, in *Dionysiaca* 40, relocates Greek myths of Heracles to the Near East in ways that suggest a source in ideologically motivated Hellenistic cultural syncretism—and that in his poem, especially, prompt a comparison with the ktistic adventures of Dionysus. The identity of conqueror that Anchises gives to Augustus wavers between Western and Eastern—or rather, takes them both in, using a well-known metaphor for world empire.[29]

Anchises' words on Caesar and Pompey (826–35) are an even more complex instance of assimilation of the ethnic self to the Oriental:

> "illae autem paribus quas fulgere cernis in armis,
> concordes animae nunc et dum nocte prementur,
> heu quantum inter se bellum, si lumina vitae
> attigerint, quantas acies stragemque ciebunt,
> 830   aggeribus socer Alpinis atque arce Monoeci
> descendens, gener adversis instructus Eois!

[26] Diodorus Siculus 1.15.6.

[27] Plutarch *Ant.* 4.2; Theocritus 17.20–27. See Cameron 1995:245, Hannah 2004:150.

[28] Hollis 1994:159–66, suggesting Euphorion (who wrote foundation poetry for Antiochus the Great: fr. 174 Powell) as the source.

[29] On the pairing of East and West in assertions of world empire see p. 144 n. 33 above. See Hollis 1992:281 on an assimilation (at 798–800) of Augustus to Hercules through Callimachus' *Hymn* 4, with gestures toward the Ptolemies and Alexander.

ne, pueri, ne tanta animis adsuescite bella
~~neu patriae validas in viscera vertite viris;~~
tuque prior, tu parce, genus qui ducis Olympo,
835   proice tela manu, sanguis meus!"

"But those souls, whom you see shining in matched armor, harmonious for now and for as long as they are held down in this night—alas! What a war, what great armies and slaughters they will rouse between themselves should the light of life touch them! The father-in-law bearing down from Alpine heights and the citadel of Monoecus, the son-in-law supported by opposing peoples of the Dawn! No, my boys, do not habituate your spirits to such great wars, nor turn your powerful might against the vitals of your country! And you first forbear, you who draw your lineage from Olympus: blood of mine, cast the weapon from your hand!"

Pompey, the "son-in-law supported by opposing peoples of the Dawn," anticipates the picture of Antony on Aeneas' Shield, a passage we discussed in chapter 4 (compare especially 8.685–86 *hinc ope barbarica variisque Antonius armis, / victor ab Aurorae populis et litore rubro*, "on this side Antony with a barbaric host and motley arms, conqueror from the nations of the Dawn and the ruddy shore"). Each Roman takes on the persona of an Eastern conqueror (each had consciously, in fact, cultivated Alexander as a model)—now assimilable to, identifiable with, their conquered peoples.[30] As Aeneas' application of *barbaricus* to his own nation (2.504) is reversed at 8.685, so his alliance during the Trojan War years with "armies of the Dawn" (1.489 *Eoasque acies*) would seem to be reversed in both the Antony passage and in Anchises' description of Pompey: something Trojan has been exorcised from Roman identity.[31] The trick mitigates civil war by making it seem like an external war; this comports with Octavian's propaganda, which made of Antony a renegade Roman in the service of Egypt and, by extension, of the Oriental world that Egypt represented most egregiously and over which Cleopatra claimed dominion. In this warning to Aeneas about the (proleptic) civil war he himself will soon be fighting, one between himself and his would-be father-in-law Latinus (7.317), Pharsalus prefigures Actium.

An implication of the parallel between Pompey and Antony is that the former, like the latter, is a throwback to the Trojanness that Romans left behind long ago. Pompey already carries such a message in his earlier, vicarious

---

[30] A version of this view is presented as Cleopatra's in the epic poem preserved on the "Bellum Actiacum" papyrus (P. Hercul. 817), col. iv, where she claims Antony has decided to conquer Parthia for Egypt and die for her people. Courtney ad loc. (1993:337) compares *Anthologia Latina* 462.1–2 Riese *venerat Eoum quatiens Antonius orbem / et coniuncta suis Parthica signa ferens* ("Mark Antony had come rattling the Eastern world and bearing Parthian standards jointly with his own").

[31] Note also 7.606 for a reference to "the Dawn" as the natural enemy of Augustan Rome (cf. p. 106 above).

appearance in the poem, the lines on the death of Priam that allude to him (2.554–58):

> "haec finis Priami fatorum, hic exitus illum
> sorte tulit Troiam incensam et prolapsa videntem
> Pergama, tot quondam populis terrisque superbum
> regnatorem Asiae. iacet ingens litore truncus,
> avulsumque umeris caput et sine nomine corpus."

"This was the end of the destiny of Priam, this death carried him away by fate, with the burning of Troy and the collapse of Pergama before his eyes—once the ruler of Asia, proud with so many peoples and lands. He lies, a great torso upon the shore, a head torn away from its shoulders and a body without a name."

On 557 Servius notes, "Saying *ingens*, not *magnus* [the title of Pompey the "Great"], he touches on the story of Pompey" (*Pompei tangit historiam, cum ingens dicit, non magnus*). Pompey, after losing the Battle of Pharsalus to Caesar in 48 B.C.E., had fled to Egypt and been beheaded on disembarking by the government of Ptolemy XIII; Lucan, recognizing the implicit subject, transferred Virgil's phrasing back to Pompey (*Bellum Civile* 1.685–86).[32] The assimilation of the dead Priam to Pompey assimilates the shore of Troy to the shore of Egypt. Indeed, Pompey is describable, like Priam, as "the ruler of Asia, once proud with so many [subject] peoples and lands" (2.556–57 *tot quondam populis terrisque superbum / regnatorem Asia*)—as is Antony, the "conqueror from the nations of the Dawn." The *imperator* who brought the East under Roman control is paradoxically identified with that East and is thrown, like Antony, back onto the side of the ethnic boundary long ago forsaken (though not yet forsaken by Aeneas, whose naive, still Trojan view both of the pageant of Roman descendants and of the Shield is always available to color this seemingly inevitable transition with a sense of contingency).

An Augustan assimilation, one might call this, using Pharsalus to endorse the expulsion of Antony from Roman nationality; but it is not only Pompey whom Anchises' words assimilate to conquered Easterners. In the *Aeneid* there is only one other army, besides that of Caesar, that descends from the Alps. We glanced at this passage already in chapter 3, in connection with the steady differentiation of Aeneas' people from Dido's (10.11–15):

> "adveniet iustum pugnae (ne arcessite) tempus,
> cum fera Karthago Romanis arcibus olim
> exitium magnum atque Alpis immittet apertas:
> tum certare odiis, tum res rapuisse licebit.
> nunc sinite et placitum laeti componite foedus."

[32] On these passages see Bowie 1990; Hinds 1998:8–10, 100.

"The right time to fight will come—do not hurry it—when savage Carthage will someday unleash upon the citadels of Rome great destruction and a breaching of the Alps. Then, then, it will be licit to vie in hatred, to plunder each other. For now let things be, and cheerfully agree to the pact that pleases me."

This is Jupiter admonishing the other Olympians not to take sides against each other over the Italian war, and incidentally giving the most explicit (though tortuous) prediction in the poem of the Punic Wars. Anchises' Orientalizing works not only against Pompey, but against Augustus' adoptive father (6.830): "the father-in-law bearing down from Alpine heights and the citadel of Monoecus." He entered Italy from Gaul, yes, but this has nothing to do with the civil war; the specification of the route is provocative. Caesar crossed the Alps and entered Cisalpine Gaul with perfect legality, as its governor; it was of course his crossing of the Rubicon—the border between Cisalpine Gaul and Italy proper—that precipitated civil war.[33] The way Anchises traces the geography irresistibly likens the heir of Iulus to Dido's avenger (4.625–26), Hannibal, who famously passed through southern Gaul (including the "citadel of Monoecus," Monaco) and came over the Alps into Italy.[34] Anchises, in his prophecy, is constructing the Civil War to encompass, figuratively, the great third-century struggle for Roman survival, but in a way that makes both sides out to be symbolic Easterners. Civil war can serve as a metaphor for inconsistency, for the fissures and differences that lurk and threaten within a seeming identity. Anchises' account evades that possibility. Whichever side of the Civil War "we" stand on, it makes us Roman by opposition to a symbolic non-Roman—at the price of estranging Roman conquerors from Rome. Depending on how one looks at it, the Civil War was symbolically an external war—or was a degeneration to, a recrudescence of, original Easternness that fulfilled both Dido's curse and, grotesquely, her dreams that the Aeneadae should meld into her realm.

It is not so easy to divorce this degeneration or recrudescence cleanly from Augustus and from the ultimate Roman self, as the *Aeneid* constructs it. The indeterminacy between Julius Caesar and Augustus that O'Hara finds in Jupiter's prediction that Venus will welcome "Julius Caesar" into heaven "loaded with the spoils of the East" (1.289 *spoliis Orientis onustum*) points up the ethnic fluidity that we are tracing.[35] In the *Aeneid* not only Julius Caesar the adoptive father, but the adopted son too—C. Julius Caesar Augustus Divi Filius—accommodates this ambivalence and assimilability to Pompey and Antony. He too is a "conqueror from the nations of the Dawn." We have

---

[33] Lucan quietly corrects Anchises (1.183–85): Caesar's crossing of the Alps was preliminary to his *meditating* civil war.

[34] On this route and its symbolism for the Romans see DeWitt 1941.

[35] O'Hara 1990:155–63; see also O'Hara 1994b. On the ethnic ambiguity in 1.289, see p. 143 above.

already noticed that Augustus, receiving tribute from Eastern peoples at the "proud," spoil-laden doors to his temple, reembodies Priam as a ruler of the rich, Oriental type (see p. 123 above). Jupiter is combining Julius and Augustus into one triumphant figure—"Trojan Caesar" (286)—who can be considered a worthy heir to Priam; and so Rome can be considered a worthy heir to Troy. The poem, despite the ethnic realignment evident on the Shield and elsewhere, does not cease to make the Trojan perspective of Venus and Aeneas available.

The national boundaries in the Punic Wars themselves are soon disturbed. The incomplete line at 835 suggests that a transition from Caesar and Pompey eluded Virgil's creative powers up until his death; as the text stands Anchises moves on to cast the Roman conquerors of Greece as the avengers of Troy (836–40). The next lines, down through the elder Marcellus, introduce Roman heroes of the Punic Wars, especially the Second (842–46):

> "quis Gracchi genus aut geminos, duo fulmina belli,
> Scipiadas, cladem Libyae . . . ?
>
> > tu Maximus ille es,
> unus qui nobis cunctando restituis rem."

"Who [would pass over] the race of Gracchus or the twin Scipiads, two lightning bolts of war, the scourge of Libya . . . ? You there are that Maximus who alone, by hesitation, are the restorer of our state."

The first two lines offer a complicated pun: *geminos, duo fulmina belli, Scipiadas*, implicitly derives the name Scipio from Greek *sképtos*, "lightning bolt," but also makes them the counterparts to the house of Barca, whose name was popularly derived from a Semitic word for lightning bolt, *brq*.[36] This folk etymology has a long history in Latin literature in connection with the Scipios, including Lucretius' "the Scipiads, lightning bolt of war" (3.1034 *Scipiadas, belli fulmen*) and Cicero's "Gnaeus and Publius Scipio, the two lightning bolts of our empire" (*Pro Balbo* 34 *duo fulmina nostri imperi . . . Cn. et P. Scipiones*); O'Hara notes that the motif may have begun with Ennius. Silius will learnedly restore the wordplay to Hannibal, "the sudden lightning bolt from Carthage" (*Punica* 15.664 *fulmen subitum Carthaginis*). The pun combines Greek, Punic, and Latin into one linguistic compound. It also provides for multinational viewpoints on the Scipios, who are not only the Roman counterpart to Hannibal's family, but become them in name and identity.

Line 846 *unus qui nobis cunctando restituis rem* ("You there are that Maximus who alone, by hesitation, are the restorer of our state," on Fabius Maximus Cunctator, who wore Hannibal down by avoiding direct engagement) also goes back to Ennius: it adapts *Annales* 363 Skutsch, also on Fabius: *unus homo*

---

[36] On the pun see O'Hara 1996:179–81. The Punic name *Barca* is in fact more likely to come from *brk*, "blessed": Brown 2000:123–24.

nobis cunctando restituit rem ("one man, by hesitation, restored our state").[37]
~~What does *nobis* mean here? "Restored *our* state," with a dative of possession,~~
or equally plausibly with a dative of interest, "restored the state *to us*" or "*for us*."
The transition to Anchises' version is interesting, particularly when one considers the relation between Ennius' speaker (it is unknown who delivers the
line) and narrator (most emphatically Ennius himself). Ennius was not originally Roman, but Messapian, a native Sabellan speaker who served the
Romans in the Second Punic War and received citizenship after establishing
himself as the major Roman poet of his age. He is a towering figure in the roster of non-native Romans who created a Latin version of Greek literature "in
the interstices" of Central and South Italian culture.[38] When Anchises appro-
priates this *nobis*, it becomes proleptic: Anchises is not a Roman, nor is Aeneas
(if *nobis* includes him), but both are proto-Romans; this is indeed Anchises'
principal message, and in a few lines, he will address his listener as *Romane*
(851). That vocative is almost predicative: "remember as a Roman—*that* you
are Roman." But Anchises does not just make the Ennian "us" proleptic; he
also extends and transfigures that single subjectivity into which Ennius had
gathered a motley Italian empire (particularly here through opposition to
Carthage).[39] That empire is bigger in Augustus' time (which is Anchises' vantage point), and that act of gathering is all the grander and more ambitious.
From a different perspective, remembrance of the Ennian narratology of "us"
undoes the subsumptive Augustan imperial identity, by reminding us of its
constituents and the process by which it was won.

Terms like *Scipiadas*—whose very patronymic form, as well as the pun made
on it, is Greek—reminds us that the Roman poetic stance itself is basically
Greek.[40] Another such example is the Greek poetic adjective[41] *Italides*, "Italian
women" (at 11.657, referring to Camilla's companions Larina, Tulla, and
Tarpeia, whose Roman-sounding names we noticed on p. 59); it is to be
compared with the *Iliades* who mourn Pallas at 35. That term goes back to
Homer: Trojan is already long interpreted in Greek terms; now Italian (implic-
itly including Roman) also is. Anchises both obscures and emphasizes the
Greek fundament of the Roman poetic stance when he says (immediately after
his notice of Fabius Maximus and immediately before Aeneas picks out
Marcellus), "Let others practice sculpture, oratory, and astronomy; you,
Roman, remember to rule the nations with imperial sway—this will be your

---

[37] Wigodsky 1972:72–73.

[38] Feeney 1998:52–53 and elsewhere, e.g. 68. Cf. p. 118 above.

[39] Skutsch inclines to Badian's idea that the lines on Fabius were part of the account of Aemilius
Paullus' campaign against the Ligurians in Cisalpine Gaul (Badian 1972:176).

[40] On the Greek vantage point in Virgilian wordplay see Bleisch 1998, especially p. 600 (noting
the relevance of national identity).

[41] In Greek it occurs at Thallus *A.P.* 7.373.2 (first century B.C.E. or C.E.) and (in prose) Dio
54.22.1 (not used of persons).

art—and to add civilized order to pacification" (847–52). His o
poetry from the catalogue of arts best left to the Greeks leaves ope
poets (as not to sculptors, orators, astronomers, and imperialists) a continu...
exchange of ethnic identity. *Excudent alii* . . . "let others cast in bronze . . .":
the passage virtually defines *alii*, and continues the Trojan-Roman identity (*tu
Romane*), opposed to Greek, that Anchises' lesson aims at. Greek is alterity—
for all but poets? For them Anchises' prohibition leaves open a dialectic of
national identity, which the *Aeneid* takes full advantage of.

III

A reading of the Elysium episode against the Punic Wars has a notable intertextual dimension, since Cicero's "Dream of Scipio" (the most substantial surviving part of his *De Re Publica*, in which it occupied Book 6), which parallels
Aeneas' visit to and education in the Underworld, is set in 149 B.C.E., during
the Third Punic War. The young Scipio Aemilianus (who is narrating)
arrives with the Roman army in North Africa and enjoys the hospitality of the
local king; in a dream that night he travels to heaven and meets his father
Aemilius Paullus and adoptive grandfather Scipio Africanus the Elder, both of
them brilliant examples of Roman conquest and expansion, the latter in
Carthage, the former in Greece. They expound to him the workings of the
universe and the eschatological rewards of great Romans, and do so in terms
that resemble Anchises' instruction of Aeneas, beginning with the grandfather's explanation: "But in order that you may be all the keener to protect the
Roman state, Africanus . . ." (13.1 *sed quo sis, Africane, alacrior ad tutandam rem
publicam* . . .).[42] The proleptic (and protreptic) *Africane* by which the younger
Scipio is constantly addressed—the title given to him after his defeat of
Carthage in 146—recalls the *Romane* that Anchises uses toward Aeneas at
Aeneid 6.851. Cicero's Scipio says that those who serve their country go to the
starry heaven after death; the characters of the *Aeneid* repeatedly state that
Roman founding heroes go the starry heaven after death (Aeneas at 1.259–60,
Dardanus at 7.210–11,[43] "Julius Caesar" at 1.289–90, unspecified Romans at
3.158), whereas those who are anti-*ktistai* in the poem (Dido, Turnus)
emphatically go elsewhere.[44]

---

[42] The metaphor of the body as prison of the soul figures in each exposition: "Dream" 15.4, *Aen.*
6.734. See Norden 1957:47–48, Lamacchia 1964:263 (citing Isaiah 42:7 as a parallel). On the
intertext, and on that of both texts with Plato, see also Feeney 1986.

[43] Latinus' report here is contradicted by the sight of Dardanus with other Trojan ancestors in the
Elysian fields (6.650). Servius on that line compares the placement of Hercules both among the
gods and in the Underworld at *Od.* 11.601–604.

[44] Note the metaphor in 4.322–23 (Dido) *exstinctus pudor et, qua sola sidera adibam, / fama prior.*
For Turnus see 12.892–93. Both characters ultimately go *sub umbras*, "down to the shades."

In each case a question from the son motivates the father's exposition of the nature of the soul in the afterlife. Aeneas's question to Anchises at 721 recalls the younger Scipio to Paullus (15.1): why should I stay on earth rather than die and come here to you as soon as I can?[45] In each case, too, the answer is that earthly life is a duty owed to the gods,[46] and in each case this duty is largely presented as a political one in service of the Roman empire. The heroes of the pageant carry this message for Anchises. In Cicero, the purpose of the whole exposition is to prepare Scipio for the Roman conquests (starting with that of Carthage) and diplomatic missions for which he will become famous, and which his grandfather enumerates at 11.4. Scipio does not use the trope of desire that emerges in Aeneas' phrase *dira cupido*, but couches the idea in the most personal terms: "Why should I linger on earth? Why not hurry here to you?" (*quid moror in terris? quin huc ad vos venire propero?*). These terms are also implicit under Aeneas' question: now that he has rejoined his father, why would he wish to go back? What desire does here in the *Aeneid*, as against the "Dream of Scipio," is to help change Cicero's vision into an Augustan one. Aeneas strikes just the right metaphor in his somber query, despite his father's hesitation to answer it. It is finally desire, *amor* (889), with which Anchises fires Aeneas with enthusiasm for his mission—a love that, from different perspectives, is both dishearteningly different from and unsettlingly close to the love he had for Dido and that threatened to merge their nations and forestall Rome altogether.

A more radical revision of Cicero's text comes about through another intertext. The introduction of reincarnation into the *Aeneid*'s vision of the afterlife represents a reaching back through Cicero to the chief model of his *De Re Publica*: Plato's *Republic*. This background was announced with the Golden Bough, Aeneas' ticket into the Underworld, which recalls Meleager's emblem for Plato;[47] as a Platonic place, Virgil's Underworld recalls both the parable of the Cave in Book 4 of the *Republic* and Er's vision of the afterlife as round after round of reincarnation in Book 10. It is this combination that forces a rereading of Cicero, and that tends to cast doubt on the unadulterated beneficence of all that young Scipio's instructors (and Anchises) predict. Anchises is at pains to make his presentation encompass both good and bad in Roman history, reaffirming his lesson that emotional disturbances of all kinds are necessarily a part

---

[45] Norden 1957:48, Feeney 1986:3–4 (pinpointing the differences between the texts: young Scipio is urged to despise *gloria*). Lamacchia 1964:263–64 paraphrases the common element in both queries: "Wie kann man wünschen, dieses Leben zu leben, wenn nur das andere das wahre, ewige und glückliche ist?" She traces the Platonic background of the idea, e.g., in *Phaedo* 80E (see also Feeney loc. cit., Zetzel 1995:232).

[46] At "Dream" 15.4 *munus humanum assignatum a deo*; see Lamacchia 1964:270–75 on the reflexes of this idea in Anchises' lesson and elsewhere in the *Aeneid*.

[47] Meleager *A.P.* 4.1.47–48; see Michels 1945, West 1987:10–13. By making it sacred to Persephone, Virgil makes this Platonic bough an Eleusinian initiatory bough.

of earthly existence (6.733 *hinc metuunt cupiuntque, dolent gaudentque*, "this is where they get fear and desire, pain and joy")—this necessity is something Aeneas has noticed, as young Scipio does too. Against the Platonic background this dubiety extends to the blessed afterlife itself. Against the Platonic background it is disturbing, not comforting, to find that the denizens of Elysium "know" their own sun and stars (641 *solemque suum, sua sidera norunt*): in Plato's *Republic*, the inability to take in the real sun is the sign of the man who has just emerged from the Cave and still cannot accept a higher level of reality than the artificial light and false images he was familiar with down there (7.515E–16B).[48]

Aeneas' exit from Elysium through the ivory Gate of False Dreams (6.893–99), of course, casts a similar doubt on the closeness to truth of all that he has seen and heard, and the philosophical intertext suggests that this doubt concerns not a factual falsehood, but something else, namely the happiness (*felicitas, fortuna, eudaimonia*, call it what you will) that, so the vision has persuaded him, Aeneas must abjure in order to fulfill his destiny.[49] Happiness is always deferred: Aeneas defers it to Ascanius; Anchises, perhaps, defers it to Augustus. In Cicero, personal satisfaction is perhaps still possible for the aspiring Roman champion. In Virgil this satisfaction must be sacrificed, and the labor that Aeneas owes to the gods and to posterity will bring him no *fortuna* of a personal kind (as he counsels Ascanius at 12.435–36, in passing down his own version of the *antiqua virtus* that Andromache had enjoined at 3.342). A pointed divergence from Cicero makes this poignantly plain: at *De Re Publica* 14.4, Scipio gets a big, gratifying hug from his father Paullus when they meet in heaven. When Aeneas meets his own father in Elysium and tries three times to embrace him, his arms pass through the ghost each time as through air (6.699–702).[50] This is the third time he has been denied physical contact with loved ones, each of whom gives him crucial information for his journey: it happened first with Creusa's spirit in a similar scene (2.792–94) and next with Venus, who walks away before she even lets herself be recognized, let alone embraced, by her son (1.402–409). These unsatisfying encounters may be conceived as synecdoches for the sacrifice of personal happiness that Aeneas makes, and metaphors for the elusiveness of his desired objects in general. It is not only "passion" that is replaced, for Aeneas, by an *amor* for a new nation, but personal satisfaction of all kinds. The Rome described by Anchises, the telos with which Aeneas is (successfully) teased, is many centuries in the future. Even after his landfall in Italy, there is a permanent truth to Aeneas' sad

---

[48] This thought owes its beginnings to a conversation with Thomas Gould in April 1986.

[49] Cf. Reed 2001:165–67.

[50] The explanations that in a dream one can hug the dead, but not in a waking encounter (so Zetzel ad loc.), or that Virgil is following *Od.* 11.206–208 do not speak to the emotional effects of the difference. In view of Aeneas' impending translation to heaven, will this in fact be the last time he and his father meet? The contradictory locations of Dardanus (n. 43 above) obscure the answer.

characterization, during his wanderings, of "the farmlands of Italy, always receding backward," whose antithesis to him is the settled life of Helenus and Andromache (3.496 *arva . . . Ausoniae semper cedentia retro*). The Pageant of Heroes, after all, proceeds from his father's perception that Aeneas needs some extra motivation to be happy even after he has reached Italy.[51]

As for sleep and the visions therein, occurring in a context connected with Plato's *Republic*, note Socrates' stern words there (8.571C–D): visions of sleep are as pernicious as the false things seen in the Cave. It was Cicero who, transforming the true vision of Er into a dream, introduced this tension; Virgil's Gates of Sleep make us press it instead of resolving it. (Virgil likewise thus retroactively introduces this tension into the version of Aeneas' foundation given by Fabius Pictor, the first writer of Roman history, who—according to Cicero, who may have taken the passage as a model for his "Dream of Scipio" episode—said Aeneas foresaw in a dream everything that he did and experienced.)[52] Relevant also in the Platonic intertext is a philosophical commentary on the poetry itself: Socrates in the *Republic* is notoriously doubtful about the wholesomeness of poetry; the Cave parable comments on poetry as much as on other matters. Servius' interpretation of the exit through the Ivory Gate—that it means that everything Virgil has said is false[53]—is an extreme, unnuanced view that nevertheless resonates against a compelling philosophical reading of the poem. Some commentators suggestively see these gestures toward philosophy as a canny acknowledgment of the poet's betrayal of philosophical truth, subsuming both sides of the old *agôn* between poetry and philosophy that Plato speaks of.[54] Such a subsumption, however, retains as much tension as any the *Aeneid* offers us.

Let us not overlook the political implications of this intertext. Plato is talking about the superiority of a philosopher king over a democracy or a tyranny; Cicero is taking up Plato's argument and coming out in favor of a republic. What is Anchises' reading of all this? Among the kings, he portrays Ancus Marcius in a distinctly negative light, as "too fond of the favor of the populace" (6.816 *nimium gaudens popularibus auris*), apparently without historical justification. Feeney sees this characterization as a familial trope: in Republican times the Marcii gloried in their popular affinities and, no doubt, traced them

---

[51] 6.717–18 *hanc prolem cupio enumerare meorum, / quo magis Italia mecum laetere reperta* ("I desire to enumerate the progeny of my people, so that you may rejoice with me the more, now that Italy has been reached").

[52] Fabius Pictor *FGrH* 809 F 1 = Cicero *Div.* 1.43. Cf. Michels 1981:143. Fabius' version is also a precedent for the dream prophecies in *Aeneid* 4, 5, and 8.

[53] Servius on 898 "The poetic sense is plain: the poet wishes for everything he has said to be understood as false" (*et poetice apertus est sensus: vult autem intellegi falsa esse omnia quae dixit*). But *falsa* (from *fallere*) can mean something closer to "deceptive" or "disappointing" than "false"—see above on the disappointment of hopes for personal happiness in Anchises' lesson.

[54] This is the sum of West's interpretation of Gate of False Dreams (West 1987:13–15); cf. Bray on the Epicureanism of Anchises' account of Lethe.

to their eponymous ancestor. If so, Virgil has followed this tradition, but has Anchises find regrettable excess in Ancus' proclivities; this is the clearest hint in the catalogue of the class struggles that periodically divided Rome.[55] Anchises' provocative displacement of the hated King Tarquin's epithet *superbus* to the spirit of Brutus at 817 goes further, suggesting a comment on the potential tyranny of a republic, given the two faces of *superbia*. Against this background the *purpurei flores* that enrobe Marcellus recall the royal purple, like that of Eastern monarchs and Roman noblemen alike, which he would have worn as Augustus' heir.

In fact the whole poem presupposes kingship. This is not only the assumption for Aeneas' mode of rulership, but for that of Augustus as well.[56] In the apostrophe to Nisus and Euryalus at 9.449 *pater Romanus* could be a poetic singular for plural, amounting to a metonymy for the senate (the *patres conscripti*) and affirming a Republican form of government as the Roman norm;[57] but even so, the literal singular asserts itself as revaluing the idea of the senatorial *patres* as a single authority, a single man, inheriting a kind of *patria potestas* over the state. Lines 7.173–76 (on the Latin kings) tend to subordinate the *patres* to the kings and emphasize (in a historical imagining) the monarchical basis of consular power.

Yet the kingship of individuals is more of a trope for Roman power in this poem, as in Anchises' display, both of which, after all, are about a nation (*populus*) that will be *late rex*, literally "king far and wide" (1.21). Anchises' lesson insists on *imperium*. He makes Augustan conquests over the East the culmination of Roman history (6.794–805); his summary of Roman success is that the city "will make its empire equal to the whole earth, its spirit to heaven" (782 *imperium terris, animos aequabit Olympo*). Imperialism underlies his suggestion at 813–15 that "breaking *otia*," making war, is a good thing; indeed the pageant is overwhelmingly about Roman wars, and in light of its Trojan perspective desiderates a reconstitution of Trojan *imperium* on grander lines. Even his crucial rhetorical question to Aeneas "Do we still hesitate to extend our valor by deeds, or does fear keep us from settling on Ausonian land?" (806–807 *an dubitamus adhuc virtutem extendere factis, aut metus Ausonia prohibet consistere terra?*) has implications of territorial expansion. With Anchises' question compare Jupiter's admonition at 10.468–69 "to extend fame by deeds—this is the work of valor" (*famam extendere factis, hoc virtutis opus*), one of his consolations of Hercules over the dead Pallas. Anchises too binds his imperialist idea of Roman *virtus* closely with that of fame, as is seen most clearly in

---

[55] Feeney 1986:9–10. Compare the ideology of the poem's first simile (1.148–56). It is interesting to note that Ancus Marcius' *gens* was that of L. Marcius Philippus, Augustus' stepfather.

[56] The *Aeneid* constantly makes Augustus heir to Aeneas' role in terms of kingship. Cairns 1989 discusses kingship as a model or paradigm in the poem, with fruitful readings against Hellenistic kingship theory.

[57] Sabbadini 1889:33.

his lesson's success in kindling Aeneas' spirit "by love of the fame that was to come" (889). Whereas the "Dream of Scipio" downgrades the value of personal *fama* or *gloria* compared to service to one's country, the *Aeneid* makes Aeneas' lack of desire for it the obstacle to his mission.[58]

The threat to his mission would seem to lie in forgetting: forgetting the Trojan past, retaining no model for future glory. *Fama* ("renown," "reputation," "report," but most basically "speech") is closely connected with memory, as in those denizens of Elysium who "who by their deeds of merit made people remember them" (664 *quique sui memores aliquos fecere merendo*). Poetry is the supreme example of this *fama*, as the poet, speaking in his own voice, suggests in his blessing over Nisus and Euryalus: "If my song has any power, no day will ever remove you from the record of time" (9.446–47); he likewise breaks out of the narrative to address Lausus as "young man who shall be remembered" (10.793 *iuvenis memorande*), in reassuring him that his deeds will be part of the poem. Quint explores the "therapeutic effects of forgetting" for the mission of the Aeneadae: breaks with the past can permit progress; there is a "need to forget Troy and escape from a debilitating cycle of repetition."[59] This is one part of the process of repetition-with-variation that Quint traces in the poem, the process that culminates in the reversal of Trojan defeat. One thing Anchises aims to teach his son is what to forget and what to remember. When at 851 he appeals to Aeneas as a "Roman" and urges on him the Roman imperial mission, his words are "You, Roman, remember." For memory is the basis of any handing-down. It is the essence of the collaborations of metaphor and metonymy that are nations, communities of individuals identifying as a group, insisting on some shared experience among them, and of the history that can serve as the foremost such commonality. Memory is at the heart of etymology, etiology, even focalization—all the metaphorical tropes that bind past to present in the *Aeneid*, and bind persons into (or cut them out of) a nationality.[60] Memory is the essence of consciousness, individual or collective: a constant comparison of past selves, moment by moment. One would not be the same, in the afterlife or reincarnated, if one did not retain past memories. The poet begins the story of the *Aeneid* by asking the Muse to give him memory, to "remind him of the causes" (1.8), to bind past to future in the style of ktistic etiology. It is significant that what he specifically asks to be reminded of, in the interests of his whole project of distinguishing a Roman self, is not exactly the origins of Rome, but of Juno's hostility to Rome, which turns out primarily to involve the story of Carthage: the Muse's power here works through antitype. But memory does not first enter the *Aeneid* there at line 8. It has already come in at line 4,

---

[58] Cf. Jupiter at 4.232–34 (see p. 201 below).

[59] See Quint 1993:55–56, 63–65.

[60] The etymology at 5.117 of Memmius from Mnestheus (whose name comes from the Greek for "remember") signposts this possibility. See Feldherr 1995:259–61.

in "the remembering anger of savage Juno" (*saevae memorem Iunonis . . . iram*). The poet is asking for memory of memory: the interchange thickens, the interplay of comparison and contrast becomes multilayered, the *fama* of Roman origins becomes fraught with the image of their opposite.

The unstated irritant in the Underworld episode lurks in unanswered questions in the account of metempsychosis and the function of Lethe—in the relation between Anchises' philosophical account at 748–51 (his initial response to Aeneas' question about *dira cupido*) and his inspirational account of Roman history. Were these future Romans once other people? According to Anchises they must have been; now they have drunk of Lethe, and are waiting (some for many centuries) to reemerge on earth as new, Roman beings. The whole idea of Lethe is unsettling: it purges the soul of all individual memory (750 *immemores*) along with fears, desires, and so on. In this underpinning there is an easily imagined allegory—connected with the questions raised at the end of the last chapter—with the process of Roman imperialism that our whole experience here expounds: existing peoples will merge into Romans and forget their individual national histories; the nations that Rome subsumes will only achieve their full potential as components of the Roman empire. This is more than an allegory: as these future Romans were recently other people with their own individual and cultural memories, so actual Romans of Virgil's time had recently been, for example, Italians fighting against Rome for their liberty in the Social Wars. What happens to their cultural memories? Are they made over into Romans by some process analogous to Lethe? This is the flip side of Virgil's enlarged vision of Roman identity. "Roman" comprehends other nations at the expense of those other nations' individual characters (Ardea, of course, is a prime example).[61] This is the nation that Marcellus represents. Questions press: who was Marcellus? We know who he will—would—be; but who was he until he drank the water of Lethe? For that matter, who is he now, this sad-eyed boy apparently standing, silent and vacant, for a thousand years? Will he be somebody else after he dies, considering that he will never really accomplish any great feat to keep him in Elysium? Or is his potential alone enough to bring him back there for good?

The *dira cupido* that Aeneas inquires about at line 721 turns out to be, in Anchises' telling, this mass loss of individual memory, and the "love of the fame that was to come" that fires Aeneas as they end their survey of Elysium seems to wash him clean, too, of his Trojan identity. And yet as we have seen again and again in the *Aeneid*, Trojanness never ceases to play a part in Roman identity (let alone in Aeneas' identity); and those conquered peoples, too, constantly threaten to reassert themselves past the uniform Romanness that has enveloped them, and to resolve that Romanness into its elements. The "antiquity" of cities that we discussed in the previous chapter carries in its themes of

[61] Cf. Parry 1963:68–69, Toll 1991 and 1997, Henderson 2000, Johnson 2001.

identity and empire a similar tension between memory and oblivion: at 8.355–58 Evander describes the abandoned settlements of Janiculum and Saturnia as "the remnants and reminders of men of old" (356 *reliquias veterumque . . . monimenta virorum*). Even here something of their past existence persists, and the term "reminders" reminds us that poetry, the anti-Lethe, is the proper medium for this persistence, through the dialectic evoked by desires and counter-desires in the text. In this light the poem's Adonis-figures, who from some angles have seemed prefigurations of the enlarged Roman nationality, are subversive of that unity: they die as Arcadian, Volscian, Etruscan, Trojan, without giving the poem a chance to make them over fully into Romans, even proleptically.[62]

[62] Compare Antores, who, dying for Aeneas, "remembers sweet Argos" (10.781–82): memory represents an unassimilated Greek element in the inchoate nation.

Chapter Seven

AENEAS

We could pursue our question into many other parts of the *Aeneid*. We shall conclude by making one such extension, focusing on a figure around whom our discussion has often circled. Where does Aeneas stand? Lacking a final nationality, he most plainly embodies the desirer of the national identity that the poem aims at. His interest to us has lain in his viewership of two of our Adonis-scenes (as well as of Marcellus in Elysium), and more generally in his role as the peculiarly vague subjective focus of the epic. As we shall see, he also has something in common with objects of the poetic gaze: ambiguities of gender and sexuality alight on him at crucial moments (as on Turnus and the Euryalus-figures of the Italian war) and complicate his narratological role. His characteristic combination of activity and passivity may underlie the sense one often finds expressed in *Aeneid* criticism that he embodies a lack, an empty space, at the center of the poem. Here is Aeneas on the future site of Rome (8.310–12):

> miratur facilisque oculos fert omnia circum
> Aeneas capiturque locis et singula laetus
> exquiritque auditque virum monimenta priorum.

Aeneas stares in wonder, sending his ready glances everywhere. He is captivated by the scene, and joyfully inquires about and hears tales about each and every reminder of earlier men.

His gaze, troped as his curiosity and desire to satisfy visually his conspicuous (especially as seen from the proleptic frame) ignorance, is immediately further troped as his passivity: he *is captivated* by the place, its individual features, its past. This passivity—almost susceptibility, vulnerability—in turn leads to his questions and the explanations of Evander. Aeneas recapitulates Dido's desire to hear and know. The series of discrete settlements that Evander narrates— almost rather a series of caesurae, each followed by a brief, obscure population— mirrors the vacuum in the questioner, which mirrors that in us. One is unsure how to fill this space; that is, how to choose an authoritative standpoint whence to read the poem and its vision of Roman history. The following readings, illustrating the way scenes of viewership shape Aeneas' role in the *Aeneid*, will neither fill that central space nor give us a definitive perspective on the poem; rather, they will reaffirm the shiftiness of the poem's viewpoint on such matters as nationality, and find in Aeneas an emblem of that shiftiness.

I

The way that a gazing persona supervenes on that of Aeneas in the Lausus and Pallas scenes, introducing ideas (there erotic and ethnic) that seem partly to bypass him and to inform us, can be traced in his gaze even from Book 1. Aeneas' first explicit view in the poem begins at 1.113, during the storm at sea, shortly after his prayer:

> unam, quae Lycios fidumque vehebat Oronten,
> ipsius ante oculos ingens a vertice pontus
> 115 in puppim ferit: excutitur pronusque magister
> volvitur in caput, ast illam ter fluctus ibidem
> torquet agens circum et rapidus vorat aequore vertex.
> apparent rari nantes in gurgite vasto,
> arma virum tabulaeque et Troia gaza per undas.

One [ship], which carried the Lycians and faithful Orontes, the immense sea smites on the stern before his own eyes. The captain is thrown off and rolls forward, head first; the wave spins the ship around three times and the rapacious whirlpool swallows it into the sea. Scattered swimmers are visible upon the vast surf, men's weapons and planks[1] and Trojan treasure among the waves.

This is a scene of national devastation, containing the seeds of national reestablishment. In chapter 4 we noted the ktistic allegory suggested by the name of Orontes. The symbolic extrusion of Orientalness from this group of former Trojans is underscored by Orontes' epithet *fidus*, soon (first in line 188) to become the epithet of Aeneas' constant companion Achates, who in this passage (120) bears the more neutral epithet *fortis*, "brave." Aeneas, of course, cannot grasp the national symbolism of this tragedy; but he does see the newly reacquired "Trojan treasure" scattered among the waves, his homeland sacked anew. Here is anticipated the wealth of Dido that will recall the lost wealth of Priam, appearing to Aeneas as a piercing reminder of the grandeur that his people once had, and simultaneously to the reader as a sign that Carthage is a detour from the true trajectory of Aeneas' nationhood and must be given up, like Troy, for a new land. This first viewership of his epitomizes a characteristic split, throughout the poem to follow, between the historical significance of what he sees and his personal reactions to it. One might recall his responses to the Pageant of Heroes in the Underworld and especially to his Shield at the very end of Book 8 (at 2.604–20 he will relate an occasion when Venus, revealing to him the gods working Troy's ruin, gives him a fuller vision for

---

[1] An anonymous reader points out to me that if *tabulae* refers not to planks from the ships but to paintings from among the treasure, we see Aeneas looking at images—ancestral portraits?—but are not permitted his view or interpretation of them (as we are in the ecphrases at 1.450–93 and 6.14–33).

once). Here in the storm, an allegory of incipient nationhood plays itself out before his eyes, yet he sees only the death of a faithful companion, made even more painful by a fresh dispersal of his city.

But it is not just that Aeneas characteristically has incomplete vision on the poem's scenes of national importance, and that our (historically and intertextually informed) view and reactions diverge from and complement his focalization. Notice how his view is curtailed—how it emerges from the text, signaled by "before his own eyes" (*ipsius ante oculos*), is picked up by "are visible" (*apparent*), and then subsides into the heaving narrative, rapidly losing affect, without leaving a distinct impression of Aeneas' attitude. The passage quoted above continues with a description, from no particular viewpoint, of the foundering of four other ships. Soon the perspective has shifted, and Neptune, *graviter commotus* (126 "gravely troubled"), has taken command of the viewpoint (literally at 127 *prospiciens* and 129 *videt*). This is also typical; one recalls the evaporation of Aeneas' viewership in the two Adonis-scenes where he is the viewer. His particular gaze seems to lose its hold on ours and yield to or dissolve into an unattached gaze without a turn signaled by the narrative. Once the verbs of seeing have stopped coming we may still be seeing with his eyes, but no sign remains that the attitudes implicit in the text are his. A similar drift occurs in the Underworld: we start seeing the ghostly heroines with Aeneas (6.446 *cernit*), so that when Dido appears we may well conceive that we are seeing her with his eyes (an explicit sign of his viewing comes at 452 *agnovitque*, parallel to the beholder in the simile: 454 *aut videt aut vidisse putat*); later with him we see the ghostly Trojans (482 *cernens*, 487 *vidisse*) and Deiphobus (495 *videt*). In between these explicit coincidences, the narrative gives no special sign of imparting his reactions or mood; most strikingly, Dido, receiving his words in marmoreal silence and stalking away, once again imposes her own reaction to Aeneas on the narrative. Is she seizing the narrative viewpoint here, edging him out, or is he still focalizing, assimilating her gaze on him? The viewpoint of Aeneas is too capacious, too easily diluted.

The second sustained view of his starts at 1.180:

> 180 Aeneas scopulum interea conscendit, et omnem
> prospectum late pelago petit, Anthea si quem
> iactatum vento videat Phrygiasque biremis
> aut Capyn aut celsis in puppibus arma Caici.
> navem in conspectu nullam, tris litore cervos
> 185 prospicit errantis; hos tota armenta sequuntur
> a tergo et longum per vallis pascitur agmen.
> constitit hic arcumque manu celerisque sagittas
> corripuit fidus quae tela gerebat Achates.

In the meantime Aeneas mounts a cliff and seeks the whole wide view over the sea, in case he might see some sign of Antheus, buffeted by the wind, and the Phrygian ships or Capys or the armor of Caicus upon the high stern. He spies no ship, but sees three stags wandering on the shore. ~~Behind them whole herds are following, and a long array is browsing~~ through the valleys. He stopped and took in hand the bow and swift arrows, the weapons that faithful Achates was carrying.

The description starts out imperious, but the narration is not in character: there is no embedded focalization or free indirect discourse. We share no more than his view; and if not for the visual element in *agmen*, "array" (186), the browsing deer might threaten to draw the viewpoint to themselves. There is much more of Jupiter in the similar scene a few dozen lines later (1.223–26):

> et iam finis erat, cum Iuppiter aethere summo
> despiciens mare velivolum terrasque iacentis
> litoraque et latos populos, sic vertice caeli
> constitit et Libyae defixit lumina regnis.

And now it was at an end, when Jupiter, looking down from highest heaven upon the sail-winged sea and the lands that lay there, and the shores and widespread peoples, settled on the peak of the sky and fixed his eyes on the realm of Libya below.

Here is a viewpoint whence to rule and conceptualize. It makes one wonder to what extent, in limning any viewpoint, a poet intrinsically emulates and simultaneously creates a god. The string of objects with their modifiers (especially *iacentis*) does not just record the view, but seems to instill the god's easy mastery, which the two *de-* prefixes ("down," "below") also reinforce. The reminiscence of Ennius in "sail-winged," *velivolum*,[2] announcing to the reader a national, historical scene, resonates well in Jupiter's own designs, as we soon learn. One is reminded of another Ennian scene: Jupiter at *Euhemerus* fr. 6 Vahlen "widely contemplating the earth" and heaven (*contemplatus est late terras . . . suspexit in caelum*) from the mountain called "the Seat of Uranus" (*sella Caeli*) upon seizing control of the world from Saturn.[3] Jupiter's gaze is described again at *Aeneid* 10.3–4, when he calls the gods to council in the "starry seat" (*sideream sedem*) from which he looks onto the whole earth and the opposed camps of Trojans and Latins.

The power implicit in a height comes out in scenes like that in which Turnus sights his victim, Pallas, from a rise in the ground (10.454, where he is compared to a lion seeing its prey "from a high vantage point"). Such heights,

---

[2] See Ennius *Andromacha* fr. 8 Ribbeck and especially *Annales* 379–80 Skutsch (on Rome's war with Antiochus III of Syria; note the expressed viewpoint) *quom procul aspiciunt hostes accedere ventis / navibus velivolis*, "when they spied the enemy approaching under the wind in sail-winged ships." The term was later used by Laevius fr. 11 Courtney (in a poem titled *Helen*) and Lucretius 5.1442.

[3] On this passage Courtney 1999:33 notes that "The notion of looking down from a height on humanity . . . was much used in Cynic literature and was probably popularized by Menippus," giving citations. On Zeus' view from a height in Homer, philosophy, and Orphic poetry, see West 1983:215. Lucian *Hist. conscr.* 49 compares Zeus' gaze to that of a historian (cf. Walker 1993, on *enargeia*).

in fact, are metaphors for the vantage point on the world that the Romans them-selves will have.[4] In the transition from Trojan to Roman, the "ramparts of high Rome" (1.7 *altae moenia Romae*) will replace and more than compensate for "the high ramparts of Troy" (3.322 *Troiae sub moenibus altis*).[5] Indeed, we could explore the metaphor of "height" as we did "antiquity" in chapter 5, as an inher-ited quality, so to speak, carrying a complex of themes and permitting a com-parative interchange of cities, or as in chapter 4 we compared as false Romes or misguided proto-Romes the different physical, architectural recreations of Troy that the poem offers. Troy is emphatically high. When at 4.312 Dido asks Aeneas what he would be doing "if ancient Troy were still remaining" (*Troia antiqua maneret*), she is assimilating and conflating his characterizations of the city at 2.363 *urbs antiqua* and 56 *Troiaque nunc staret Priamique arx alta maneret* ("and Troy would still be standing and the high citadel of Priam would abide [had not the gods opposed it]"). To her he responds that if fate permitted, "Priam's high halls would abide" (4.343 *Priami tecta alta manerent*). Carthage itself is *alta* at 4.97 (in the words of Juno) and 265 (in those of Mercury): a potential substitute for Troy (and Rome). At 10.374 Pallanteum, on the same site as "high Rome" (and specifically on the same eminence as the residence of Augustus), is Pallas' "high homeland," *patria alta*. Latinus' city presents "lofty buildings" (*ardua tecta*) to the approaching Trojans at 7.160–61 and likewise to Allecto at 342–43 (*tecta . . . celsa*). Compare the "lofty dwelling" in Ardea (7.413 *tectis in altis*) where we first encounter Turnus—indeed, note the potential pun between "Ardea" and *ardua*, "lofty, towering, steep."[6] Implicit in the shared height of these cities is their similar vantage point. Even the settlement of Helenus and Andromache at Buthrotum is announced as a "lofty city" by Aeneas (3.293 *celsam Buthroti accedimus urbem*): it has both a protected position and a view like Troy's, to dominate the little plain of the substitute Simois and Xanthus.

Another view from a height is the Pageant of Heroes in Book 6, which Anchises "reads" (*legere*, which can mean "read" or "select") to Aeneas from a hill (6.752–55):

> dixerat Anchises natumque unaque Sibyllam
> conventus trahit in medios turbamque sonantem,

---

[4] Cf. Fredrick 1995:269 on the ideology of a commanding view from a wealthy man's villa (and by his extension of one painted on a wall inside): "The studies of Bek, Clarke, Dwyer, and Wallace-Hadrill have shown that power and status were strongly associated in the Roman house with a privileged view: . . . or the view of landscape and sea from the luxury villa." Cf. Bergmann 1991, Newlands 2002:172–74.

[5] A textual consideration: *altae* at line end (yielding the sense "ramparts of high Troy") would make the phrase even closer to that in 1.7, and would be liable to corruption to the abl. after *moenibus*. The name of Corythus, the Dardanids' ancestral place (see pp. 10–12), through its connection with Greek *korus* (genitive *koruthos*), "helmet," also carries the suggestion of a settlement situated on a height.

[6] On the pun see Maltby 1991:48–49, O'Hara 1996:190 (it is noted by Servius on 7.412). Some further, passing examples are the "high homeland" of Arruns (11.797 *patria alta*) and the "lofty cities" whence the Tiber rises (8.65 *celsis urbibus*)—both in the hill country of Etruria.

et tumulum capit unde omnis longo ordine posset
~~adversos legere et venientum discere vultus.~~

Having spoken [of the the wish of the spirits to return to earthly bodies],
Anchises leads his son together with the Sibyl into the middle of the
gathering and the noisy crowd, and occupies a mound whence he might
read all comers in a long series and teach [his guests] about the faces of
those who approached.

Intertextually, Anchises' modest hill replicates the far greater height of heaven
in Cicero's "Dream of Scipio," whence Scipio looks down upon the earth—to
the vexation of his grandfather, who urges him to direct his gaze rather to the
realities of heaven (just as he warns young Scipio away from the *gloria* of
human fame that is the precise object of Anchises' instruction). The Scipios'
view is that of Jupiter, and the knowledge they impart figures the power of
the godlike philosopher. So, in a smaller way, does the hill from which Anchises
surveys and imparts his eschatological philosophy; but in a programmatic
addition to the Ciceronian model, his vantage point is also a temporal vantage
point: Anchises views (and speaks) from the standpoint of the Augustan
empire.[7] A place is troped as a time, the consummation of Roman history (one
recalls the spatio-temporal prolepsis in 1.13–14 *Italiam contra Tiberinaque
longe / ostia*, discussed on p. 130). The suggestion of such a temporal vantage
point is also present in Jupiter's gaze at 1.223–26, since the lines that follow
recount his prophetic speech to Venus.

Another view from a height illustrates the way Dido's viewership, as we
remarked in chapter 3, tends to involve her own feelings more insistently than
that of Aeneas does. The ant simile at 4.402–405 (on which see pp. 98–99) is
followed by a more definitive account of Dido's viewership (408–15):

> quis tibi tum, Dido, cernenti talia sensus,
> quosve dabas gemitus, cum litora fervere late
> 410 prospiceres arce ex summa, totumque videres
> misceri ante oculos tantis clamoribus aequor?
> improbe Amor, quid non mortalia pectora cogis?
> ire iterum in lacrimas, iterum temptare precando
> cogitur et supplex animos summittere amori,
> 415 ne quid inexpertum frustra moritura relinquat.

What feelings did you have then, Dido, as you watched such a scene;
what groans did you utter, when from the top of your citadel you per-
ceived the shore seething far and wide, and saw before your eyes the

---

[7] The elder Scipio, to be sure, accurately predicts his grandson's future life. Leach 1999:114 suggests that Anchises' pageant demands that the reader become a new kind of spectator, with "a new
kind of involvement suitable to the transition Aeneas himself is making" (cf. 117). We should
insist upon the ideological aspect of this spectatorship.

whole sea disturbed with great shouts? Cruel Love, to what extreme do you not force mortal hearts? She is driven to fall back into tears, to entreat him again with prayers and subject her spirit in supplication to love, so as not to leave anything untried and die in vain.

Here is another broad prospect (*late prospiceres*) from on high, but one whose subject, gazing on a scene whose description foreshadows Roman conquest, herself feels a helpless victim. Yet Dido colonizes the narrative. The apostrophe, which necessarily distances her from the narrator and reader, nevertheless imparts to the reader the narrator's urge to understand, sympathize with, assimilate her feelings at this sight, as well as to share her literal view on the scene. The feelings, themselves unstated, thus emerge with peculiar vividness, especially in the knowing exclamation *improbe Amor* and the recitation of her final, desperate actions. Aeneas' mindset throughout the exchanges of this book, by contrast, are so elusive that critics can argue (for example) over whether he "really loves" Dido or not.

A telling example of Aeneas' evanescent, or diluted, viewpoint occurs in his own narration at 2.483–84. Pyrrhus breaks his way into the royal palace of Troy: "There appears the interior of the house, and long halls open up [before him]; there appear the inner quarters of Priam and the kings of old" (*apparet domus intus et atria longa patescunt; / apparent Priami et veterum penetralia regum*). We have a right to doubt whether Aeneas is describing something he could see from his rooftop perch; in any case, the viewpoint is far more suited to Pyrrhus. Then it swings around to the Trojan inmates: "they see them standing in full armor on the first threshold" (485 *armatosque vident stantis in limine primo*). On the one hand, we could say that Virgil temporarily removes the authority for viewpoint from Aeneas and gives it to Pyrrhus, then to the Trojans in the palace.[8] On the other hand, if Aeneas is narrator, how does Pyrrhus become the focalizer? Aeneas must be imagining Pyrrhus' view, then the Trojans'; now the questions arise thick and fast over Aeneas' shifting self-identification at this catastrophic moment, his fluid drawing and redrawing of the boundaries between self, enemy, and ally. And what of the bestowal of this viewpoint on Dido, the reader's proxy as audience? And what of Virgil, the prime viewer behind all these masks? Concern over focalization is left behind as it ramifies and transmutes into concern over other problems in the narrative.

There are two sides to Aeneas' focalizing capacity. If his view is characteristically an almost passive organ—capacious to the point of obliteration, potentially dissolving into that of others—it is in the same regard a colonizing force analogous to the colonist he is and the Roman imperialist he prefigures, suggestively melding the gaze of others to itself. Even if the final episode of Book 12 shows much more of Turnus' viewpoint than Aeneas', and Turnus' subjectivity threatens to replace that of his conqueror, this is not a final, negative

---

[8] Cf. Kenney 1979:116 and 228 n. 55.

verdict on Aeneas' focalizing power. He is a kind of cipher, but perhaps only because he is so often a proxy for ourselves, seeing what we must see and identifying and symphathizing with characters (like Dido) whose aims are in conflict with his. If Aeneas' gaze seldom seems to stick, if it vanishes into the narrative or gives way to the gaze of this or that other character, that does not necessarily make Aeneas a weak, certainly not an unmemorable or unsympathetic character. Let us say rather that, as a focalizer, he is more open than other characters, as perhaps befits the central character of a poem that takes in so many personalities and attitudes, and the founder of a race that must—in the picture of Roman nationhood that the *Aeneid* offers—somehow encompass the whole world, and provide a common national identity to members of many races. Such a role demands of a character an almost vanishingly broad capacity.

We have come close to saying that Aeneas' is a kind of default focalization in the poem, to be invoked whenever another is not readily forthcoming. This would be mistaken; quite apart from the difficulty of places where the tenor of the narrative is clearly at odds with Aeneas' sympathies, the positivism in such a fingering of viewpoint—the need to attach the gazing persona always to a specific character—is, once again, too ham-handed for Virgil's metaphoric of narrative personae. Yet it is possible to speak, more tentatively, of a passive-aggressiveness in his viewpoint, a recessiveness that on the one hand yields the scene to other viewpoints and attitudes, but on the other does not plainly disappear altogether. We observed something like this in the welcoming scene at Carthage in Book 1. When Dido enters the scene Aeneas is the explicit viewer (of the decorations on the temple: 494–95); his view expressly picks up again at 510, where he sees (*videt*) his fellow Trojans approach. Even there he shares the focalization with Achates, whose emotions are indeed more clearly expressed than his are.[9] Can Aeneas see the activities inside the temple? Or how does the poetic gaze here map onto his? As he observes, unseen, the speeches between Ilioneus and Dido, the reception she gives his people reprises and confirms all the hopes he expressed in the preceding lines, keeping his viewpoint in our minds and making us imagine his relief—in fact, making us impersonate Aeneas by generating specifically his reactions—until his consciousness returns explicitly to the text at line 580. This is not to impute omniscience to Aeneas; the often-noted irony in the setting—his divine enemy's temple—should alone remind us of the limits of his awareness in this scene. Rather, it is always worth observing the seepage of Aeneas' attitudes into, or difficulty of excluding them from, parts of the narrative where they are not explicitly signaled.

[9] 1.513–15 *obstipuit simul ipse, simul percussus Achates / laetitiaque metuque; avidi coniungere dextras / ardebant, sed res animos incognita turbat* ("He himself was dumbstruck, and at the same time Achates was smitten with both joy and fear. They burned with eager desire to join hands [with the other Trojans], but the uncertainty of the situation troubled their minds").

Herein lies part of his strangely blunted portrayal in the poem. There is no need to rehearse the complaints of readers who find him regrettably colorless, unsympathetic, and devoid of personality for the hero of an epic poem. In his own narration in Books 2 and 3 he often seems to miss the chance to impress us with his own view of things (in contrast to the Odysseus of the *Odyssey*, whose four books of narration are so strong that one tends to remember the other twenty by his lights); as in the Pyrrhus scene, this vagueness can some-times be plotted naratologically. If in Books 2 and 3 the vanishingly capacious narrative persona that he gives himself serves a rhetorical purpose, gathering in the whole story from all sides, elsewhere in the poem the focalizing persona he is given accommodates other necessary ironies. Lyne, noticing that Aeneas is often cut off in speech, hears "further voices" intrude upon his.[10] The inter-views with Dido in Book 4 leave him speechless, as also does his last meeting with her in the Underworld. Perhaps we can construe these silences as open-ings for new voices or feelings.

Another example from the Underworld episode shows how his responses, foreclosed on the surface of the narrative, can impose themselves nonetheless. His vain wish at 6.697–702 to embrace his father (for whom he had come down) is fraught with the desires he has entertained throughout the poem:

> "da iungere dextram,
> da, genitor, teque amplexu ne subtrahe nostro."
> sic memorans largo fletu simul ora rigabat.
> ter conatus ibi collo dare bracchia circum;
> ter frustra comprensa manus effugit imago,
> par levibus ventis volucrique simillima somno.

"Let me join hands, let me, father, and do not withdraw fom my embrace." Speaking thus, he simultaneously drenched his face with copious tears. There and then he tried thrice to put his arms around his neck; thrice the simulacrum, grasped in vain, escaped from his hands like sporting winds or a fleeting dream.

Aeneas is thereupon deluded of an embrace for the third time (after his meet-ings with Creusa's ghost at 2.792–94 and Venus at 1.407–409). What is remarkable, but altogether characteristic, is that the text reports no reaction on his part, but simply resumes the narrative at 6.703 with Aeneas' view of the valley of Lethe (*interea videt Aeneas. . .*).[11] This explicit view, however, should signal that his attitude is not far away, and indeed his melancholy returns as suddenly as the sight of his father had raised his spirits. We soon find him

---

[10] Lyne 1987:55–56; cf. Feeney 1990:176–77. Aeneas himself cuts off a victim's speech at 10.599.

[11] This narrative omission is especially noteworthy in contrast with the conversation between Odysseus and Anticlea on the emotional effects and physiological causes of the failed embrace in Virgil's model (*Od.* 11.209–24).

horrified, for some reason, at the sight (710 *horrescit visu*) of the spirits floating and flitting on the riverbank, and asking what "terrible desire" drives them
"to revert again to slow bodies" (720–21). The sluggishness of his own body
must still be on his mind, coloring his reaction to all he sees. His feelings are
vividly imaginable, though not plainly expressed in the text.

Perhaps we can now cast a fresh eye on the Adonis-scenes that he explicitly
views and understand his role in them better. We have already noted (in
chapter 1) the narratological complications inherent in his gaze on the corpse
of Pallas—the possible insinuation of the viewpoint of the mourning Trojan
women, sympathetically assimilated by Aeneas—and warned that a reader
attentive to the rhetoric of focalization will leave such complications open, and
not let them explain definitively the unexpected sensual imagery. When
Aeneas, saying *miserande puer* over Lausus and Pallas (10.825, 11.42), echoes
his father over Marcellus (6.882), he announces another such assimilation. In
the case of Pallas, *lacrimis ita fatur obortis* at the end of 11.41 echoes the opening of Anchises' speech, *lacrimis ingressus obortis*, at 6.867: Aeneas over Pallas
telescopes his father's lament over Marcellus. He expresses his view on the
deaths of Lausus and Pallas with Anchises' words over Marcellus, thus assimilating his father's sense of sorrow for a lost paradigm of Roman heroism and
casting each boy, Etruscan and Arcadian, as a prototypical Roman (though
with his limited knowledge he would not describe them that way). His viewpoint tropes generational succession and the crucial transmission of culture
and ideals from Troy to Italy and down to the future nation: he has accepted
Anchises' viewpoint on the Pageant of Heroes and in a sense taken on the role
of his father.[12] The heavy emphasis on Lausus' and Pallas' fathers in the narrative (and particularly in Aeneas' own words) underscores the importance of
paternity here, and in the Lausus passage Aeneas' parallel to the boy is brought
out by his designation as *Anchisiades* (10.822), as the humanist de la Cerda
noticed long ago.[13] Aeneas' viewpoint does not just carry a message about him
or its objects; it *is* a message about the transmission from Troy to Rome.

And since we are exploring viewpoint as metaphor there is no warrant to
ignore the slippage between his father's view in Book 6 and his own in these
places, or to ignore the transformation that a handing down inevitably entails:
that too is part of the message. Let us consider more closely the thoughts to
which the sight of snowy Pallas' smooth, mortally wounded chest move him
(11.42–58):

> "tene," inquit "miserande puer, cum laeta veniret,
> invidit Fortuna mihi, ne regna videres
> nostra neque ad sedes victor veherere paternas?
> 45 non haec Evandro de te promissa parenti

---

[12] Reed 2001:148–49, 163–64.
[13] Johnson 1976:72–73; cf. Clausen 2002:207, with n. 56.

discedens dederam, cum me complexus euntem
mitteret in magnum imperium metuensque moneret
acris esse viros, cum dura proelia gente.
et nunc ille quidem spe multum captus inani
50   fors et vota facit cumulatque altaria donis,
nos iuvenem exanimum et nil iam caelestibus ullis
debentem vano maesti comitamur honore.
infelix, nati funus crudele videbis!
hi nostri reditus exspectatique triumphi?
55   haec mea magna fides? at non, Evandre, pudendis
vulneribus pulsum aspicies, nec sospite dirum
optabis nato funus pater. ei mihi quantum
praesidium, Ausonia, et quantum tu perdis, Iule!"

"Has Fortune then begrudged me you," he said, "pitiable boy, though she
came in happiness, so that you would not see my realm or be conveyed
back to your father's home victorious? This is not what I promised your
father Evander concerning you as I departed, when he embraced me as I
went away and sent me upon a great mission of command, and fearfully
warned me that these were fierce men, that the battle was with a tough
people. Even now, held by an empty hope, he may be making vows and
piling altars with gifts; while we in sorrow and with empty pomp attend a
lifeless boy who owes nothing more to any powers of heaven. Unhappy
man, you will see the cruel funeral of your son! Is this the homecoming
and triumphal procession you looked forward to? Is this the great trust you
placed in me? Yet never, Evander, will you look upon a boy struck down
by a shameful wound nor will you pray for accursed death because of your
son's survival. Alas, what a bulwark you lose, Ausonia, and you, Iulus!"

(Let it be noted that after this speech, as usual, clear signs of Aeneas' feelings
disappear from the narrative.)

In addressing Pallas as *miserande puer*, Aeneas (with perhaps no more than
partial understanding of what he is doing) is potentially casting him as such a
youth, full of thwarted promise, as Marcellus is to Anchises, a lost hope of his
family line and of his nation. Indeed he strikes all these notes in the speech,
and in so doing echoes even more of his father's speech in Book 6. Line 53
infelix, nati funus crudele videbis! ("Unhappy man, you will see the cruel funeral
of your son!") is a reminiscence of Anchises over Brutus, executioner of his
own sons (6.822): *infelix, utcumque ferent ea facta minores* ("unhappy, however
posterity will judge his deed"); it also picks up the various other deaths of sons,
sometimes at their fathers' hands, in the Pageant of Heroes. Aeneas begins
with regret that Pallas will not live to see his regime and ends with regret for
the loss suffered by Italy and Iulus: a nod to the coming order, not as farsighted
as Anchises' extravaganza, but Anchises-like in its quasi-proleptic form and

near-tendentiousness.[14] He has accepted his father's lesson about the Roman future (as 6.889 suggested: *incenditque animum famae venientis amore*; Anchises "kindled his son's spirit with love of the coming fame").[15] Yet in this mimesis—or better, synthesis—his own earlier melancholy abides. It is the tearfulness of his father's message that he seems to have taken most to heart; his words on "sorrow" and "empty pomp" set this tone, and his vision of the beguiled old man "piling up altars with gifts" in "empty hope" is a projection of Anchises' final words on Marcellus: "I will heap up the soul of my descendant with these gifts at least, and fulfill the empty duty" (6.884–86 *animamque nepotis / his saltem accumulem donis, et fungar inani / munere*).

The whole speech (or the mindset behind it) is structured by a sort of generational syllepsis, most clearly suggested by his understandable obsession with Evander's reaction and his own sense of guilt and need to justify himself. The apostrophe beginning at 56 *Evandre* should be remarked on: it is as if he were already rehearsing what he will say to the stricken father. Oddities abound in the reminiscences. We never heard, at their departure from Pallanteum in Book 8, that Evander embraced Aeneas, or that he sent him on a mission of command, or that he gave him any particular information about the Rutulian host, or that Aeneas made Evander any promises concerning Pallas. All of this might have happened, yet the text at that point does not encourage us to think it did (8.554–84). What Aeneas remembers sounds much more like his departure in the Underworld from Anchises, who did give him detailed warnings about the coming war and the peoples of Latium (6.890–92), and who most certainly did send him on a mission of command. In his lament over Pallas, Aeneas combines the foreknowledge of the father with the anxiety of the son—this is one face of the synthesis, one form that his capacity for focalization takes here. Even more mysteriously, his dubious recollections appropriate the embrace (substituting here for the embrace his father could not give him?) and words that Pallas received from Evander at 8.558–84, as if he were taking on the identity and responsibilities of the boy whose body lies before him. He seems to reverse the mirroring envisioned by Evander as he commits his son to Aeneas' care (8.514–17):

> "hunc tibi praeterea, spes et solacia nostri,
> Pallanta adiungam; sub te tolerare magistro
> militiam et grave Martis opus, tua cernere facta
> adsuescat, primis et te miretur ab annis."

[14] Whom is he teaching? His addressee is dead, and bystanders are underemphasized; it is as if he were reviewing his father's instruction to himself.

[15] Cf. 11.24–26 *"ite" ait "egregias animas, quae sanguine nobis / hanc patriam peperere suo, decorate supremis / muneribus"* ("'Go,' he said, 'adorn with the supreme rites these extraordinary spirits who have brought forth for us this homeland by their blood'"), which picks up Anchises' promise of a new polity.

"In addition, to you I will attach Pallas, our hope and consolation. Under your tutelage let him learn to endure warfare and the grievous work of Mars, to observe your deeds; and let him look upon you from his early youth."

Even as Aeneas takes on the role of Anchises over Marcellus, his lament in Book 11 remembers and conflates the words of his own and of Pallas' father, and responds to them with the doubly heavy consciousness of a son mindful of duty.

At this point we might revisit and test the relationship between Aeneas' literal view on the dead Pallas and the desirous gaze of the virtual viewer. To ascribe that gaze to Aeneas, making him for the moment a desirer or lover of Pallas, not only heightens the sense of loss at the latter's death, but rings true against a certain subtext of the poem, again involving a generational syllepsis. Putnam (1985) comes very close to affirming that Aeneas does love Pallas; that might be too literal a reading of the signs of Aeneas' affection, but Putnam is probably right to read in Pallas' affection for Aeneas, signaled everywhere by nuptial language and imagery, a boyish crush. Lloyd so interprets, convincingly, Evander's remembrance of his own youthful feelings for Anchises when they met in Arcadia: "My mind was on fire with a young man's love to call out to the man. . . . I went up to him and, full of desire, led him to the walls of Pheneus' city" and so on (8.163–65 *mihi mens iuvenali ardebat amore / compellare virum . . . accessi et cupidus Phenei sub moenia duxi*). Evander's words, saturated with the topoi of *amor* and the *sermo amatorius*, forewarn us (and Aeneas) how to understand Pallas' attitude. It is interesting that in both pairs the younger man makes the first move. This is not what we expect from the conventions of a Greek-style paiderastic relationship, but it emphasizes the ardor of Evander and Pallas respectively for Anchises and Aeneas, and also recalls the admiration of Euryalus toward Nisus. To set Aeneas in the role of a loving gazer upon a desirable young man (a role like that of Nisus) allows him to assimilate the viewpoint of Pallas on their relationship, and thus to emphasize again the breadth of his focalizing sympathies. That this happens on Pallas' death underscores the consummational nature of this exchange of personae, its eulogistic nature, the way it enforces teleology and hindsight (analogously to Aeneas' reworking of Anchises' speech over Marcellus).

The openness of Aeneas' focalization facilitates these speculations, some of which simply lead to suggestions that lead to more suggestions before vanishing, while others send the reader into an inescapable loop of potentially assimilable personae. It is paramount, however, for one who reads the *Aeneid* rhetorically to forbear simply to accept exchanges of personae without reading primarily the points of interchange: metaphor is not synecdoche, and Pallas, for example, does not in *all* respects reward reading as a trope on Aeneas (or on Dido, or on any of his fellow Adonis-figures). In any such reading, the cooperation of similarity and difference yields a message of its own. With this warning in mind we can extend the assimilation between Pallas and Aeneas a little further. Commentators discern an Iliadic subtext in the climax of the poem: Aeneas has become Achilles, killing Turnus who has become Hector, to avenge Pallas who is Patroclus—whose armor the slayer is wearing. We should add the further Iliadic equation, the sense that Achilles is destroying himself, both literally and figuratively (because Hector is wearing Achilles' own armor, borrowed by the ill-fated Patroclus).[16] This intertextual note might not resonate in the *Aeneid* were it not for Aeneas' implicit, fleeting identification with Pallas in Book 11, picked up by 12.948–49 (*Pallas te hoc vulnere, Pallas immolat* etc.); as it is, it resonates enough to urge a pointed contrast between the death wish of the *Iliad* and the nation-founding climax of the *Aeneid*. Aeneas seems to have assumed on behalf of Pallas the savagery of Dido's curse (4.607–29), bending it to his own mission. The token of this multiple interchange, the swordbelt engraved with the Danaids and the slaughtered sons of Aegyptus, stamps it yet more clearly with implications of dynastic frustration and an East-West ktistic death match. What stimulates the identification with Pallas is Aeneas' sight of the belt (12.941 *apparuit*, 945–46 *oculis . . . hausit*), which simultaneously—however much Aeneas and Turnus may otherwise function as doublets in the poem (in their half-mortal, half-divine parentage; their tortuous ancestral origins; their slow exchange of roles as Achilles-figure and Hector-figure)—casts Turnus far across the boundary line of identity for Aeneas, and puts an end both to the assimilation with himself that Turnus' final speech had awakened and to the poem.[17]

II

In the passages quoted above, Aeneas' responses, the attitudes ascribed to him or otherwise attributable to him, are usually melancholy. More: he tends to respond to events reflexively, with self-pity, always with some implied consciousness not just of sorrow, but of himself as a victim. Such is the import of his remarks on the "slow bodies" and of his reproaches to Venus in Book 1; an anxious defensiveness about his own circumstances is also traceable, for example, in his response to the loss of Palinurus (5.869–71).[18] This tone is especially evident in the first half of the poem (and might therefore be supposed to have found a bracing remedy in Anchises' lesson), but it perhaps most memorably comes out in his words to Ascanius before he goes to battle with Turnus: "My

[16] Cf. Gould 1990:101–102.

[17] On Aeneas' assimilation to Turnus see Thomas 1998 and Quint 1993:79–80, who—warning us against finding definitive closure here—interprets Aeneas as killing his mirror image in a scene premonitory of civil war.

[18] Reed 2001:149–50.

boy, learn valor and true toil from me—fortune from others" (12.435–36 *disce, puer, virtutem ex me verumque laborem, / fortunam ex aliis*). It is noteworthy that this self-consciousness has a narratological correlative in his treatment as both subject and object of a gaze (reminiscent of the case of Dido), and also a thematic correlative: the themes of generational succession, nation building, and ethnic difference operate through the metaphor of love in scenes that superimpose on him the persona of a lovelorn heroine of Hellenistic epic.

A complex example comes at 8.18–30, after a few lines about the beginnings of the Italian War:

> talia per Latium. quae Laomedontius heros
> cuncta videns magno curarum fluctuat aestu,
> 20   atque animum nunc huc celerem nunc dividit illuc
> in partisque rapit varias perque omnia versat,
> sicut aquae tremulum labris ubi lumen aënis
> sole repercussum aut radiantis imagine lunae
> omnia pervolitat late loca, iamque sub auras
> 25   erigitur summique ferit laquearia tecti.

Such things were taking place in Latium, and the Laomedontian hero, seeing it all, fluctuates on a great surge of anxieties, and splits his swift thoughts now one way, now another, sending them swiftly in various directions and putting them through every turn, as when the wavering light cast by water within a brazen rim, reflected by the sun or by the image of the beaming moon, flitters through every nook and cranny far and wide, and now rises aloft and strikes the uppermost panels of the ceiling.

The bizarrely concrete metaphors for thought in lines 20–21, the core of his distress ("and divides his swift thoughts . . . and puts them through all turns"— he is like a virtuosic animal trainer), repeat 4.285–86, where Aeneas worries over his stay in Carthage and the gods' commands to leave. But as in that place the proximity of Dido's own sleepless worry (4.80–85) invites comparison and contrast, around this passage the text elaborates an image that melds him with Dido in her distressed-heroine persona:[19] line 19 *magno curarum fluctuat aestu* picks up Dido at 4.531–32 *ingeminant curae rursusque resurgens / saevit amor magnoque irarum fluctuat aestu* ("her anguish redoubles, and love, flooding back, rages and fluctuates on a great surge of anger")—via Ariadne at Catullus 64.62 *magnis curarum fluctuat undis* ("she fluctuates on great waves of anguish").[20] Note the revaluation of *curae* at 8.19, from "anguish" in the sense "love cares" in the

---

[19] Cf. Lyne 1987:125–32 (who holds that in these echoes of Apollonius, Medea functions strictly as a medium for comparing Aeneas and Dido).

[20] We might notice here that Aeneas' reproach of his mother at 1.409—a principal example of Aeneas' self-consciousness, not to say self-pity—follows Ariadne's complaint at Catullus 64.166 *nec missas audire queunt* [the winds] *nec reddere voces.*

Dido passages to the more general meaning "cares, anxiety."[21] The whole phrase will again be strikingly revalued in the thick of battle at 12.486 (where the free indirect discourse signaled by the deliberative subjunctive aligns us with Aeneas' viewpoint): "Alas, what is [Aeneas] to do? He fluctuates on a changeful surge to no purpose, and various anxieties call his mind in different directions" (*heu quid agat? vario nequiquam fluctuat aestu / diversaeque vocant animum in contraria curae*).[22]

The simile at the beginning of Book 8 comes from Apollonius of Rhodes, *Argonautica* 3.755–59, where it describes the wakeful cares of the lovelorn Medea:

> πυκνὰ δέ οἱ κραδίη στηθέων ἔντοσθεν ἔθυιεν,
> ἠελίου ὥς τίς τε δόμοις ἔνι πάλλεται αἴγλη
> ὕδατος ἐξανιοῦσα, τὸ δὴ νέον ἠὲ λέβητι
> ἠέ που ἐν γαυλῷ κέχυται, ἡ δ' ἔνθα καὶ ἔνθα
> ὠκείῃ στροφάλιγγι τινάσσεται ἀίσσουσα.

Her heart beat rapidly within her breast, as sunlight shimmers inside a house when it bounces off water that has just been poured into a basin, or perhaps a pail, and here and there on the swift whirlpool it races and quivers.[23]

Virgil's addition of "the image of the beaming moon" to the sun as source of light sends us back to 6.454, where Aeneas' sight of Dido in the Underworld evokes a comparison to one who "sees or thinks he sees" the moon appear through clouds.[24] Moreover, Virgil's architectural addition to the simile—which transforms Apollonius' light to "a trembling, fitful splendor, moving at random, overwhelmed by a space whose magnitude it can suggest but cannot illumine"[25]—conflates Medea with Dido: *laquearia* appears in Virgil elsewhere only at 1.726, where it denotes the gold-coffered ceiling of Dido's opulent palace—the panels that participate in an allusion to Ennius' Andromacha and a cross-textual dialogue on what it means to be Roman.[26] One could, for

---

[21] For the erotic sense of *cura*, see *TLL* IV.1474–75 s.v. *cura* II.B.1. Cf. Gk. *melô* and its cognates, e.g. *meledêmasi* at Apollonius *Arg.* 3.4, in the passage introducing the love of Medea for Jason.

[22] Cf. 12.527 (on Aeneas and Turnus) *fluctuat ira intus*.

[23] It is obligatory to wonder, however inconclusively, about how Varro of Atax, who included this passage in his translation (fr. 8 Morel; see p. 61 above), handled the simile and whether Virgil has incorporated any of his text here.

[24] Gransden on 22–25 notes another engagement with Apollonius' text: Virgil's *tremulum* presupposes that the water has been freshly poured, as in the Greek.

[25] Johnson 1976:87. Note how the almost hapless image in the simile contrasts with the greater control the external text gives Aeneas over his thoughts (20–21).

[26] See p. 107 above. Let us remember that Andromacha is originally a Euripidean heroine of the distressed type (cf. Euripides *Andr.* 394 and 400 for parts of her lament that Ennius uses in his version). It is noteworthy that as he leaves behind her (feminine) persona, Aeneas also becomes more distant from Trojan identity.

example, read into this detail a pertinent regret for the empire Aeneas could have shared, abandoned for the one he is now, doubtfully and with great anguish, about to attempt. What is most striking for our purposes is that the addition of the Didonian ceiling insinuates a viewpoint, that of someone looking up at the ceiling, an Aeneas standing apart from his own thoughts and observing their effects in metaphor mixed with memory (of the banquet that first night in Carthage). This Aeneas, whose viewpoint is given to us through the simile's language, is like Dido or her literary model Medea; we are invited to see his character as inhabited by the Dido who left that banquet besotted and unable to sleep.

The superimposed persona of the heroine tropes Aeneas' ktistic doubts and anxieties as love—which the wording conflates here, as often, with the "concern" to found a nation. The simile in *Aeneid* 8 leads immediately, at lines 26–30, into a version of the sleeplessness motif that is commonly given to lovelorn heroines (for example Medea, in the same passage as her light simile):[27]

> nox erat et terras animalia fessa per omnis
> alituum pecudumque genus sopor altus habebat,
> cum pater in ripa gelidique sub aetheris axe
> Aeneas, tristi turbatus pectora bello,
> procubuit seramque dedit per membra quietem.

It was night, and over the whole earth deep slumber held weary creatures, the race of winged things and of herds, when father Aeneas, troubled in his breast by the dismal war, sank down on the riverbank beneath the axis of a cool heaven and let sleep go late through his limbs.

For a moment Aeneas remains the lovelorn heroine—but he does fall asleep. The motif yields to a prophetic dream, a vision of the god of the river Tiber; the intertextual suggestion of love flows directly into the theme of foundation. A similar transition occurs at 10.215–18:

> iamque dies caelo concesserat almaque curru
> noctivago Phoebe medium pulsabat Olympum:
> Aeneas (neque enim membris dat cura quietem)
> ipse sedens clavumque regit velisque ministrat.

Now daylight had retreated from the sky and the kindly moon goddess was striking the midst of heaven in her night-wandering chariot. Aeneas himself (for anxiety gives no rest to his limbs) sits and both directs the tiller and tends to the sails.

Line 216 introduces a literary statement: modeled on the first or (as Skutsch argues) second line of Ennius' *Annales* (*Musae quae pedibus magnum pulsatis*

---

[27] See p. 61 above. The phrase "it was night" and the report of sleeping animals is typical.

Olympum), it at least heralds a ktistic subtext.[28] The phrasing in 217 revalues 4.5, Dido's first moment of nocturnal inquietude (*nec placidam membris dat cura quietem*), which uses language from Varro's scene of Medea's sleepless night. As at the opening of Book 8, the heroine-derived wakefulness betokens Aeneas' dutifulness, and here too yields to divine prophecy: immediately the newly created nymphs who until recently were the Trojans' ships swim up and offer advice and encouragement from the gods.

In at least a few other places Aeneas' connection to distressed-heroine language has ktistic import. Io's divine enemy was Juno, who pursued her with violence through her journeys, and this fact already likens Aeneas to her, especially when we recall the foundational import of Io's story and its exploitation by Alexandrian writers (it is worth remembering that distressed mythological heroines typically end up giving birth to the founder of a dynasty or the like; their stories are normally readable as ktistic in some way).[29] In Aeneas' view of the central panel in Juno's temple at Carthage, between the dragging of Troilus and that of Hector, an intertextual suggestion raises this association (1.479–82):

> interea ad templum non aequae Palladis ibant
> crinibus Iliades passis peplumque ferebant
> suppliciter, tristes et tunsae pectora palmis;
> diva solo fixos oculos aversa tenebat.

> Meanwhile the Trojan women were going to the temple of hostile Minerva with their hair undone, grieving and beating their breasts with their hands, and they were bringing a robe in suppliant fashion; the goddess, turning away, kept her eyes fixed on the ground.

Thomas shows that the offering of the *peplum* comes from Calvus' miniature epic *Io*, and O'Hara brings this intertext to bear upon the situation of Aeneas.[30] Through the common mythological connection, the intertext identifies Aeneas (as an Io figure) with the Trojan women with whom he is sympathetically identifying as he peruses the pictures; moreover, one now recalls the Trojan women who mourn Pallas at 11.35—*et maestum Iliades crinem de more solutae*—and the close identification of Aeneas' attitude and view with theirs in that passage. If Aeneas is like Io, then he is also (as in other ways) like Turnus, and both are like Dido.[31] Moreover, comparison with the scene at

[28] Ennius *Ann.* 1 Skutsch; see Skutsch 1985:143–44. He sees Virgil's line as at most a "merely acoustic echo" of Ennius (p. 146), but the themes of the *Annales* are relevant here, and every literate Roman would have attached significance to an echo of the opening of that poem.

[29] Cf. Stephens 2003:8–9, 25–26.

[30] Thomas 1999:316–20 (first published in 1983), O'Hara 1990:36–39. Cf. Lyne 1978:109–10.

[31] The latter two are apparently descended from Io (one recalls the complicated association of Augustus with Hercules, ancestor of both Antony and Cleopatra, at 6.801). See p. 69 above. On Aeneas' assimilation to Turnus through Io, cf. O'Hara 1990:78–80.

11.479 where Lavinia and Latin women approach Minerva with offerings not only indirectly assimilates Aeneas to his future bride (as her downcast eyes as she approaches the altar in the same scene liken Turnus at 12.220 to her), but blurs the normally stark distinctions between actual and averted Roman ancestries by suggesting that the line that eventually did proceed from Lavinia is somehow as Io-like (and so latently Greek, Oriental, Ptolemaic, and so on) as the one that might have. This equation not only works through a distressed heroine and raises all the suggestions we have been discussing, but also complicates the overall picture of Aeneas' ethnicity, insofar as this wandering Dardanid, descendant of an Italian emigrant and ancestor of the Romans, is likened to an Inachid, a Greek ancestor of Easterners, and one whose wanderings became foundational for that ancestry. This mirror effect can be more easily accommodated if we accept that at this point in the narrative Aeneas' ethnicity is fluid, and his merging with the Oriental line still a live possibility, never more so than at this moment (which immediately precedes Dido's welcoming speeches, with their erasure of distinctions between the two peoples). Yet as we observed in earlier chapters, an ethnic foil always retains its power to assimilate as well as differentiate, and so the questions that the central panel of Juno's temple raises remain active.

Another assimilation is more direct. The first distressed heroine in Latin epic is Ennius' Ilia, in her account of the prophetic dream of her rape by Mars that will produce Romulus and Remus. The central part is at *Annales* 38–40 Skutsch:

> "nam me visus homo pulcer per amoena salicta
> et ripas raptare locosque novos. ita sola
> postilla, germana soror, errare videbar."

"For I dreamed that a handsome man carried me away over pleasant willow groves and riverbanks and places strange to me. Afterward, sister, I dreamed that I wandered alone."

Dido's nightmare at at 4.465–68 is densely comparable with Ennius' whole passage (*Annales* 34–50 Skutsch) in wording and in circumstances like the dream, the terror, and the address to a sister (which occurs upon her waking, at 476):[32]

> agit ipse furentem
> in somnis ferus Aeneas, semperque relinqui
> sola sibi, semper longam incomitata videtur
> ire viam et Tyrios deserta quaerere terra.

"In her sleep cruel Aeneas himself drives her raving, and she dreams that she is constantly left alone, constantly left to travel a long journey without companions and search for the Tyrians in a desert land."

---

[32] Krevans 1993 discusses the allusions to Ennius in Dido's nightmare.

This is what results when this lovelorn heroine manages to fall asleep. By investing her trajectory from Tyre to Carthage with a hallucinatory futility, the nightmare makes what had seemed teleological a mere wandering (her onomastic destiny) and pointedly replaces the sexual violence that will produce a new nation with a barren violence, and loneliness without compensation. The replacement of "new places" by "a desert land" reverses the ktistic import of Ilia's dream and works to subvert Dido's role as a foundress. Not only does Aeneas' dream of the Tiber contrast with this, but Ennius' passage is reused for his approach to Elysium (6.637–39):

> his demum exactis, perfecto munere divae,
> devenere locos laetos et amoena virecta
> fortunatorum nemorum sedesque beatas.

> These rites performed and their duty to the goddess fulfilled, they went down to happy places, and the pleasant greeneries of the groves of the fortunate, and the blessed abodes.

This time Ilia's role is taken by Aeneas: the foundational aspect of the intertext, which was pointedly erased from the passage on Dido's dream, now makes itself felt (this contrast is especially piquant after the recent meeting with Dido's shade). The passing echo rings true: both Ilia and Aeneas, especially as he approaches the scene of his indoctrination by Anchises, are unknowing conduits of the Roman race. On the other hand, the whole Underworld episode (not to say the whole poem) casts him as a more active ancestor of Rome, like Mars in the *Annales* (his intertextual role in Dido's nightmare). Amata, for one, might not hesitate to characterize Aeneas as a ktistic rapist. He is in fact the active enabler of those prophecies that Anchises would make of him, and that he in fact becomes in the remaining books of the *Aeneid*.[33]

One final example touches the problem of Italy, and its unity with Rome (and with itself), that surfaced at the end of the last chapter. The first two lines of the poem oddly announce its subject as "the first [man] who came from the shores of Troy to Italy" (*Troiae qui primus ab oris / Italiam . . . venit*). Why this accomplishment (as opposed to his founding the Roman nation, or being the "first Roman" in some sense) should justify an epic about him is unclear.[34] It is hastily followed by ". . . and the Lavinian shores," as if by correction. In any case the claim may not even be true. *Primus* is a provocation. In her complaint to Jupiter at 1.247–49, Venus contrasts with the much-buffeted Aeneas his countryman Antenor, who has already founded a settlement:

> "hic tamen ille urbem Patavi sedesque locavit
> Teucrorum et genti nomen dedit armaque fixit
> Troia, nunc placida compostus pace quiescit."

---

[33] Reed 2001:157–59.
[34] Cf. Galinsky 1969:3–6.

"But here he has laid the city of Padua as an abode for the Teucrians, and given a name to his people and hung up Trojan arms; now he rests, settled in placid peace."

Referring to this passage on 1.1, Servius explains that this city is not in Italy proper, but in Cisalpine Gaul (Virgil's homeland too), which was not politically united with Italy until after the death of Julius Caesar. Aeneas is *primus* only if we imagine ourselves back before that date and deny the subsequent unification. He was the first Trojan to reach an "Italy" that lacked everything between the Rubicon and the Alps. But this unseaming of the poem's Italy is not the main issue now; our focus is the distressed-heroine language in *placida . . . pace quiescit*, "he rests in placid peace."[35] Venus' image makes quiet sleep a metaphor for successful foundation, as the love that troubles the heroine, and keeps her from *quies*, is a metaphor for the foundational effort. In a sense Antenor has escaped the trouble that plagues Turnus and Dido. Turnus' troubles in this regard symbolize his failure to found a nation. Antenor is the model for Aeneas. He too must find the repose of a successful *ktistês*.

Thus Aeneas is comparable to Dido and Turnus as a heroine figure; or to put it more aptly, he and Turnus in the latter part of the poem rework Dido's distressed-heroine persona, with love sliding under ktisis and the ethnic and foundational implications of her story coming to the fore by the metaphorical operation we are by now familiar with. In this regard, as in many, he and Turnus are doublets—foils for each other, with Turnus' more helpless heroine-scene (sent away by Juno on an empty ship at 10.659–88; see pp. 65–68 above) in telling contrast to Aeneas' more promising ones, which typically end up casting him not as the pawn of the gods, but as their favorite, and as the ancestor of the future nation.[36] And yet it would be unwise to read the heroine-persona of Aeneas merely as a figure for another theme, without looking at the way it casts him, whether resonantly or contrastively, as feminized, passive, prey to emotions. We find in him, at key moments in the last stage of his toils, the kind of gender ambiguity we saw in our fallen warriors. He himself is never an Adonis-figure, of course; he neither dies nor endures an elaboration of his supernal beauty[37] into a sensual appraisal. Yet there is at least one point at which he approaches being one, and that is the point where he is most vulnerable: wounded, in fact, penetrated by an enemy weapon, and under the care of the physician Iapyx. Like that of Adonis, Aeneas' wound is apparently on

---

[35] Cf. pp. 61–63. *Pace* here refers especially to the harmonious relations Antenor's people have with their neighbors; there is a contrast with the war Aeneas is going to have to fight in Italy.

[36] Note, however, that this distinction is blurred by the ambiguities in the prophecies to Aeneas by Father Tiber and the nymph Cymodocea; see O'Hara 1990:31–35, 39–47.

[37] At 4.141 *ipse ante alios pulcherrimus omnis*, "himself most beautiful of them all" (cf. Turnus at his first mention, 7.55: *ante alios pulcherrimus omnis*).

his thigh (12.386); and the same anxious goddess presides over both scenes.[38]
When at 413–14 the dittany that Venus adds to Iapyx' brew is said to produce
a "crimson flower" (*flore purpureo*), with a phrase that can be a periphrasis for
the hyacinth (and thus has associations with a dying god), we recall the prominence of crimson flowers in Bion's *Epitaph on Adonis* and in the similes at the
deaths of Euryalus and Pallas, as well as the crimson flowers (*purpureos flores*)
with which Anchises proposes to strew the corpse of Marcellus.[39] We should
again think of Dido, and the mixture of subjectivity and passivity that her
dying-god background, as well as the heroine persona, lend her, and bring this
persona to bear on the question of Aeneas' gaze in the poem.[40] In this regard
his resemblance to a lovelorn heroine of Hellenistic and Roman epic allegorizes his loose grasp on the narrative viewpoint, the combination of pervasive-
ness and unassertiveness in his gaze.

It is time to acknowledge that the Adoniac subtext of the *Aeneid* activates
a powerful analogy between Venus as mourner of Adonis and Venus as mother
of Aeneas, and of Rome. Our Adonis-scenes superimpose her keening over
her dead beloved onto her care for Rome—Venus the lover of Adonis (and
of Anchises for that matter) onto Venus *genetrix*, the mother of the Roman
race and in particular of the Julian line. In general it should be noted that
Venus, with her strong identification not only with Greek Aphrodite, but also
with local Aphrodites plainly syncretistic with Near Eastern great goddesses,
is an even more commodious divine emblem of Rome's embrace of other cultures than is Cybele in Anchises' simile (see p. 157 above). She (like Adonis)
represents both Greek and Oriental, and the adoption of both into Roman
religion and cultural identity. Leaving Aeneas after their encounter near
Carthage, she enacts a Sapphoesque fantasy of a Near Eastern goddess of love
(1.415–17):

> ipsa Paphum sublimis abit sedesque revisit
> laeta suas, ubi templum illi, centumque Sabaeo
> ture calent arae sertisque recentibus halant.

The goddess herself departs on high for Paphos and in contentedness
resorts to her abode there, where she has a temple, and a hundred altars
smolder with the frankincense of Sheba and breathe forth the perfume of
fresh garlands.

---

[38] Imperial-era sarcophagi exploit this analogy: Koortbojian 1995:49–62 identifies Aeneas
sarcophagi as models for the analogous scenes on the Adonis sarcophagi.

[39] The passage on Aeneas' wound also contains tantalizing suggestions of Bion's poem on Hyacinthus (fr. 1); see Reed 2004:39–40. For "crimson" (Lat. *purpureus*) as an epithet of the hyacinth
see Sappho (?) fr. 105B Voigt, Euphorion fr. 40.1 Powell, Meleager *A.P.* 5.147.3–4, Ovid *Met.*
13.395 (cf. 10.212–13), Manilius 5.257, Pancrates fr. 3.1–2 Heitsch. Cf. Brenk 1990:223 n. 16.

[40] An analogous construction is Aeneas' status as both narrator (of Books 2 and 3) and narrated in
the *Aeneid* (cf. Clay 1988:200).

Her very abode in a city of Cyprus, here redolent of both the ancient opulence of the East and its freshest flowers, is at the historical crossroads of Greek and Near Eastern cultures, and is the supreme locus for the syncretistic goddess of love. Paphos was the mythological seat of Cinyras, the father of Adonis in a widespread myth. We are given an appreciative Greek-derived view of an Oriental goddess who is the ancestor of the Romans—an identification with the Orient, adapted from Greek culture by a Roman poet. Even more crucially than in the passages on Cybele, the three ethnic identities share a standpoint.

I suggest that Aeneas' easily diluted viewpoint, on Pallas and in general, and his subtextual transformation into a distressed heroine at critical moments both reflect his dual role as conquered and redresser of that conquest, the vehicle of passage from Trojan to Roman, the synecdochic achiever of Rome's teleology. As Virgil needs him to encompass many viewpoints—even to the point of losing a distinctive one—the heroine figure provides an analogue to that same imperial receptivity in sexual as well as in ethnic terms (especially because of the particular heroines he takes after and their reflexes in Dido and Turnus). Both modes usefully complicate his subjectivity. The heroine is erotically conquered (emotionally or physically), sometimes physically objectified, yet so full-bloodedly subjective that her viewpoint compels the reader. It takes over a shorter narrative poem like the *Epitaph on Adonis*, commandeers the memorability of Catullus 64, and transforms Apollonius' *Argonautica* (and with it, arguably, Greco-Roman epic). That Aeneas must do battle over and over with Dido, and then Turnus, for the sympathies and viewpoint of the reader may have as its symptom or emblem the fact that all three are calqued on the figure of the epic heroine—or perhaps it is that to compete with them for our sympathies he needs the heroine-model. It is significant that distressed mythological heroines (like Io, Europa, and Danae) typically produce the founders of nations and national dynasties, as in the Greek mythological complex that the *Aeneid* mirrors in the transgenerational migrations of its chief founding figures.[41] Not only does this persona effect a system of ethnic exchanges that is most congenial to Virgil's foundational and imperial interests, but as a long-lived literary motif the heroine allows him a conversion from political to literary terms and back again.

Amor is the governing metaphor in these exchanges. There is one use Virgil makes of this metaphor that might have fit in chapter 3, but that we can now assess better, having traced to some extent the the open-endedness of Aeneas' gaze and the general role of his viewpoint in the poem. At the end of Book 1 Dido asks to hear Aeneas' adventures; at the beginning of Book 2 he complies

---

[41] A primary text for this complex of themes would have been the Hesiodic *Catalogue of Women* (cf. p. 10 above). Herodotus opens his *Histories* by tracing the relations between Greeks and Eastern peoples—and Greek self-differentiation from the East—up to the Trojan War as a series of literal exchanges (kidnappings and counter-kidnappings) of mythological heroines.

after a masterly show of reluctance (2.3–9), announcing in lines 10–13 his role as narrator:

> "sed si tantus amor casus cognoscere nostros
> et breviter Troiae supremum audire laborem,
> quamquam animus meminisse horret luctuque refugit,
> incipiam."

"But if you have such great desire [*amor*] to know our misfortunes and to hear briefly of the final struggle of Troy, although my spirit shudders at the remembrance and shrinks from the grief, I shall commence."

On Aeneas' interpretation of Dido's wishes, an erotics of reading launches Books 2 and 3, his account of the fall of Troy and his people's wanderings over the next seven years. From the very start of his narration he is implicitly a reciprocal reader of his audience, which includes Dido, the other Carthaginians of the court, and by implication Virgil's readers, ourselves.[42] He reads them (and us) as lovers.

Aeneas reads astutely. Dido "drinks in desire"[43] as she follows his conversation (1.748–50):

> nec non et vario noctem sermone trahebat
> infelix Dido longumque bibebat amorem,
> multa super Priamo rogitans, super Hectore multa.

And unfortunate Dido also drew out the night with varied conversation, and drank in long desire [*amorem*], asking many questions about Priam, many about Hector.

More samples of her questions follow, culminating, in direct speech, in her invitation to Aeneas to tell his adventures from the beginning. At 4.77–79 her repeated requests for retellings are a sign of her love:

> nunc eadem labente die convivia quaerit,
> Iliacosque iterum demens audire labores
> exposcit pendetque iterum narrantis ab ore.

Now, at the close of the day, she seeks those same banquets and in her madness demands again to hear his exploits, and hangs from his lips as he narrates.

---

[42] One could profitably read Aeneas here as an "interpreting character" against Dido in that capacity (see O'Hara 1993, who employs Schor's concept and terminology).

[43] The locution has its closest precedent, interestingly, in Bion *Ad.* 49 ἐκ δὲ πίω τὸν ἔρωτα ("I will drink desire"), where Aphrodite identifies her passionate last kiss with drinking and Adonis' last breath with love, and vows to "keep that kiss as Adonis himself," assimilating him within herself. There is an analogue there to Aeneas' assimilation of Pallas' persona in the gaze on the latter's body, as interpreted above; but it is also part of Bion's constant assimilation of the goddess to her mortal lover.

Listening as kissing: an apt catachresis. She drinks in love with his story; he transmits love by narrating as surely as by a kiss. At 4.83–85 this narrative *amor* is characterized as unsatisfiable. She constantly asks to hear and rehear his stories; then:

> illum absens absentem auditque videtque
> aut gremio Ascanium genitoris imagine capta
> detinet, infandum si fallere possit amorem.

Apart from him, she sees and hears him apart from her, or detains Ascanius on her lap, captivated by his father's likeness, in the hope that she could fool her unspeakable love.

His narrating presence is never enough; and the sublimation of her *amor* from something narrative into something maternal (compare her wish for a "little Aeneas," *parvulus Aeneas*, at 328–29) suggests a necessary deferral. In listening over and over to the same tales, she seems to be trying to reach a satisfactory definitiveness that narrative ultimately cannot offer, any more than her desire can be but asymptotic. For Aeneas' story too the metaphor in 2.10 has life, though he may not consciously know it yet: he initially resists giving in to her *tantus amor* in this matter as, finally, in the matter of staying with her and merging their nations. That he nominally resists gratifying Dido's *amor* in lines 2–9, citing the grief it brings him and the sinking stars, which, he susurratingly concludes, counsel sleep (9 *suadentque cadentia sidera somnos*), makes him like Odysseus at *Odyssey* 7.241 and 9.12–13—not only in the reluctance to reopen old grief, but in the Odyssean dissembling and craft of speech that he displays elsewhere too, for example in his bracing optimism after the storm at sea (1.198–207). The touch of manipulation is a rhetorical correlative to his narratological passive-aggressiveness and also to the halfway commitment in his actual relations with Dido.

Dido's situation brings to life Brooks's metaphor, in his chapter on "Narrative Transaction and Transference," of narrative infection: the love with which Cupid infects her (1.717–19) melds with a readerly desire.[44] Pursuing Brooks's insight, one might ask: How does Dido respond to the narration, discharge the energies of desire that it creates in her? To what extent are the Punic Wars the story that she creates in answer to his, the trajectory of a thwarted readerly love? How do those wars finally misread his narration as mere chaos or contingency, imposing a counter-viewpoint to take in history from a different ethnic angle? We are of course not to accept this figure unquestioningly as a definition of the reader of the *Aeneid*; rather, let us test it against other figures of reading in the poem. It recalls most of all our point of departure, in chapter 1, from the lover that the erotic death imagery in the last four books makes of every reader, and insinuates that trope allegorically at the poem's premier moment of narrative self-reflection.

[44] Brooks 1984:216–37.

Imperialism and reading allegorize each other—as dialectics, with the reader not just subject, but also the recipient of the action. The poet's narrative personae, already occupied by those of earlier poets, colonize our own readerly personae—not without the resistence and change inevitable in imperialist syncretism, or the ironies they entail. The vehicle of this allegory is love.

Aeneas, then, fits into our network of personae in his versatile viewpoint, which is typical for him throughout the poem and which typically accommodates the viewpoint of the reader, and in the way the figure of the epic heroine lends him a useful indeterminacy in gender and ethnicity. The obsessive compromising of Aeneas' subjectivity can serve a similar purpose: his viewpoint is paradoxically not restricted, but enlarged. As with the images we started from, Virgil achieves these effects by narratological and intertextual means, which are not discrete processes in the text, but are always coinvolved, indeed often interchangeable (as when a focalization adapts a precursor's focalization)—but interchangeable in the way metaphors are, with difference always ready to assert new meaning. And the themes Aeneas, and our four warriors, thus carry have to do (not surprisingly) with Roman identity and nationhood, especially the divine mission to develop from Trojan to Roman. Virgil's gaze, which he gives his reader, is active on levels of both form and content. Aeneas is a model for this reader—except when he becomes a foil too; for as a character he works in different ways. Thus Roman nationality emerges as a dialectic, endlessly accommodating and adaptable to the needs of empire.

III

We end by closely reading a scene that exhibits a number of our themes as they concern Aeneas. We have been talking about the shifts in Aeneas' viewing character through the poem, which we can tie to the representation of nationhood in the poem and theorize in terms of narrative metaphor. The theoretical point we return to here is prolepsis, and more broadly the metaphorical relationship between the opening and close of narrative. Aeneas personifies this relationship, perhaps most conspicuously in national terms: he starts out Trojan and ends up Roman. Or rather, he personifies it incompletely, since he does not himself end up Roman except in the most schematic, symbolic, proleptic way. As an asymptote of Roman national identity, he is paralleled by Mercury in Book 4, who also embodies a viewpoint, and who upon first touching down at Carthage delivers a message about the end of Aeneas' ktistic journey. What does this say about the eventual "touching-down" of the Aeneadae: will their national identity ever be really firmly established? How does the case of Mercury predict the fixity of that trope?

In Book 4 Jupiter, his gaze turned by Iarbas' prayer to the activities in Carthage, sends Mercury to speed Aeneas on his way. A dressing scene describes his winged sandals and the rod by which he summons the dead to and from the Underworld, "gives and removes sleep, and seals eyes closed in death" (244 *dat somnos adimitque, et lumina morte resignat*)—the last phrase imagining death as a loss of vision. He takes off, and becomes the explicit viewer (246–58):

> iamque volans apicem et latera ardua cernit
> Atlantis duri caelum qui vertice fulcit,
> Atlantis, cinctum adsidue cui nubibus atris
> piniferum caput et vento pulsatur et imbri,
> 250 nix umeros infusa tegit, tum flumina mento
> praecipitant senis, et glacie riget horrida barba.
> hic primum paribus nitens Cyllenius alis
> constitit; hinc toto praeceps se corpore ad undas
> misit avi similis, quae circum litora, circum
> 255 piscosos scopulos humilis volat aequora iuxta.
> haud aliter terras inter caelumque volabat
> litus harenosum ad Libyae, ventosque secabat
> materno veniens ab avo Cyllenia proles.

And now in his flight he spies the summit and steep sides of rugged Atlas, which supports the heavens on its crown—Atlas, whose pine-covered head is continually surrounded by dark clouds and beaten by wind and rain, and whose shoulders are covered with snowfalls. Rivers rush headlong from the old man's chin, and his bristling beard is rigid with ice. Here first the Cyllenian stops, balancing on matched wings; from this point he launches himself headlong with his whole body, like a bird that flies low around the shores, around the fishy crags, near the sea surface. In the same way the scion of Cyllene flew between earth and heaven toward the sandy shore of Libya and cut through the winds, coming from [his] maternal grandfather.

As the messenger god bears Aeneas a message from Jupiter, Aeneas' maternal grandfather, he encounters his own maternal grandfather (258 *materno veniens ab avo* can refer to either Atlas or Jupiter).[45] Parallel messages of ancestry operate here; notice also the characterization of Mercury as *proles*, "offspring." At 8.134–42 Aeneas will cite Atlas as a common ancestor uniting Trojans and Arcadians (grandfather of Dardanus through Electra and thence a Trojan forebear, grandfather of Mercury through Maia and thence an Arcadian forebear), so that genealogy binds Evander's people, Greek though they are, to the Dardanid mission.

[45] Note the pun in 254 *avi similis*, which can mean "like a bird" or "like his grandfather": the latter characterization resonates mildly with the titles Mercury is given here, *Cyllenius* and *Cyllenia proles*, from Mount Cyllene in Arcadia where he was born, and more pointedly with Mercury's role as messenger from—and, in his speech, impersonator of—*Aeneas'* grandfather.

This winged asymptote, master of his loft and swerve, never lands on solid earth. Mercury skims, hovers. He stops momentarily on Mount Atlas, apparently not even touching it with his feet but only pausing in midair "on matched wings"; likewise when he arrives in Carthage he seems to perch on the *magalia*, the temporary housing amid the construction of the city, and to call down to Aeneas from there (4.259–61):

> ut primum alatis tetigit magalia plantis,
> Aenean fundantem arces ac tecta novantem
> conspicit.

As soon as he touched the shelters with his winged feet, he spied Aeneas in the act of laying foundations for the citadel and creating new buildings.

In *conspicit*, the gaze passes to the young god from Jupiter (who at 220–21 *oculosque ad moenia torsit regia*, "twisted his eyes [or "launched his gaze"] toward the city walls of the queen"). What we see, with Mercury, is an Aeneas dressed by Dido in the purple-dyed, gold-embroidered robe we have noticed already in connection with its twin robe, in which Aeneas shrouds Pallas in Book 11. This detail perhaps excites the indignation he has assimilated from Jupiter (who at 224 had spoken to him of Aeneas' lingering in "Tyrian Carthage"), and he "immediately attacks" Aeneas (265 *continuo invadit*) with the words "Are you now laying the foundations of high Carthage and uxoriously building a beautiful city?" (265–67 *tu nunc Karthaginis altae / fundamenta locas pulchramque uxorius urbem / exstruis?*). This characterization may actually represent the suppression of a divine syncretism: Brown compares a Punic term "Rosh Melqart" ("promontory [literally "head"] of Melqart," that is, one adorned with a shrine of the god) with a "Promunturium Mercurii" in Africa, and wonders "whether *Mercurius* is elsewhere a Latinization of Melqart."[46] The parallel hints at some sort of syncretism on at least a topographical level, and the involvement of promontories, lookouts onto the sea from Africa (the exact opposite of the view from the mouths of Tiber toward Carthage that 1.13–14 gave us), recalls the Virgilian Mercury's journey along the African coast, his pause on Mount Atlas, and the relevance of his viewpoint in this episode. Depending on what these hints of syncretism would lead to, his viewpoint might become a diplopic ethnic viewpoint in the subtext, complementing and complicating his view of Aeneas. In any case, this is a god privileged with ethnic foresight (which, again, he has derived from Jupiter), who knows that Rome, not Carthage, is the destiny of these Trojans and who cannot behold a Carthaginianized Aeneas without dismay.

---

[46] Livy 29.27.8, Pliny *N.H.* 5.24; see Brown 2000:109. On Mercury at pre-Roman Carthage see Ribichini 1985:95–112. Hercules is Melqart's usual equivalent in Greco-Roman theology. On Punic-Roman divine syncretism in the *Aeneid* (with special attention to what is suppressed or unstated) cf. Henderson 1999:8; Hexter 1992:346–47, 351–52.

Mercury is a surrogate for Jupiter, largely repeating Jupiter's words to Aeneas in his message (in the style of divine messengers' speeches in Homeric poetry too). He is also both viewer of Aeneas and double for Aeneas (in their parallel ancestries). As a kind of go-between, translating fate into desire, Mercury is virtually a metaphor *for* metaphor; this episode thus encapsulates the complex semantics of the Virgilian persona. Jupiter passes to Mercury an idea of Aeneas' mission couched in an architectural trope. He complains that Aeneas is dallying in "Tyrian Carthage" when he should be heading to Italy in order to fulfill a greater destiny (232–34):

> "si nulla accendit tantarum gloria rerum
> nec super ipse sua molitur laude laborem,
> Ascanione pater Romanas invidet arces?"

"If the glory of so great an empire does not set him afire, and he is not laboring at any effort for his own renown, does he, a father, begrudge Ascanius the Roman citadel?"

The usual notes are struck: generational succession, in Jupiter's view, should trump even love of Roman fame—with which we will indeed see Aeneas set afire at 6.889. The citadel Jupiter envisions (*Romanas . . . arces*) is that of "high Rome" (1.7), the city whose name is so readily interpretable as Phoenician for "high place."[47] Mercury leaves out this phrase, but his translation of it into "high" Carthage (265), spoken in mockery of Aeneas' architectural pursuits— already sarcastically enough, for one who has just descended from heaven via earth's loftiest mountain—focuses the irony carried by the prolepsis, or teleology. Jupiter and he both know what is meant by "high Carthage": what Rome should and will be, the city on a height, taking in the world with its infinitely responsive gaze.

Typically here, Aeneas' response is to fall mute, but his viewpoint suffuses the narrative (279–83):

> at vero Aeneas aspectu obmutuit amens,
> arrectaeque horrore comae et vox faucibus haesit.
> ardet abire fuga dulcisque relinquere terras,
> attonitus tanto monitu imperioque deorum.
> heu quid agat?

"But at this vision Aeneas, out of his mind, went mute, and his hair stood on end with fear and his voice stuck in his throat. He burns to go away in flight and leave these sweet lands, thunderstruck by such a mighty admonishment and by the command of the gods. Alas, what should he do?"

---

[47] See above, p. 140.

And so on. Mercury seems to have imparted something of Jupiter's vision. Aeneas is persuaded primarily by brute terror, but there is at least a stark emotional ambivalence in line 281: he "burns" (the strongest word for desire in the Virgilian vocabulary) to leave a land that is sweet to him.[48] Here is the choice between his god-appointed destiny and his old self, cast (characteristically) as one between obedience and happiness. The "kindling" of his desire for Rome that will come to fullness at the end of Book 6 has begun. In his subsequent interview with Dido he will declare that his *amor* is Italy (347). And yet the precarious balance insinuated in line 281 between ardor for his mission and attachment to his past persists, explicit or sublimated, in Aeneas' own attitude and is even projected into the poem's reconciliations of Trojan, Italian, Oriental, and Greek in a multivalent Roman identity. Airborne Mercury, even as he communicates the need to break with a former nationality, allegorizes Aeneas' and the poem's resistance to the idea of a definitive Roman.

[48] Fowler 2000b:47–48 notes Aeneas' focalization in *dulcis*, following Servius' (unfortunately corrupt) note.

BIBLIOGRAPHY

Adams, J. N. 1982. *The Latin Sexual Vocabulary*. London.

Ahl, F. 1976. *Lucan: An Introduction*. Ithaca.

———. 1985. *Metaformations: Soundplay and Wordplay in Ovid and Other Classical Poets*. Ithaca.

Alfonsi, L. 1963. "Pulchra Mors." *Latomus* 22:85–86.

Anderson, W. S. 1957. "Vergil's Second *Iliad*." *TAPA* 88:17–30.

Arrigoni, G. 1982. *Camilla: Amazzone e sacerdotessa di Diana*. Milan.

Austin, R. G. 1960. *M. Tulli Ciceronis pro M. Caelio Oratio*. 3rd ed. Oxford.

———. 1971. *P. Vergili Maronis Aeneidos Liber Primus*. Oxford.

Babcock, C. L. 1992. "*Sola . . . multis e matribus:* A Comment on Vergil's Trojan Women." In R. M. Wilhelm and H. Jones, eds., *The Two Worlds of the Poet: New Perspectives on Vergil*, pp. 39–50. Detroit.

Badian, E. 1972. "Ennius and His Friends." In O. Skutsch, ed., *Ennius*. Entretiens sur l'antiquité classique 17, pp. 149–99. Geneva.

Bal, M. 1977. *Narratologie*. Paris.

Barchiesi, A. 1978. "Il lamento di Giuturna." *MD* 1:99–121.

———. 1994. "Rappresentazioni del dolore e interpretazione nell'Eneide." *A&A* 40:109–24.

———. 1997. "Virgilian Narrative: Ecphrasis." In Martindale 1997:271–81.

———. 2001. *Speaking Volumes: Narrative and intertext in Ovid and other Latin poets*. Ed., trans. M. Fox and S. Marchesi. London.

———. 2002. "Narrative technique and narratology in the *Metamorphoses*." In P. Hardie, ed., *The Cambridge Companion to Ovid*, pp. 180–99. Cambridge.

Barthes, R. 1973. *Le plaisir du texte*. Paris.

Bauer, H. 1917. "Kanaanäische Miszellen." *ZDMG* 71:410–13.

Benz, F. L. 1972. *Personal Names in the Phoenician and Punic Inscriptions* (Studia Pohl 8). Rome.

Berchem, D. van. 1959–60. "Hercule Melqart à l'Ara Maxima." *RPAA* 32:61–68.

Bergmann, B. 1991. "Painted Perspectives of a Villa Visit: Landscape as Status and Metaphor." In E. Gazda, ed., *Roman Art in the Private Sphere*, pp. 49–70. Ann Arbor.

Bickerman, E. J. 1952. "*Origines gentium*." *CP* 47:65–81.

Bleisch, P. R. 1998. "Altars Altered: The Alexandrian Tradition of Etymological Wordplay in *Aeneid* 1.108–12." *AJP* 119:599–606.

Boella, U. 1979. "Virgilio e Bione di Smirne." *RSC* 27:326–28.

Bonanno, M. G. 1989. "Candido Ila (Theocr. XIII 49)." In *Mnemosynum: Studi in onore di Alfredo Ghiselli*, pp. 51–53. Bologna.

Bonfanti, M. 1985. *Punto di vista e modi della narrazione nell'Eneide*. Pisa.

Bowersock, G. W. 1965. *Augustus and the Greek World*. Oxford.

Bowie, A. M. 1990. "The Death of Priam: Allegory and History in the *Aeneid*." *CQ* 40:470–481.

Bray, J. J. 1966. "The Ivory Gate." In M. Kelly, ed., *For Service to Classical Studies: Essays in Honour of Francis Letters*, pp. 55–69. Melbourne.

Brenk, F. E. 1986. "*Auorum spes et purpurei flores*: The Eulogy for Marcellus in *Aeneid* VI." *AJP* 107:218–28 = *Clothed in Purple Light* (Stuttgart 1999), pp. 76–86.

———. 1990. "'Purpureos spargam flores': A Greek Motif in the *Aeneid*?" *CQ* 40:218–23 = *Clothed in Purple Light* (Stuttgart 1999), pp. 87–92.

Brooks, P. 1984. *Reading for the Plot*. New York.

———. 1993. *Body Work*. Harvard.

Brown, J. P. 1995. *Israel and Hellas*. Berlin.

———. 2000. *Israel and Hellas. Volume II. Sacred Institutions with Roman Counterparts*. Berlin.

———. 2001. *Israel and Hellas. Volume III. The Legacy of Iranian Imperialism and the Imdividual*. Berlin.

Brown, J. P., and S. Levin. 1986. "The Ethnic Paradigm as a Pattern for Nominal Forms in Greek and Hebrew." *General Linguistics* 26:71–105.

Burkert, W. 1979. *Structure and History in Greek Mythology and Ritual*. Berkeley.

Cairns, F. 1989. *Virgil's Augustan Epic*. Cambridge.

Cameron, A. 1995. *Callimachus and His Critics*. Princeton.

Champion, C. 2000. "Romans as βάρβαροι: Three Polybian Speeches and the Politics of Cultural Indeterminacy." *CP* 95:425–44.

Chuvin, P. 1991. *Mythologie et géographie dionysiaques*. Clermont-Ferrand.

Clarke, K. 1956. *The Nude*. New York.

Clausen, W. 1987. *Virgil's* Aeneid *and the Tradition of Hellenistic Poetry*. Berkeley.

———. 2002. *Virgil's* Aeneid: *Decorum, Allusion, and Ideology*. Beiträge zur Altertumskunde 162. Leipzig.

Clay, D. 1988. "The Archaeology of the Temple to Juno in Carthage (*Aen.* 1. 446–93)." *CP* 83:195–205.

Clua, J. A. 1988. "El *Traci* d'Euforió: mitemes, male diccions, estructures." *Ítaca* 4:83–96.

Conington, J. 1883. *P. Vergili Maronis Opera*. Vol. 3. 3rd ed., rev. H. Nettleship. London.

Connolly, J. 2001. "Picture Arcadia: The Politics of Representation in Vergil's *Eclogues*." *Vergilius* 47:89–116.

Conte, G. B. 1986. *The Rhetoric of Imitation*. Trans. and ed. C. Segal. Cornell.

Courtney, E. 1988. "Vergil's Military Catalogues and Their Antecedents." *Vergilius* 34:3–8.

———. 1993. *The Fragmentary Latin Poets*. Oxford.

———. 1995. *Musa Lapidaria*. Atlanta.

———. 1999. *Archaic Latin Prose*. Atlanta.

Davies, G. 1997. "Gender and Body Language in Roman Art." In T. Cornell and K. Lomas, eds., *Gender and Ethnicity in Ancient Italy*, pp. 97–107. London.

Dewar, M. 1991. *Statius. Thebaid IX*. Oxford.

DeWitt, N. J. 1941. "Rome and the 'Road of Hercules.'" *TAPA* 72:59–69.

Dufallo, B. 2007. *The Ghosts of the Past: Latin Literature, the Dead, and Rome's Transition to a Principate*. Columbus.

Egan, R. B. 1980. "Euryalus' Mother and *Aeneid* 9–12." In R. Bardon, ed. *Collection Latomus* 168, pp. 157–76. Paris.

Eichhoff, F. G. 1825. *Etudes grecques sur Virgile*. Vol. 3. Paris.

Empson, W. 1935. *Some Versions of Pastoral*. London.

Erskine, A. 2001. *Troy between Greece and Rome: Local Tradition and Imperial Power.* Oxford.

Feeney, D. C. 1984. "The Reconciliations of Juno." *CQ* 34:179–84.

———. 1986. "History and Revelation in Vergil's Underworld." *PCPS* 212:1–24.

———. 1991. *The Gods in Epic.* Oxford.

———. 1998. *Literature and Religion at Rome.* Cambridge.

Feldherr, A. 1995. "Ships of State: *Aeneid* 5 and Augustan Circus Spectacle." *ClAnt* 14:245–65.

———. 1998. *Spectacle and Society in Livy's History.* Berkeley.

———. 1999. "Putting Dido on the Map: Genre and Geography in Vergil's Underworld." *Arethusa* 32:85–122.

Fletcher, K.F.F. 2005. *Ovid, Mythography, and the Translation of Myth.* Diss. University of Michigan. Ann Arbor.

———. 2006. "Vergil's Italian Diomedes." *AJP* 127:219–59.

Fowler, D. 1987. "Vergil on Killing Virgins." In M. Whitby et al., eds., *Homo Viator: Classical Essays for John Bramble.* Bristol, pp. 185–98.

———. 1997. "The Virgil commentary of Servius." In Martindale 1987:73–78.

———. 2000a. "Epic in the Middle of the Wood: *Mise en Abyme* in the Nisus and Euryalus Episode." In A. Sharrock and and H. Morales, eds., *Intratextuality,* pp. 89–113. Oxford.

———. 2000b. *Roman Constructions: Readings in Postmodern Latin.* Oxford.

Fowler, W. W. 1919. *The Death of Turnus.* Oxford.

Fraenkel, E. 1954. "Urbem quam statuo vestra est." *Glotta* 33:157–59.

Frazer, J. G. 1914. *The Golden Bough.* Pt. 4: "Adonis Attis Osiris." 2 vols. 3rd ed. London.

Fredrick, D. 1995. "Erotic Painting and Visual Pleasure in the Roman House." *ClAnt* 14:266–87.

———., ed. 2002. *The Roman Gaze: Vision, Power, and the Body.* Baltimore.

Galinsky, G. K. 1969. "*Troiae qui primus ab oris . . . , (Aen.* I, 1)." *Latomus* 28:3–18.

———. 1996. *Augustan Culture.* Princeton.

Genette, G. 1980. *Narrative Discourse: An Essay in Method.* Trans. J. E. Lewin. Ithaca.

———. 1988. *Narrative Discourse Revisited.* Trans. J. E. Lewin. Ithaca.

Gesenius, W. 1837. *Scripturae linguaeque Phoeniciae monumenta.* Leipzig.

Gillis, D. 1983. *Eros and Death in the* Aeneid. Rome.

Girard, R. 1978. *Des choses cachées depuis la fondation du monde.* Paris.

Goldberg, S. 1995. *Epic in Republican Rome.* Oxford.

Goold, G. P. 1992. "The Voice of Virgil: The Pageant of Rome in *Aeneid* 6." In T. Woodman and J. Powell, eds., *Author and Audience in Latin Literature.* Cambridge, pp. 110–23.

Gould, T. 1990. *The Ancient Quarrel between Poetry and Philosophy.* Princeton.

Gransden, K. W. 1976. *Virgil: Aeneid Book VIII.* Cambridge.

———. 1984. *Virgil's Iliad: An essay on epic narrative.* Cambridge.

———. 1991. *Virgil: Aeneid Book XI.* Cambridge.

Greene, E. 2000. "Gender Identity and the Elegiac Hero in Propertius 2.1." *Arethusa* 33:241–61.

Griffin, J. 1980. *Homer on Life and Death.* Oxford.

Gruen, E. S. 1992. *Culture and National Identity in Republican Rome.* Ithaca.

Habinek, T. 1998. *The Politics of Latin Literature: Writing, Identity, and Empire in Ancient Rome*. Princeton.

Haggerty, G. E. 2004. "Love and Loss: An Elegy." *GLQ* 10:385–405.

Hall, E. 1989. *Inventing the Barbarian*. Oxford.

Hallett, J. P., and M. B. Skinner, eds., 1997. *Roman Sexualities*. Princeton.

Halperin, D. M. 2006. "The Best Lover." In B. Dufallo and P. McCracken, eds., *Dead Lovers: Erotic Bonds and the Study of Premodern Europe*, pp. 8–21. Ann Arbor.

Hannah, B. 2004. "Manufacturing Descent: Virgil's Genealogical Engineering." *Arethusa* 37:141–64.

Hardie, P. 1986. *Virgil's* Aeneid: *Cosmos and Imperium*. Oxford.

———. 1993. *The Epic Successors of Virgil*. Cambridge.

———. 1994. *Virgil: Aeneid Book IX*. Cambridge.

———. 1997. "Virgil and tragedy." In Martindale 1997:312–26.

———. 2002. *Ovid's Poetics of Illusion*. Cambridge.

Harrison, E. L. 1976. "Virgil's Location of Corythus." *CQ* n.s. 26:293–95.

Harrison, S. J. 1991. *Vergil: Aeneid 10*. Oxford.

Heinze, R. 1915. *Virgils epische technik*. 3rd ed. Leipzig.

Henderson, J. 1999. *Writing Down Rome*. Oxford.

———. 2000. "The Camillus Factory: *per astra ad Ardeam*." *Ramus* 29:1–26.

Henry, J. 1873. *Aeneidea*. Vol. I. Dublin.

Heuzé, P. 1985. *L'image du corps dans l'œuvre de Virgile* (Collection de l'école française de Rome 86). Rome.

Hexter, R. 1990. "What Was the Trojan Horse Made Of?: Interpreting Virgil's *Aeneid*." *YJC* 3.2:109–31.

———. 1992. "Sidonian Dido." In R. Hexter and D. Selden, eds., *Innovations of Antiquity*. New York.

Heyne, C. G. 1797. *P. Virgilius Maro varietate lectionis et perpetua adnotatione illustratus*. 3rd ed. 4 vols. Leipzig.

Hinds, S. 1998. *Allusion and Intertext: Dynamics of Appropriation in Roman Poetry*. Cambridge.

Hollis, A. S. 1992. "Hellenistic Colouring in Virgil's *Aeneid*." *HSCP* 94:269–85.

———. 1994. "[Oppian] Cyn. 2.100–158 and the Mythical Past of Apamea-on-the-Orontes." *ZPE* 102:153–66.

Honeyman, A. M. 1947. "Varia Punica." *AJP* 68:77–82.

Horsfall, N. M. 1987. "Corythus Re-examined." In J. N. Bremmer and N. M. Horsfall, *Roman Myth and Mythography*. Institute of Classical Studies Bulletin Supplement 52, pp. 89–104. London.

———. 1989a. "Virgil and Marcellus' Education." *CQ* n.s. 39:266–67.

———. 1989b. "Aeneas the Colonist." *Vergilius* 35:8–27.

———. 1990. "Dido in the Light of History." In Harrison 1990:127–44 = *PVS* 13 (1973–74), 1–13.

———., ed. 1995. *A Companion to the Study of Virgil* (*Mnem.* Suppl. 152). Leiden.

———. 2000. *Virgil, Aeneid 7: A Commentary* (*Mnem.* Suppl. 198). Leiden.

How, W. W., and J. Wells, 1928. *A Commentary on Herodotus*. 2 vols. Rev. ed. Oxford.

Huss, W. 1985. *Geschichte der Karthager*. Munich.

Innocenti, B. 1994. "Towards a Theory of Vivid Description as Practiced in Cicero's *Verrine* Orations." *Rhetorica* 12:355–81.

Jackson Knight, W. F. 1933. *"Animamque superbam."* *CR* 46:55–57.

James, S. L. 1995. "Establishing Rome with the Sword: *Condere* in the *Aeneid.*" *AJP* 116: 623–37.

Janko, R. 1992. *The Iliad: A Commentary. Volume IV: Books 13–16.* Cambridge.

Jocelyn, H. D. 1967. *The Tragedies of Ennius.* Cambridge.

———. 1991. "Virgil and Aeneas' Supposed Italic Ancestry." *Sileno* 17:77–100.

Johnson, W. R. 1976. *Darkness Visible.* Berkeley.

———. 2001. "Imaginary Romans: Vergil and the Illusion of National Identity." In S. Spence, ed., *Poets and Critics Read Virgil,* pp. 3–16. New Haven.

Jong, I.J.F. de 1987. *Narrators and Focalizers: The Presentation of the Story in the* Iliad. Amsterdam.

Kenney, E. J. 1979. *"Iudicium transferendi:* Virgil, *Aeneid* 2.469–505 and Its Antecedents." In West and Woodman 1979:103–20.

Klingner, F. 1967. *Virgil: Bucolica Georgica Aeneis.* Zürich.

Koenen, L. 1976. "Egyptian Influence in Tibullus." *ICS* 1:127–59.

Koortbojian, M. 1995. *Myth, Meaning, and Memory on Roman Sarcophagi.* Berkeley.

Krevans, N. 1993. "Ilia's Dream: Ennius, Virgil, and the Mythology of Seduction." *HSCP* 95:257–71.

Kurke, L. 1992. "The Politics of ἀβροσύνη in Archaic Greece." *ClAnt* 11:91–120.

Kvíčala, J. 1878. *Vergil-Studien.* Prague.

Laird, A. 1997. "Approaching characterisation in Virgil." In Martindale 1997:282–93.

Lamacchia, R. 1964. "Ciceros Somnium Scipionis und das sechste Buch der Aeneis." *RhM* 107:261–78.

Leach, E. W. 1999. "Viewing the *Spectacula* of *Aeneid* 6." In C. Perkell, ed., *Reading Vergil's* Aeneid*: An Interpretive Guide,* pp. 111–27. Norman, OK.

Lennox, P. 1977. "Virgil's Night-Episode Re-examined (Aeneid IX, 176–449)." *Hermes* 105:331–42.

Lloyd, C. 1999. "The Evander-Anchises Connection: Fathers, Sons, and Homoerotic Desire in Vergil's *Aeneid.*" *Vergilius* 45:3–21.

Lloyd, R. B. 1972. "Superbus in the *Aeneid.*" *AJP* 93:125–32.

Loraux, N. 1989. *Les expériences de Tirésias.* Paris.

Lyne, R.O.A.M. 1978. *Ciris: A Poem Attributed to Vergil.* Cambridge.

———. 1987. *Further Voices in Vergil's* Aeneid. Oxford.

Mackie, C. J. 1993. "A Note on Dido's Ancestry in the *Aeneid.*" *CJ* 88:231–33.

Makowski, J. F. 1989. "Nisus and Euryalus: A Platonic Relationship." *CJ* 85:1–15.

Malkin, I. 1998. *The Returns of Odysseus: Colonization and Ethnicity.* Berkeley.

Maltby, R. 1991. *A Lexicon of Ancient Latin Etymologies.* Leeds.

Martindale, C., ed. 1997. *The Cambridge Companion to Virgil.* Cambridge.

Mastronarde, D. 1994. *Euripides: Phoenissae.* Cambridge.

Michels, A. K. 1945. "The Golden Bough of Plato." *AJP* 66:59–63.

———. 1981. "The *Insomnium* of Aeneas." *CQ* n.s. 31:140–46.

Mitchell, R. N. 1992. "The Violence of Virginity in the *Aeneid.*" *Arethusa* 24: 219–38.

Momigliano, A. 1975. *Alien Wisdom: The Limits of Hellenization.* Cambridge.

Müller, H.-P. 1988. "Pygmaion, Pygmalion und Pumaijaton: Aus der Geschichte einer mythischen Gestalt." *Orientalia* 57:192–205.

Newlands, C. 2002. *Statius' Silvae and the Poetics of Empire.* Cambridge.

Nifadopoulos, C., ed. 2003. *Etymologica: Studies in Ancient Etymology. Proceedings of the Cambridge Conference on Ancient Etymology 25–27 September 2000.* Münster.

Norden, E. 1957. *P. Vergilius Maro: Aeneis Buch VI.* 4th ed. Stuttgart.

Obbink, D. 2002. "Vergil, Philodemus, and the Lament of Iuturna." In J. F. Miller et al., eds., *Vertis in usum: Studies in Honor of Edward Courtney.* Beiträge zur Altertumskunde 161, pp. 90–113. Leipzig.

O'Hara, J. J. 1990. *Death and the Optimistic Prophecy in Vergil's* Aeneid. Princeton.

———. 1993. "Dido as 'Interpreting Character' at *Aeneid* 4.56–66." *Arethusa* 26:99–114.

———. 1994a. "They Might Be Giants: Inconsistency and Indeterminacy in Vergil's War in Italy." *Colby Quarterly* 30:206–32.

———. 1994b. "Temporal Distortions, 'Fatal' Ambiguity, and *Iulius Caesar* at *Aeneid* 1.286–96." *SO* 69:72–82.

———. 1996. *True Names: Vergil and the Alexandrian Tradition of Etymological Wordplay.* Ann Arbor.

———. 2005. "Trying Not to Cheat: Responses to Inconsistencies in Roman Epic." *TAPA* 135:15–33.

Otis, B. 1963. *Virgil: A Study in Civilized Poetry.* Oxford.

Page, T. E. 1894. *The Aeneid of Virgil: Books I–VI.* London. Repr. 1967.

Parry, A. 1963. "The Two Voices of Virgil's *Aeneid.*" *Arion* 2.4:66–80.

Petrini, M. 1997. *The Child and the Hero: Coming of Age in Catullus and Vergil.* Ann Arbor.

Pichon, R. 1902. *De sermone amatorio apud Latinos elegiarum scriptores.* Paris. Pp. 75–303 repr. as *Index verborum amatoriorum.* Hildesheim 1966.

Prato, C. 1968. *Tyrtaeus.* Rome.

Pucci, P. 1978. "Lingering on the Threshold." *Glyph* 3:52–73.

——— 1987. *Odysseus Polutropos: Intertextual Readings in the* Odyssey *and the* Iliad. Ithaca.

Putnam, M. C. J. 1965. *The Poetry of the Aeneid.* Harvard.

——— 1985. "Possessiveness, Sexuality and Heroism in the *Aeneid.*" *Vergilius* 31:1–21 = *Vergil's Aeneid: Interpretation and Influence* (Chapel Hill 1995) 27–49.

——— 2001. "Ovid, Virgil and Myrrha's Metamorphic Exile." *Vergilius* 47:171–93.

Quint, D. 1993. *Epic and Empire: Politics and Generic Form from Virgil to Milton.* Princeton.

Reed, J. D. 1997. *Bion of Smyrna: The Fragments and the* Adonis. Cambridge.

——— 1998. "The Death of Osiris in *Aeneid* 12.548." *AJP* 119:399–418.

——— 2001. "Anchises Reading Aeneas Reading Marcellus." *SyllClass* 12:146–68.

——— 2004. "A Hellenistic influence in *Aeneid* IX." *Faventia* 26/1:27–42.

Rehm, B. 1932. *Das geographische Bild des alten Italien in Vergils Aeneis.* Wiesbaden.

Ribichini, S. 1985. *Poenus advena: gli dei fenici e l'interpretazione classica.* Rome.

Ross, D. O. 1975. *Backgrounds to Augustan Poetry.* Cambridge.

Russell, D. A. 1979. "De Imitatione." In West and Woodman 1979:1–16.

Sabbadini, R. 1889. *Studi critici sulla Eneide.* Lonigo.

Sanderlin, G. 1969. "Point of View in Virgil's Fourth *Aeneid.*" *CW* 63:81–5.

Saunders, C. 1940. "Sources of the Names of Trojans and Latins in Virgil's *Aeneid.*" *TAPA* 71:537–55.

Schor, N. 1980. "Fiction as Interpretation / Interpretation as Fiction." In S. Suleiman and I. Crosman, eds. *The Reader in the Text. Essays on Audience and Interpretation*, pp. 165–182. Princeton.

Scodel, R., and R. Thomas. 1984. "Virgil and the Euphrates." *AJP* 105:339.

Shackleton Bailey, D. R. 2001. *Cicero: Letters to His Friends*. Vol. 2. Harvard.

Silverman, K. 1992. *Male Subjectivity at the Margins*. New York.

Skinner, M. B. 1997. "Ego mulier: The Construction of Male Sexuality in Catullus." In Hallett and Skinner 1997:129–50.

Skulsky, S. 1985. "Aeneas and the Love of Rome." *AJP* 106:447–55.

Skutsch, O. 1985. The *Annals* of Q. Ennius. Oxford.

Smith, M. S. 1994. *The Ugaritic Baal Cycle*. Vol. 1. Suppl. to *Vetus Testamentum* 55. Leiden.

Stahl, H.-P., ed. 1998. *Vergil's* Aeneid: *Augustan Epic and Political Context*. London.

Stanley, K. 1963. "Rome, Ἔρως, and the *Versus Romae*." *GRBS* 4:237–49.

Starks, J. H., Jr. 1999. "*Fides Aeneia*: The Transference of Punic Stereotypes in the *Aeneid*." *CJ* 94:255–83.

Stephens, S. A. 2003. *Seeing Double: Intercultural Poetics in Ptolemaic Alexandria*. Berkeley.

Stocks, H. 1936. "Adoniskult in Nordafrika." *Berytus* 3:31–50.

Stok, F. 1989. "Le guance di Turno." *Seminari Sassaresi*, pp. 29–52. Sassari.

Tatham, G. 1990. "Ariadne's Mitra: A Note on Catullus 64.61–4." *CQ* 40:560–61.

Thomas, R. F. 1988. *Virgil: Georgics*. 2 vols. Cambridge.

———— 1998. "The Isolation of Turnus: *Aeneid* Book 12." In Stahl 1998:271–302.

———— 1999. *Reading Virgil and His Texts: Studies in Intertextuality*. Ann Arbor.

Toll, K. 1991. "The *Aeneid* as an Epic of National Identity: *Italiam laeto socii clamore salutant*." *Helios* 18:3–14.

———— 1997. "Making Roman-ness and the *Aeneid*." *ClAnt* 16:34–56.

Traina, A. 1997. *Virgilio: L'utopia e la storia*. Turin.

Vasaly, A. 1993. *Representations: Images of the World in Ciceronian Oratory*. Berkeley.

Vermeule, E. 1979. *Aspects of Death in Early Greek Art and Poetry*. Berkeley.

Vernant, J.-P. 1991. "A 'Beautiful Death' and the Disfigured Corpse in Homeric Epic." In *Mortals and Immortals: Collected Essays*, pp. 50–74. Princeton.

Vidal-Naquet, P. 1989. *Mythe et tragédie deux*. Paris.

Walker, A. D. 1993. "*Enargeia* and the Spectator in Greek Historiography." *TAPA* 123:353–77.

Walters, J. 1997. "Invading the Roman Body: Manliness and Impenetrability in Roman Thought." In Hallett and Skinner 1997:29–43.

Webb, R. 1999. "*Ekphrasis* Ancient and Modern: The Invention of a Genre." *Word and Image* 15:7–18.

West, D. 1987. *The Bough and the Gate*. Exeter.

West, D., and T. Woodman, eds. 1979. *Creative Imitation and Latin Literature*. Cambridge.

West, M. L. 1983. *The Orphic Poems*. Oxford.

———— 1985. *The Catalogue of Women*. Oxford.

———— 1997. *The East Face of Helicon*. Oxford.

Westermann, A. 1839. Παραδοξογράφοι: *Scriptores rerum mirabilium Graeci*. Brunswick.

Wigodsky, M. 1965. "The Arming of Aeneas." *C&M* 26:192–221.

Wigodsky, M. 1972. *Vergil and Early Latin Poetry* (*Hermes* Einzelschriften 24). Wiesbaden.

Williams, C. A. 1999. *Roman Homosexuality*. Oxford.

Williams, G. W. 1968. *Tradition and Originality in Roman Poetry*. Oxford.

——— 1980. *Figures of Thought in Roman Poetry*. New Haven.

——— 1983. *Technique and Ideas in the* Aeneid. New Haven.

Williams, R. D. 1972. *The Aeneid of Virgil: Books 1–6*. Basingstoke.

Wills, J. 1996. *Repetition in Latin Poetry: Figures of Allusion*. Oxford.

——— 1998. "Divided Allusion: Virgil and the *Coma Berenices*." *HSCP* 98:277–305.

Wiltshire, S. F. 1989. *Public and Private in Vergil's* Aeneid. Amherst.

Zaffagno, E. 1973. "Nomi di Rutuli nell'*Eneide*." *Atti della Accademia Ligure di Scienze e Lettere*. 29:304–13.

Zanker, G. 1981. "Enargeia in the Ancient Criticism of Poetry." *RhM* 124:297–311.

Zeitlin, F. 1990. "Thebes: Theater of Self and Society in Athenian Drama." In J. Winkler and F. Zeitlin, eds. *Nothing to Do with Dionysus? Athenian Drama in Its Social Context*, pp. 130–67. Princeton.

——— 1993. "Staging Dionysus between Thebes and Athens." In T. H. Carpenter and C. A. Faraone, eds., *Masks of Dionysus*, pp. 147–82. Ithaca.

Zetzel, J. E. G. 1989. "*Romane memento:* Justice and Judgment in *Aeneid* 6." *TAPA* 119:263–84.

——— 1995. *Cicero: De Re Publica. Selections*. Cambridge.

INDEX OF TEXTS CITED

(Individual Greek epigrammatists are listed under the *Anthologia Palatina*.)

GENERAL INDEX